Air Fryer Cookbook

550 Easy-to-Remember and Quick-to-Make Air Fryer Recipes For Smart and Busy People

Olivia Harrington

TABLE OF CONTENTS

Introduction

Air Fryer is an ultra-modern kitchen invention that has introduced a revolutionary way of cooking foods by using hot air. It is invented to prepare meals using as much as 80% less amount of oil as compared to traditional method. It is the perfect solution to enjoy crispy foods at home every day

While we all love having fried-foods, but it comes at a cost of weight gain issues. Less consumption of cooking oil automatically curbs use of calories and promotes the process of fat burning. Air Fryer recipes are healthy to eat and takes control over your weight gain issues

This cookbook is comprised of a delicious collection of 550 recipes that are suitable for all tastes. Each recipe is simple to make, full of flavor, and offers a healthier alternative to traditionally fried foods. This book is made to help ensure you get the most out of your Air Fryer

As some healthy foods, tend to have a knock-off taste from the real deal, air fryers produce foods with a delicious taste and feel in your mouth

The air fryer can be used in many ways to help make your hectic, daily life more manageable. Whether you want to fry, bake, grill or roast ingredients, the air fryer can do it all. It can cook without oil, prepare multiple dishes at once and its parts can be easily removed for cleaning

In this cookbook, you will discover a variety of sweet, savory, salty, citrusy, and other delicious recipes. These flavorful dishes are hand-picked to ensure you have a hearty collection of the best recipes on hand at all times. As a result, this cookbook is the ultimate companion book to any Air Fryer. You are guaranteed to find a wonderful selection of traditional, modern and alternative recipes inside to suit any palette

Get started to explore the exciting world of Air Fryer. Get ready to welcome a revolutionary way of preparing healthy fried recipes for your whole family.

Happy cooking!

The Benefits of Using an Air Fryer

First and foremost, the air fryer became popular for its numerous health benefits. The convenience and ease of use area close second and this combination makes it and easy choice for those who want a healthy, delicious meal in a fraction of the time. For those who doubt the air fryer capabilities and prefer conventional cooking methods, perhaps the following points will be enough to convince them to make the switch to efficient cooking.

Protect The Food's Nutrients:

Unlike deep frying, Air Fryers do not deconstruct the food's good nutrients and add on bad fats. If you think your yasai tempura (deep fried battered vegetables) are healthy, here is news for you; while they may look like they are full of nutritious elements, the deep-frying process would have destroyed the beneficial vitamins and minerals contained in the vegetables.

Keeping Cancer at Bay:

For some oils (e.g. olive and flaxseed), their chemical structure changes in high heat causing them to transform into bad forms of fat. Additionally, since there is little oil used, there is little chances for food to produce carcinogens that activate cancer cells.

Build A Fortress for Your Heart:

Eating food fried with an Air Fryer reduces the risk of heart diseases and protects your body by helping you absorb necessary nutrients. Since minimal amount of oil is used to prepare food, you can be sure that your body will not accumulate excessive fats in the long run. Instead, the optimal amount of oil used will help your body protect your heart.

Keeping Your Kidneys Clear:

Consuming excess amounts of deep-fried food will impair your kidney's ability to filter our harmful fats. Therefore, eating food fried by an Air Fryer can help you lower your risks of getting kidney disease. If you are finding it difficult to quit deep-fried food cold turkey, using an Air Fryer will ease your transition to a healthier diet.

Fat Is Not All Bad:

Fat is a macronutrient – it is essential to help control inflammation, blood clotting, maintaining healthy hair and skin, prevent heart diseases, provide energy and assist in the absorption of vitamins A, D, E and K. While it is important to your bodily functions, too much of it is detrimental to health. An Air Fryer is a modern kitchen appliance that fries food using heated hot air by using at most a tablespoon of oil. This way, you are able to eat fried food without worrying about the negative effects of fatty food on your health.

How Does the Air Fryer Work?

Take it easy It is Very simple to use an Air Fryer just follow these steps.

Step 1: The first step is to prepare the air fryer. For this, start by picking the right attachment to be used. You have to place the attachment the right way in order for the air fryer to work.

Step 2: Preheat the air fryer so that it reaches the right temperature for your food. You can look up the instructional manual provided with your machine to check which temperature suits what food the best. Generally speaking, meats and hard vegetables require the highest temperature to cook.

Step 3: Brush a little oil over the food and place it inside the attachment before fixing it on to the air fryer.

Step 4: Choose the right timing and wait patiently. Once done, you can serve the dish hot.

Tips to Prepare Healthy Foods in Air Fryer

1. Vegetables are one of the easiest foods to cook in Air Fryer. A wide variety of plants can be cooked, be it delicate beans to root vegetables. For the best cooking experience, firstly, soak the vegetables, especially the harder ones, in cold water for 15 - 20 minutes. Then after, dry them using a clean kitchen towel.

2. Re-heating leftovers: There's no hard and fast rule for time and temperature when re-heating leftovers because leftovers vary so significantly. I suggest re-heating in the air fryer at 350 degrees Fahrenheit and doing so for as long as it takes for the food to be re-heated to a food safety temperature of 165 degrees Fahrenheit. This is especially important for any potentially hazardous foods like chicken and beef.

3. Roasting with air is a new cooking trend you have to try because you can finally prepare your winter favorites

4. Flip foods over halfway through the cooking time; Just as you would if you were cooking on a grill or in a skillet, you need to turn foods over so that they brown evenly.

5. You can bake your favorite recipes in your Air Fryer but always check with the machine's manual before using new baking ware with Air Fryer

6. Keep in mind that you should always aim to cook your food to desired doneness because the recipes are flexible and they are designed for all Air Fryer models. If you feel that the food needs more cooking time, then adjust it and cook for a few more minutes. It is not a thumb rule to stick to recipe time only as certain ingredients can vary in their size and firmness from one country to another

7. When it comes to the cooking time, it changes depending on particular Air Fryer model, the size of food, food pre-preparation and so on. For shorter cooking cycles, you should preheat Air Fryer for about 3 - 4 minutes. otherwise, if you put the ingredients into the cold cooking basket, the cooking time needs to be increased to 3 additional minutes.

8. Use a good quality oil spray to brush food and cooking basket, it is also helpful for easy cleanup

Breakfast Recipes

Special Hash Browns

(Prep + Cooking Time: 30 Minutes **| Servings:** 6)

Ingredients:
- 2-pound hash browns
- 1 cup whole milk
- 6 eggs
- 9-ounce cream cheese
- 1 yellow onion; chopped
- 1 cup cheddar cheese; shredded.
- 6 green onions; chopped
- 8 bacon slices; chopped
- Salt and black pepper to the taste
- Cooking spray

Directions:
1. Heat up your air fryer at 350°F and grease it with cooking spray
2. In a bowl; mix eggs with milk, cream cheese, cheddar cheese, bacon, onion, salt and pepper and whisk well.
3. Add hash browns to your air fryer; add eggs mix over them and cook for 20 minutes. Divide among plates and serve

Easy Egg Muffins

(Prep + Cooking Time: 25 Minutes **| Servings:** 4)

Ingredients:
- 1 egg
- 2 tablespoons olive oil
- 3 tablespoon milk
- 3.5-ounce white flour
- 1 tablespoon baking powder
- 2-ounce parmesan; grated
- A splash of Worcestershire sauce

Directions:
1. In a bowl; mix egg with flour, oil, baking powder, milk, Worcestershire and parmesan; whisk well and divide into 4 silicon muffin cups
2. Arrange cups in your air fryer's cooking basket; cover and cook at 392°F, for 15 minutes. Serve warm for breakfast

Morning Egg Bowls

(Prep + Cooking Time: 30 Minutes **| Servings:** 4)

Ingredients:
- 4 eggs
- 4 dinner rolls; tops cut off and insides scooped out
- 4 tablespoon parmesan; grated
- 4 tablespoon heavy cream
- 4 tablespoon mixed chives and parsley
- Salt and black pepper to the taste

Directions:
1. Arrange dinner rolls on a baking sheet and crack an egg in each
2. Divide heavy cream, mixed herbs in each roll and season with salt and pepper.
3. Sprinkle parmesan on top of your rolls; place them in your air fryer and cook at 350°F, for 20 minutes. Divide your bread bowls on plates and serve for breakfast

Potatoes with Bacon

(Prep + Cooking Time: 30 Minutes | Servings: 4)

Ingredients:

- 4 potatoes; peeled and cut into medium cubes
- 6 garlic cloves; minced
- 2 rosemary springs; chopped
- 1 tablespoon olive oil
- 2 eggs; whisked
- 4 bacon slices; chopped
- Salt and black pepper to the taste

Directions:

1. In your air fryer's pan, mix oil with potatoes, garlic, bacon, rosemary, salt, pepper and eggs and whisk. Cook potatoes at 400°F, for 20 minutes; divide everything on plates and serve for breakfast.

Quick Turkey Burrito

(Prep + Cooking Time: 20 Minutes | Servings: 2)

Ingredients:

- 4 slices turkey breast already cooked
- 1/2 red bell pepper; sliced
- 1 small avocado; peeled; pitted and sliced
- 2 tablespoon salsa
- 2 eggs
- 1/8 cup mozzarella cheese; grated
- Salt and black pepper to the taste
- Tortillas for serving

Directions:

1. In a bowl; whisk eggs with salt and pepper to the taste, pour them in a pan and place it in the air fryer's basket
2. Cook at 400°F, for 5 minutes; take pan out of the fryer and transfer eggs to a plate.
3. Arrange tortillas on a working surface, divide eggs on them; also divide turkey meat, bell pepper, cheese, salsa and avocado
4. Roll your burritos and place them in your air fryer after you've lined it with some tin foil. Heat up the burritos at 300°F, for 3 minutes; divide them on plates and serve

Potato Frittata

(Prep + Cooking Time: 30 Minutes | Servings: 6)

Ingredients:

- 6-ounce jarred roasted red bell peppers; chopped.
- 12 eggs; whisked
- 1/2 cup parmesan; grated
- 3 garlic cloves; minced
- 2 tablespoon parsley; chopped.
- 2 tablespoon chives; chopped.
- 16 potato wedges
- 6 tablespoon ricotta cheese
- Salt and black pepper to the taste
- Cooking spray

Directions:

1. In a bowl; mix eggs with red peppers, garlic, parsley, salt, pepper and ricotta and whisk well
2. Heat up your air fryer at 300°F and grease it with cooking spray.
3. Add half of the potato wedges on the bottom and sprinkle half of the parmesan all over
4. Add half of the egg mix; add the rest of the potatoes and the rest of the parmesan.
5. Add the rest of the eggs mix; sprinkle chives and cook for 20 minutes. Divide among plates and serve for breakfast.

Veggie Burritos Breakfast

(Prep + Cooking Time: 20 Minutes | Servings: 4)

Ingredients:

- 1/2 cup sweet potatoes; steamed and cubed
- 1/2 small broccoli head; florets separated and steamed
- 2 tablespoon liquid smoke
- 2 tablespoon water
- 8 roasted red peppers; chopped
- 4 rice papers
- 7 asparagus stalks
- 2 tablespoon cashew butter
- 2 tablespoon tamari
- A handful kale; chopped

Directions:

1. In a bowl; mix cashew butter with water, tamari and liquid smoke and whisk well.
2. Wet rice papers and arrange them on a working surface
3. Divide sweet potatoes, broccoli, asparagus, red peppers and kale; wrap burritos and dip each in cashew mix.
4. Arrange burritos in your air fryer and cook them at 350°F, for 10 minutes. Divide veggie burritos on plates d serve

Bacon and Tomato Breakfast

(Prep + Cooking Time: 40 Minutes | Servings: 6)

Ingredients:

- 1-pound smoked bacon; cooked and chopped.
- 1-pound white bread; cubed
- 28-ounce canned tomatoes; chopped
- 1/2 teaspoon red pepper; crushed
- 1/2-pound cheddar; shredded.
- 1/4 cup olive oil
- 2 tablespoon chives; chopped
- 1/2-pound Monterey jack; shredded.
- 2 tablespoon stock
- 1 yellow onion; chopped
- Salt and black pepper to the taste
- 8 eggs; whisked

Directions:

1. Add the oil to your air fryer and heat it up at 350 degrees F.
2. Add bread, bacon, onion, tomatoes, red pepper and stock and stir
3. Add eggs, cheddar and Monterey jack and cook everything for 20 minutes. Divide among plates; sprinkle chives and serve

Cream Breakfast Tofu

(Prep + Cooking Time: 35 Minutes | Servings: 4)

Ingredients:

- 1 block firm tofu; pressed and cubed
- 1 tablespoon potato starch
- 2 teaspoon sesame oil
- 1 teaspoon rice vinegar
- 2 tablespoon soy sauce
- 1 cup Greek yogurt

Directions:

1. In a bowl; mix tofu cubes with vinegar, soy sauce and oil, toss, and leave aside for 15 minutes
2. Dip tofu cubes in potato starch, toss, transfer to your air fryer; heat up at 370°F and cook for 20 minutes shaking halfway. Divide into bowls and serve for breakfast with some Greek yogurt on the side

Mixed Bell Peppers Frittata

(Prep + Cooking Time: 30 Minutes | Servings: 4)

Ingredients:

- 1/2-pound chicken sausage; casings removed and chopped
- 1 orange bell pepper; chopped
- 1/2 cup mozzarella cheese; shredded.
- 1 green bell pepper; chopped
- 8 eggs; whisked
- 1 sweet onion; chopped
- 1 red bell pepper; chopped
- 2 tablespoon olive oil
- 2 teaspoon oregano; chopped
- Salt and black pepper to the taste

Directions:

1. Add 1 tablespoon oil to your air fryer; add sausage, heat up at 320°F and brown for 1 minute
2. Add the rest of the oil, onion, red bell pepper, orange and green one; stir and cook for 2 minutes more.
3. Add oregano, salt, pepper and eggs; stir and cook for 15 minutes. Add mozzarella, leave frittata aside for a few minutes; divide among plates and serve

Banana Oatmeal Casserole

(Prep + Cooking Time: 30 Minutes | Servings: 8)

Ingredients:

- 2 cups rolled oats
- 1 teaspoon baking powder
- 2/3 cup blueberries
- 1/2 cup chocolate chips
- 2 cups milk
- 1 eggs
- 2 tablespoon butter
- 1 banana; peeled and mashed
- 1/3 cup brown sugar
- 1 teaspoon cinnamon powder
- 1 teaspoon vanilla extract
- Cooking spray

Directions:

1. In a bowl; mix sugar with baking powder, cinnamon, chocolate chips, blueberries and banana and stir
2. In a separate bowl; mix eggs with vanilla extract and butter and stir.
3. Heat up your air fryer at 320 degrees F; grease with cooking spray and add oats on the bottom
4. Add cinnamon mix and eggs mix; toss and cook for 20 minutes. Stir one more time, divide into bowls and serve for breakfast.

Tasty Scrambled Eggs

(Prep + Cooking Time: 20 Minutes | Servings: 2)

Ingredients:

- 2 eggs
- 1 red bell pepper; chopped
- 2 tablespoon butter
- Salt and black pepper to the taste
- A pinch of sweet paprika

Directions:

1. In a bowl; mix eggs with salt, pepper, paprika and red bell pepper and whisk well
2. Heat up your air fryer at 140 degrees F; add butter and melt it
3. Add eggs mix; stir and cook for 10 minutes. Divide scrambled eggs on plates and serve for breakfast.

Fried Sandwich

(Prep + Cooking Time: 16 Minutes **| Servings:** 2)

Ingredients:
- 2 eggs
- 2 English muffins; halved
- 2 bacon strips
- Salt and black pepper to the taste

Directions:
1. Crack eggs in your air fryer, add bacon on top; cover and cook at 392°F, for 6 minutes
2. Heat up your English muffin halves in your microwave for a few seconds; divide eggs on 2 halves, add bacon on top, season with salt and pepper; cover with the other 2 English muffins and serve for breakfast

Simple Breakfast

(Prep + Cooking Time: 23 Minutes **| Servings:** 4)

Ingredients:
- 7-ounce baby spinach
- 8 chestnuts mushrooms; halved
- 4 eggs
- 4 chipolatas
- 4 bacon slices; chopped.
- 8 tomatoes; halved
- 1 garlic clove; minced
- Salt and black pepper to the taste
- Cooking spray

Directions:
1. Grease a cooking pan with the oil and add tomatoes, garlic and mushrooms
2. Add bacon and chipolatas, also add spinach and crack eggs at the end.
3. Season with salt and pepper; place pan in the cooking basket of your air fryer and cook for 13 minutes at 350 degrees F. Divide among plates and serve for breakfast

Breakfast Raspberry Rolls

(Prep + Cooking Time: 50 Minutes **| Servings:** 6)

Ingredients:
- 1 cup milk
- 4 tablespoon butter
- 3 ¼ cups flour

For the filling:
- 8-ounce cream cheese; soft
- 1 teaspoon vanilla extract
- 5 tablespoon sugar
- 1/4 cup sugar
- 1 egg
- 2 teaspoon yeast

- 1 tablespoon cornstarch
- 12-ounce raspberries
- Zest from 1 lemon; grated

Directions:
1. In a bowl; mix flour with sugar and yeast and stir
2. Add milk and egg, stir until you obtain a dough, leave it aside to rise for 30 minutes; transfer dough to a working surface and roll well
3. In a bowl; mix cream cheese with sugar, vanilla and lemon zest; stir well and spread over dough
4. In another bowl; mix raspberries with cornstarch, stir and spread over cream cheese mix
5. Roll your dough, cut into medium pieces, place them in your air fryer; spray them with cooking spray and cook them at 350°F, for 30 minutes. Serve your rolls for breakfast.

Breakfast Ham Dish

(Prep + Cooking Time: 25 Minutes | **Servings:** 6)

Ingredients:
- 10-ounce ham; cubed
- 6 cups French bread; cubed
- 4-ounce cheddar cheese; shredded.
- 1 tablespoon mustard
- 4-ounce green chilies; chopped
- 2 cups milk
- 5 eggs
- Salt and black pepper to the taste
- Cooking spray

Directions:
1. Heat up your air fryer at 350°F and grease it with cooking spray.
2. In a bowl; mix eggs with milk, cheese, mustard, salt and pepper and stir
3. Add bread cubes in your air fryer and mix with chilies and ham
4. Add eggs mix; spread and cook for 15 minutes. Divide among plates and serve.

Eggs and Tomatoes

(Prep + Cooking Time: 15 Minutes | **Servings:** 4)

Ingredients:
- 4 eggs
- 8 cherry tomatoes; halved
- 2-ounce milk
- Salt and black pepper to the taste
- 2 tablespoon parmesan; grated
- Cooking spray

Directions:
1. Grease your air fryer with cooking spray and heat it up at 200 degrees F
2. In a bowl; mix eggs with cheese, milk, salt and pepper and whisk.
3. Add this mix to your air fryer and cook for 6 minutes. Add tomatoes; cook your scrambled eggs for 3 minutes, divide among plates and serve

Smoked Sausage Breakfast

(Prep + Cooking Time: 40 Minutes | **Servings:** 4)

Ingredients:
- 1 ½-pound smoked sausage; chopped and browned
- 1/4 teaspoon garlic powder
- 4 ½ cups water
- 4 eggs; whisked
- 16-ounce cheddar cheese; shredded.
- 1 cup milk
- 1 ½ cups grits
- 1 ½ teaspoon thyme; chopped.
- Cooking spray
- A pinch of salt and black pepper

Directions:
1. Put the water in a pot; bring to a boil over medium heat, add grits, stir and cover, cook for 5 minutes and take off heat
2. Add cheese, stir until it melts and mix with milk, thyme, salt, pepper, garlic powder and eggs and whisk really well
3. Heat up your air fryer at 300 degrees F; grease with cooking spray and add browned sausage.
4. Add grits mix; spread and cook for 25 minutes. Divide among plates and serve for breakfast

Cheesy Bread

(Prep + Cooking Time: 18 Minutes **| Servings:** 3)

Ingredients:
- 6 bread slices
- 6 teaspoon sun dried tomato pesto
- 5 tablespoon butter; melted
- 3 garlic cloves; minced
- 1 cup mozzarella cheese; grated

Directions:
1. Arrange bread slices on a working surface
2. Spread butter all over; divide tomato paste, garlic and top with grated cheese
3. Add bread slices to your heated air fryer and cook them at 350°F, for 8 minutes. Divide among plates and serve for breakfast.

Breakfast Potatoes

(Prep + Cooking Time: 45 Minutes **| Servings:** 4)

Ingredients:
- 3 potatoes; cubed
- 2 tablespoon olive oil
- 1 teaspoon garlic powder
- 1 teaspoon sweet paprika
- 1 teaspoon onion powder
- 1 yellow onion; chopped
- 1 red bell pepper; chopped
- Salt and black pepper to the taste

Directions:
1. Grease your air fryer's basket with olive oil; add potatoes, toss and season with salt and pepper
2. Add onion, bell pepper, garlic powder, paprika and onion powder, toss well, cover and cook at 370°F, for 30 minutes. Divide potatoes mix on plates and serve for breakfast

Delicious Hash

(Prep + Cooking Time: 25 Minutes **| Servings:** 6)

Ingredients:
- 16-ounce hash browns
- 1/4 cup olive oil
- 1 egg; whisked
- 1/2 teaspoon paprika
- 1/2 teaspoon garlic powder
- 2 tablespoon chives; chopped
- 1 cup cheddar; shredded.
- Salt and black pepper to the taste

Directions:
1. Add oil to your air fryer; heat it up at 350°F and add hash browns
2. Also add paprika, garlic powder, salt, pepper and egg; toss and cook for 15 minutes. Add cheddar and chives, toss; divide among plates and serve.

Biscuits Casserole Delight

(Prep + Cooking Time: 25 Minutes **| Servings:** 8)

Ingredients:
- 12-ounce biscuits; quartered
- 2 ½ cups milk
- 3 tablespoon flour
- 1/2-pound sausage; chopped.
- A pinch of salt and black pepper
- Cooking spray

Directions:
1. Grease your air fryer with cooking spray and heat it over 350 degrees F
2. Add biscuits on the bottom and mix with sausage.
3. Add flour, milk, salt and pepper; toss a bit and cook for 15 minutes. Divide among plates and serve for breakfast

Delicious Creamy Eggs

(Prep + Cooking Time: 22 Minutes | **Servings:** 4)

Ingredients:
- 4 eggs
- 2 teaspoon chives; chopped
- 2 tablespoon heavy cream
- 2 teaspoon butter; soft
- 2 ham slices
- 3 tablespoon parmesan; grated
- Salt and black pepper to the taste
- A pinch of smoked paprika

Directions:
1. Grease your air fryer's pan with the butter; line it with the ham and add it to your air fryer's basket
2. In a bowl; mix 1 egg with heavy cream, salt and pepper, whisk well and add over ham.
3. Crack the rest of the eggs in the pan, sprinkle parmesan and cook your mix for 12 minutes at 320 degrees F. Sprinkle paprika and chives all over; divide among plates and serve for breakfast

Delightful Eggs Casserole

(Prep + Cooking Time: 35 Minutes | **Servings:** 6)

Ingredients:
- 12 eggs
- 1-pound turkey; ground
- 1 tablespoon olive oil
- 1/2 teaspoon chili powder
- 1 sweet potato; cubed
- 1 cup baby spinach
- 2 tomatoes; chopped for serving
- Salt and black pepper to the taste

Directions:
1. In a bowl; mix eggs with salt, pepper, chili powder, potato, spinach, turkey and sweet potato and whisk well.
2. Heat up your air fryer at 350 degrees F; add oil and heat it up
3. Add eggs mix, spread into your air fryer; cover and cook for 25 minutes. Divide among plates and serve for breakfast

Tasty Tuna Sandwiches

(Prep + Cooking Time: 15 Minutes | **Servings:** 4)

Ingredients:
- 16-ounce canned tuna; drained
- 1/4 cup mayonnaise
- 2 tablespoon mustard
- 1 tablespoon lemon juice
- 2 green onions; chopped
- 3 English muffins; halved
- 3 tablespoon butter
- 6 provolone cheese

Directions:
1. In a bowl; mix tuna with mayo, lemon juice, mustard and green onions and stir
2. Grease muffin halves with the butter, place them in preheated air fryer and bake them at 350°F, for 4 minutes. Spread tuna mix on muffin halves; top each with provolone cheese, return sandwiches to air fryer and cook them for 4 minutes; divide among plates and serve for breakfast right away

Tofu Scramble

(Prep + Cooking Time: 35 Minutes **| Servings:** 4)

Ingredients:

- 4 cups broccoli florets
- 1/2 teaspoon onion powder
- 2 tablespoon soy sauce
- 2 tablespoon extra-virgin olive oil
- 1 tofu block; cubed
- 1 teaspoon turmeric; ground
- 1/2 teaspoon garlic powder
- 2½ cup red potatoes; cubed
- 1/2 cup yellow onion; chopped
- Salt and black pepper to the taste

Directions:

1. Mix tofu with 1 tablespoon oil, salt, pepper, soy sauce, garlic powder, onion powder, turmeric and onion in a bowl; stir and leave aside
2. In a separate bowl; combine potatoes with the rest of the oil, a pinch of salt and pepper and toss to coat.
3. Put potatoes in your air fryer at 350°F and bake for 15 minutes; shaking once
4. Add tofu and its marinade to your air fryer and bake for 15 minutes
5. Add broccoli to the fryer and cook everything for 5 minutes more. Serve right away.

Fish Tacos Breakfast

(Prep + Cooking Time: 23 Minutes **| Servings:** 4)

Ingredients:

- 4 big tortillas
- 1 yellow onion; chopped
- 1 cup corn
- 1 red bell pepper; chopped
- 1/2 cup salsa
- 4 white fish fillets; skinless and boneless
- A handful mixed romaine lettuce; spinach and radicchio
- 4 tablespoon parmesan; grated

Directions:

1. Put fish fillets in your air fryer and cook at 350°F, for 6 minutes
2. Meanwhile; heat up a pan over medium high heat, add bell pepper, onion and corn; stir and cook for 1 - 2 minutes
3. Arrange tortillas on a working surface, divide fish fillets, spread salsa over them; divide mixed veggies and mixed greens and spread parmesan on each at the end.
4. Roll your tacos; place them in preheated air fryer and cook at 350°F, for 6 minutes more. Divide fish tacos on plates and serve for breakfast

Veggie Mix

(Prep + Cooking Time: 35 Minutes **| Servings:** 6)

Ingredients:

- 1 yellow onion; sliced
- 8-ounce brie; trimmed and cubed
- 12-ounce sourdough bread; cubed
- 1 red bell pepper; chopped.
- 8 eggs
- 2 tablespoon mustard
- 3 cups milk
- 1 gold potato; chopped.
- 2 tablespoon olive oil
- 4-ounce parmesan; grated
- Salt and black pepper to the taste

Directions:

1. Heat up your air fryer at 350 degrees F; add oil, onion, potato and bell pepper and cook for 5 minutes.
2. In a bowl; mix eggs with milk, salt, pepper and mustard and whisk well
3. Add bread and brie to your air fryer; add half of the eggs mix and add half of the parmesan as well.
4. Add the rest of the bread and parmesan; toss just a little bit and cook for 20 minutes
5. Divide among plates and serve for breakfast

Cheesy Sandwich

(Prep + Cooking Time: 18 Minutes | Servings: 1)

Ingredients:
- 2 bread slices
- 2 teaspoon butter
- 2 cheddar cheese slices
- A pinch of sweet paprika

Directions:
1. Spread butter on bread slices, add cheddar cheese on one, sprinkle paprika, top with the other bread slices, cut into 2 halves; arrange them in your air fryer and cook at 370°F, for 8 minutes; flipping them once, arrange on a plate and serve

Cheese Fried Bake

(Prep + Cooking Time: 30 Minutes | Servings: 4)

Ingredients:
- 4 bacon slices; cooked and crumbled
- 1-pound breakfast sausage; casings removed and chopped
- 2 cups milk
- 2 ½ cups cheddar cheese; shredded.
- 1/2 teaspoon onion powder
- 3 tablespoon parsley; chopped.
- 2 eggs
- Salt and black pepper to the taste
- Cooking spray

Directions:
1. In a bowl; mix eggs with milk, cheese, onion powder, salt, pepper and parsley and whisk well.
2. Grease your air fryer with cooking spray; heat it up at 320°F and add bacon and sausage
3. Add eggs mix; spread and cook for 20 minutes. Divide among plates and serve

Ham Pie

(Prep + Cooking Time: 35 Minutes | Servings: 6)

Ingredients:
- 2 cups ham; cooked and chopped
- 16-ounce crescent rolls dough
- 2 eggs; whisked
- 1 tablespoon parmesan; grated
- 2 cups cheddar cheese; grated
- Salt and black pepper to the taste
- Cooking spray

Directions:
1. Grease your air fryer's pan with cooking spray and press half of the crescent rolls dough on the bottom
2. In a bowl; mix eggs with cheddar cheese, parmesan, salt and pepper; whisk well and add over dough
3. Spread ham, cut the rest of the crescent rolls dough in strips, arrange them over ham and cook at 300°F, for 25 minutes. Slice pie and serve for breakfast

Protein Rich Egg White Omelet

(Prep + Cooking Time: 25 Minutes | Servings: 4)

Ingredients:
- 1 cup egg whites
- 2 tablespoon chives; chopped
- 1/4 cup tomato; chopped
- 2 tablespoon skim milk
- 1/4 cup mushrooms; chopped
- Salt and black pepper to the taste

Directions:
1. In a bowl; mix egg whites with tomato, milk, mushrooms, chives, salt and pepper; whisk well and pour into your air fryer's pan. Cook at 320°F, for 15 minutes; cool omelet down, slice, divide among plates and serve

Buttermilk Biscuits

(Prep + Cooking Time: 18 Minutes | **Servings:** 4)

Ingredients:

- 4 tablespoon butter; cold and cubed+ 1 tablespoon melted butter
- 1/2 cup self-rising flour
- 1/4 teaspoon baking soda
- 1/2 teaspoon baking powder
- 3/4 cup buttermilk
- 1 ¼ cup white flour
- 1 teaspoon sugar
- Maple syrup for serving

Directions:

1. In a bowl; mix white flour with self-rising flour, baking soda, baking powder and sugar and stir.
2. Add cold butter and stir using your hands
3. Add buttermilk, stir until you obtain a dough and transfer to a floured working surface.
4. Roll your dough and cut 10 pieces using a round cutter.
5. Arrange biscuits in your air fryer's cake pan; brush them with melted butter and cook at 400°F, for 8 minutes. Serve them for breakfast with some maple syrup on top

Fried Tomato Quiche

(Prep + Cooking Time: 40 Minutes | **Servings:** 1)

Ingredients:

- 2 tablespoon yellow onion; chopped
- 2 eggs
- 1/4 cup milk
- 1/2 cup gouda cheese; shredded.
- 1/4 cup tomatoes; chopped.
- Salt and black pepper to the taste
- Cooking spray

Directions:

1. Grease a ramekin with cooking spray.
2. Crack eggs, add onion, milk, cheese, tomatoes, salt and pepper and stir. Add this in your air fryer's pan and cook at 340°F, for 30 minutes

Cream Cheese Oats

(Prep + Cooking Time: 35 Minutes | **Servings:** 4)

Ingredients:

- 1 cup steel oats
- 3 cups milk
- 2-ounce cream cheese; soft
- 3/4 cup raisins
- 1 tablespoon butter
- 2 tablespoon white sugar
- 1 teaspoon cinnamon powder
- 1/4 cup brown sugar

Directions:

1. Heat up a pan that fits your air fryer with the butter over medium heat, add oats; stir and toast them for 3 minutes
2. Add milk and raisins; stir, introduce in your air fryer and cook at 350°F, for 20 minutes.
3. Meanwhile; in a bowl, mix cinnamon with brown sugar and stir.
4. In a second bowl; mix white sugar with cream cheese and whisk. Divide oats into bowls and top each with cinnamon and cream cheese

Breakfast Cherries Risotto

(Prep + Cooking Time: 22 Minutes | Servings: 4)

Ingredients:
- 1 ½ cups Arborio rice
- 3 cups milk
- 1/2 cup cherries; dried
- 1/3 cup brown sugar
- 1 ½ teaspoon cinnamon powder
- 1 cup apple juice
- A pinch of salt
- 2 tablespoon butter
- 2 apples; cored and sliced

Directions:
1. Heat up a pan that fist your air fryer with the butter over medium heat, add rice; stir and cook for 4 - 5 minutes
2. Add sugar, apples, apple juice, milk, cinnamon and cherries; stir, introduce in your air fryer and cook at 350°F, for 8 minutes. Divide into bowls and serve for breakfast

Potato Hash

(Prep + Cooking Time: 35 Minutes | Servings: 4)

Ingredients:
- 1 ½ potatoes; cubed
- 2 teaspoon olive oil
- 2 eggs
- 1/2 teaspoon thyme; dried
- 1 yellow onion; chopped
- 1 green bell pepper; chopped
- Salt and black pepper to the taste

Directions:
1. Heat up your air fryer at 350 degrees F; add oil, heat it up, add onion, bell pepper, salt and pepper; stir and cook for 5 minutes.
2. Add potatoes, thyme and eggs, stir, cover and cook at 360°F, for 20 minutes. Divide among plates and serve for breakfast

Blackberry French Style Toast

(Prep + Cooking Time: 30 Minutes | Servings: 6)

Ingredients:
- 1 cup blackberry jam; warm
- 2 cups half and half
- 12-ounce bread loaf; cubed
- 8-ounce cream cheese; cubed
- 4 eggs
- 1/2 cup brown sugar
- 1 teaspoon vanilla extract
- 1 teaspoon cinnamon powder
- Cooking spray

Directions:
1. Grease your air fryer with cooking spray and heat it up at 300 degrees F
2. Add blueberry jam on the bottom, layer half of the bread cubes, then add cream cheese and top with the rest of the bread.
3. In a bowl; mix eggs with half and half, cinnamon, sugar and vanilla; whisk well and add over bread mix. Cook for 20 minutes; divide among plates and serve for breakfast

Tasty Polenta Bites

(Prep + Cooking Time: 30 Minutes | Servings: 4)

Ingredients:

For the polenta:
- 1 cup cornmeal
- 1 tablespoon butter
- 3 cups water
- Salt and black pepper to the taste

For the polenta bites:
- 2 tablespoon powdered sugar
- Cooking spray

Directions:
1. In a pan; mix water with cornmeal, butter, salt and pepper, stir, bring to a boil over medium heat; cook for 10 minutes, take off heat; whisk one more time and keep in the fridge until it's cold
2. Scoop 1 tablespoon of polenta, shape a ball and place on a working surface.
3. Repeat with the rest of the polenta; arrange all the balls in the cooking basket of your air fryer, spray them with cooking spray; cover and cook at 380°F, for 8 minutes. Arrange polenta bites on plates; sprinkle sugar all over and serve for breakfast

Eggs, Sausage and Cheese Mix

(Prep + Cooking Time: 30 Minutes | Servings: 4)

Ingredients:
- 10-ounce sausages; cooked and crumbled
- 1 cup cheddar cheese; shredded.
- 1 cup mozzarella cheese; shredded.
- 8 eggs; whisked
- 1 cup milk
- Salt and black pepper to the taste
- Cooking spray

Directions:
1. In a bowl; mix sausages with cheese, mozzarella, eggs, milk, salt and pepper and whisk well
2. Heat up your air fryer at 380 degrees F; spray cooking oil, add eggs and sausage mix and cook for 20 minutes. Divide among plates and serve

Bread Rolls

(Prep + Cooking Time: 22 Minutes | Servings: 4)

Ingredients:
- 5 potatoes; boiled; peeled and mashed
- 1/2 teaspoon turmeric powder
- 1 coriander bunch; chopped
- 2 green chilies; chopped
- 2 small yellow onions; chopped.
- 2 curry leaf springs
- 1/2 teaspoon mustard seeds
- 8 bread slices; white parts only
- 2 tablespoon olive oil
- Salt and black pepper to the taste

Directions:
1. Heat up a pan with 1 teaspoon oil; add mustard seeds, onions, curry leaves and turmeric, stir and cook for a few seconds
2. Add mashed potatoes, salt, pepper, coriander and chilies, stir well; take off heat and cool it down.
3. Divide potatoes mix into 8 parts and shape ovals using your wet hands
4. Wet bread slices with water; press in order to drain excess water and keep one slice in your palm
5. Add a potato oval over bread slice and wrap it around it.
6. Repeat with the rest of the potato mix and bread
7. Heat up your air fryer at 400 degrees F; add the rest of the oil, add bread rolls; cook them for 12 minutes. Divide bread rolls on plates and serve for breakfast

Baked Eggs

(**Prep + Cooking Time:** 30 Minutes | **Servings:** 4)

Ingredients:

- 1-pound baby spinach; torn
- 4 eggs
- 1 tablespoon olive oil
- 7-ounce ham; chopped
- Cooking spray
- 4 tablespoon milk
- Salt and black pepper to the taste

Directions:

1. Heat up a pan with the oil over medium heat; add baby spinach, stir cook for a couple of minutes and take off heat
2. Grease 4 ramekins with cooking spray and divide baby spinach and ham in each.
3. Crack an egg in each ramekin, also divide milk, season with salt and pepper; place ramekins in preheated air fryer at 350°F and bake for 20 minutes. Serve baked eggs for breakfast

Leek and Potato Frittata

(**Prep + Cooking Time:** 28 Minutes | **Servings:** 4)

Ingredients:

- 2 gold potatoes; boiled, peeled and chopped
- 1/4 cup whole milk
- 5-ounce fromage blanc; crumbled
- 2 tablespoon butter
- 2 leeks; sliced
- 10 eggs; whisked
- Salt and black pepper to the taste

Directions:

1. Heat up a pan that fits your air fryer with the butter over medium heat, add leeks; stir and cook for 4 minutes.
2. Add potatoes, salt, pepper, eggs, cheese and milk, whisk well; cook for 1 minute more, introduce in your air fryer and cook at 350°F, for 13 minutes. Slice frittata, divide among plates and serve

Rice, Almonds Pudding

(**Prep + Cooking Time:** 13 Minutes | **Servings:** 4)

Ingredients:

- 1 cup brown rice
- 1/2 cup maple syrup
- 1/4 cup raisins
- 1/4 cup almonds
- 1/2 cup coconut chips
- 1 cup milk
- 2 cups water
- A pinch of cinnamon powder

Directions:

1. Put the rice in a pan that fits your air fryer, add the water, heat up on the stove over medium high heat; cook until rice is soft and drain
2. Add milk, coconut chips, almonds, raisins, cinnamon and maple syrup; stir well, introduce in your air fryer and cook at 360°F, for 8 minutes. Divide rice pudding in bowls and serve

Special Shrimp Sandwiches

(Prep + Cooking Time: 15 Minutes | **Servings:** 4)

Ingredients:

- 1 ¼ cups cheddar; shredded.
- 6-ounce canned tiny shrimp; drained
- 3 tablespoon mayonnaise
- 2 tablespoon green onions; chopped
- 4 whole wheat bread slices
- 2 tablespoon butter; soft

Directions:

1. In a bowl; mix shrimp with cheese, green onion and mayo and stir well
2. Spread this on half of the bread slices; top with the other bread slices, cut into halves diagonally and spread butter on top.
3. Place sandwiches in your air fryer and cook at 350°F, for 5 minutes. Divide shrimp sandwiches on plates and serve them for breakfast

Broccoli Quiches

(Prep + Cooking Time: 30 Minutes | **Servings:** 2)

Ingredients:

- 1 broccoli head; florets separated and steamed
- 3 carrots; chopped and steamed
- 2-ounce cheddar cheese; grated
- 2-ounce milk
- 1 teaspoon parsley; chopped
- 1 tomato; chopped
- 1 teaspoon thyme; chopped
- 2 eggs
- Salt and black pepper to the taste

Directions:

1. In a bowl; mix eggs with milk, parsley, thyme, salt and pepper and whisk well
2. Put broccoli, carrots and tomato in your air fryer.
3. Add eggs mix on top, spread cheddar cheese; cover and cook at 350°F, for 20 minutes. Divide among plates and serve for breakfast

Spinach Parcels

(Prep + Cooking Time: 14 Minutes | **Servings:** 2)

Ingredients:

- 1-pound baby spinach leaves; roughly chopped
- 4 sheets filo pastry
- 2 tablespoon pine nuts
- 1 eggs; whisked
- 1/2-pound ricotta cheese
- Zest from 1 lemon; grated
- Greek yogurt for serving
- Salt and black pepper to the taste

Directions:

1. In a bowl; mix spinach with cheese, egg, lemon zest, salt, pepper and pine nuts and stir
2. Arrange filo sheets on a working surface, divide spinach mix; fold diagonally to shape your parcels and place them in your preheated air fryer at 400 degrees F. Bake parcels for 4 minutes; divide them on plates and serve them with Greek yogurt on the side

Yummy Ham Rolls

(Prep + Cooking Time: 20 Minutes | Servings: 4)

Ingredients:
- 1 sheet puff pastry
- 8 ham slices; chopped
- 4 handful gruyere cheese; grated
- 4 teaspoon mustard

Directions:
1. Roll out puff pastry on a working surface, divide cheese, ham and mustard, roll tight and cut into medium rounds.
2. Place all rolls in air fryer and cook for 10 minutes at 370 degrees F. Divide rolls on plates and serve for breakfast

Breakfast Burger

(Prep + Cooking Time: 55 Minutes | Servings: 4)

Ingredients:
- 1-pound beef; ground
- 1 yellow onion; chopped
- 1 teaspoon tomato puree
- 1 teaspoon garlic; minced
- 1 teaspoon mustard
- 1 teaspoon basil; dried
- 1 tablespoon cheddar cheese; grated
- 1 teaspoon parsley; chopped
- Salt and black pepper to the taste
- 4 bread buns; for serving

Directions:
1. In a bowl; mix beef with onion, tomato puree, garlic, mustard, basil, parsley, cheese, salt and pepper; stir well and shape 4 burgers out of this mix
2. Heat up your air fryer at 400 degrees F; add burgers and cook them for 25 minutes.
3. Reduce temperature to 350°F and bake burgers for 20 minutes more. Arrange them on bread buns and serve for a quick breakfast.

Special Long Beans Omelet

(Prep + Cooking Time: 20 Minutes | Servings: 3)

Ingredients:
- 4 long beans; trimmed and sliced
- 1 tablespoon olive oil
- 3 eggs; whisked
- 4 garlic cloves; minced
- 1/2 teaspoon soy sauce
- A pinch of salt and black pepper

Directions:
1. In a bowl; mix eggs with a pinch of salt, black pepper and soy sauce and whisk well.
2. Heat up your air fryer at 320 degrees F; add oil and garlic, stir and brown for 1 minute.
3. Add long beans and eggs mix; spread and cook for 10 minutes. Divide omelet on plates and serve for breakfast

Healthy Asparagus Frittata

(Prep + Cooking Time: 15 Minutes | Servings: 2)

Ingredients:
- 4 eggs; whisked
- 4 tablespoon milk
- 10 asparagus tips; steamed
- 2 tablespoon parmesan; grated
- Salt and black pepper to the taste
- Cooking spray

Directions:
1. In a bowl; mix eggs with parmesan, milk, salt and pepper and whisk well
2. Heat up your air fryer at 400°F and grease with cooking spray.
3. Add asparagus, add eggs mix; toss a bit and cook for 5 minutes. Divide frittata on plates and serve for breakfast

Walnuts Pear Oatmeal

(Prep + Cooking Time: 17 Minutes | **Servings:** 4)

Ingredients:
- 1 tablespoon butter; soft
- 1/2 teaspoon cinnamon powder
- 1 cup rolled oats
- 1/2 cup walnuts; chopped
- 1/4 cups brown sugar
- 1 cup water
- 1/2 cup raisins
- 2 cups pear; peeled and chopped.

Directions:
1. In a heat proof dish that fits your air fryer; mix milk with sugar, butter, oats, cinnamon, raisins, pears and walnuts; stir, introduce in your fryer and cook at 360°F, for 12 minutes. Divide into bowls and serve

Breakfast Soufflé

(Prep + Cooking Time: 18 Minutes | **Servings:** 4)

Ingredients:
- 4 eggs; whisked
- 2 tablespoon chives; chopped
- 4 tablespoon heavy cream
- 2 tablespoon parsley; chopped
- A pinch of red chili pepper; crushed
- Salt and black pepper to the taste

Directions:
1. In a bowl; mix eggs with salt, pepper, heavy cream, red chili pepper, parsley and chives; stir well and divide into 4 soufflé dishes
2. Arrange dishes in your air fryer and cook soufflés at 350°F, for 8 minutes. Serve them hot

Delicious Doughnuts

(Prep + Cooking Time: 28 Minutes | **Servings:** 6)

Ingredients:
- 1/2 cup sugar
- 2 ¼ cups white flour
- 1 teaspoon cinnamon powder
- 2 egg yolks
- 1/3 cup caster sugar
- 4 tablespoon butter; soft
- 1 ½ teaspoon baking powder
- 1/2 cup sour cream

Directions:
1. In a bowl; mix 2 tablespoon butter with simple sugar and egg yolks and whisk well
2. Add half of the sour cream and stir.
3. In another bowls; mix flour with baking powder, stir and also add to eggs mix
4. Stir well until you obtain a dough, transfer it to a floured working surface; roll it out and cut big circles with smaller ones in the middle.
5. Brush doughnuts with the rest of the butter; heat up your air fryer at 360 degrees F; place doughnuts inside and cook them for 8 minutes
6. In a bowl; mix cinnamon with caster sugar and stir. Arrange doughnuts on plates and dip them in cinnamon and sugar before serving.

Cinnamon Toast

(**Prep + Cooking Time:** 15 Minutes | **Servings:** 6)

Ingredients:
- 1 stick butter; soft
- 1 ½ teaspoon vanilla extract
- 1 ½ teaspoon cinnamon powder
- 12 bread slices
- 1/2 cup sugar

Directions:
1. In a bowl; mix soft butter with sugar, vanilla and cinnamon and whisk well
2. Spread this on bread slices; place them in your air fryer and cook at 400°F, for 5 minutes; divide among plates and serve for breakfast

Special Corn Flakes Casserole

(**Prep + Cooking Time:** 18 Minutes | **Servings:** 5)

Ingredients:
- 1/3 cup milk
- 1/4 cup blueberries
- 1 ½ cups corn flakes; crumbled
- 3 teaspoon sugar
- 4 tablespoon cream cheese; whipped
- 1/4 teaspoon nutmeg; ground
- 2 eggs; whisked
- 5 bread slices

Directions:
1. In a bowl; mix eggs with sugar, nutmeg and milk and whisk well
2. In another bowl; mix cream cheese with blueberries and whisk well
3. Put corn flakes in a third bowl.
4. Spread blueberry mix on each bread slice; then dip in eggs mix and dredge in corn flakes at the end.
5. Place bread in your air fryer's basket; heat up at 400°F and bake for 8 minutes. Divide among plates and serve for breakfast

Breakfast Shrimp Frittata

(**Prep + Cooking Time:** 25 Minutes | **Servings:** 4)

Ingredients:
- 4 eggs
- 1/2 teaspoon basil; dried
- 1/2 cup rice; cooked
- 1/2 cup shrimp; cooked, peeled, deveined and chopped
- 1/2 cup baby spinach; chopped
- 1/2 cup Monterey jack cheese; grated
- Cooking spray
- Salt and black pepper to the taste

Directions:
1. In a bowl; mix eggs with salt, pepper and basil and whisk.
2. Grease your air fryer's pan with cooking spray and add rice, shrimp and spinach
3. Add eggs mix, sprinkle cheese all over and cook in your air fryer at 350°F, for 10 minutes. Divide among plates and serve for breakfast

Mushrooms and Tofu

(Prep + Cooking Time: 20 Minutes **| Servings:** 2)

Ingredients:
- 1 tofu block; pressed and cut into medium pieces
- 1/2 tablespoon flour
- 1 egg
- 1 cup panko bread crumbs
- 1 tablespoon mushrooms; minced
- Salt and black pepper to the taste

Directions:
1. In a bowl; mix egg with mushrooms, flour, salt and pepper and whisk well
2. Dip tofu pieces in egg mix; then dredge them in panko bread crumbs; place them in your air fryer and cook at 350°F, for 10 minutes. Serve them for breakfast right away

Espresso Oatmeal

(Prep + Cooking Time: 27 Minutes **| Servings:** 4)

Ingredients:
- 1 cup steel cut oats
- 1 teaspoon espresso powder
- 2 teaspoon vanilla extract
- 2 ½ cups water
- 1 cup milk
- 2 tablespoon sugar

Directions:
1. In a pan that fits your air fryer, mix oats with water, sugar, milk and espresso powder; stir, introduce in your air fryer and cook at 360°F, for 17 minutes
2. Add vanilla extract, stir; leave everything aside for 5 minutes; divide into bowls and serve for breakfast

Tasty Artichoke Frittata

(Prep + Cooking Time: 25 Minutes **| Servings:** 6)

Ingredients:
- 3 canned artichokes hearts; drained and chopped
- 1/2 teaspoon oregano; dried
- 6 eggs; whisked
- 2 tablespoon olive oil
- Salt and black pepper to the taste

Directions:
1. In a bowl; mix artichokes with oregano, salt, pepper and eggs and whisk well
2. Add the oil to your air fryer's pan; add eggs mix and cook at 320°F, for 15 minutes. Divide frittata on plates and serve for breakfast

Bread Pudding

(Prep + Cooking Time: 32 Minutes **| Servings:** 4)

Ingredients:
- 1/2-pound white bread; cubed
- 3/4 cup milk
- 2 teaspoon cornstarch
- 1/2 cup apple; peeled; cored and roughly chopped.
- 5 tablespoon honey
- 3/4 cup water
- 2 teaspoon cinnamon powder
- 1 ⅓ cup flour
- 3/5 cup brown sugar
- 1 teaspoon vanilla extract
- 3-ounce soft butter

Directions:
1. In a bowl; mix bread with apple, milk with water, honey, cinnamon, vanilla and cornstarch and whisk well.
2. In a separate bowl; mix flour with sugar and butter and stir until you obtain a crumbled mixture
3. Press half of the crumble mix on the bottom of your air fryer; add bread and apple mix, add the rest of the crumble and cook everything at 350°F, for 22 minutes. Divide bread pudding on plates and serve

Dates Millet Pudding

(Prep + Cooking Time: 25 Minutes | **Servings:** 4)

Ingredients:
- 14-ounce milk
- 4 dates; pitted
- 2/3 cup millet
- 7-ounce water
- Honey for serving

Directions:
1. Put the millet in a pan that fits your air fryer; add dates, milk and water; stir, introduce in your air fryer and cook at 360°F, for 15 minutes. Divide among plates; drizzle honey on top and serve for breakfast

Pea Tortilla

(Prep + Cooking Time: 17 Minutes | **Servings:** 8)

Ingredients:
- 8 eggs
- 1/2-pound baby peas
- 1 ½ cup yogurt
- 1/2 cup mint; chopped
- 4 tablespoon butter
- Salt and black pepper to the taste

Directions:
1. Heat up a pan that fits your air fryer with the butter over medium heat, add peas; stir and cook for a couple of minutes
2. Meanwhile; in a bowl, mix half of the yogurt with salt, pepper, eggs and mint and whisk well
3. Pour this over the peas, toss, introduce in your air fryer and cook at 350°F, for 7 minutes. Spread the rest of the yogurt over your tortilla; slice and serve.

Breakfast Spanish Omelet

(Prep + Cooking Time: 20 Minutes | **Servings:** 4)

Ingredients:
- 3 eggs
- 1/2 chorizo; chopped
- 1 potato; peeled and cubed
- 1/2 cup corn
- 1 tablespoon olive oil
- 1 tablespoon parsley; chopped
- 1 tablespoon feta cheese; crumbled
- Salt and black pepper to the taste

Directions:
1. Heat up your air fryer at 350°F and add oil
2. Add chorizo and potatoes; stir and brown them for a few seconds.
3. In a bowl; mix eggs with corn, parsley, cheese, salt and pepper and whisk
4. Pour this over chorizo and potatoes; spread and cook for 5 minutes. Divide omelet on plates and serve for breakfast

Mushroom Quiches

(Prep + Cooking Time: 20 Minutes | **Servings:** 4)

Ingredients:

- 2 button mushrooms; chopped
- 2 tablespoon ham; chopped
- 1/2 teaspoon thyme; dried
- 1/4 cup Swiss cheese; grated
- 1 small yellow onion; chopped.
- 1/3 cup heavy cream
- 3 eggs
- 1 tablespoon flour
- 1 tablespoon butter; soft
- 9-inch pie dough
- A pinch of nutmeg; ground
- Salt and black pepper to the taste

Directions:

1. Dust a working surface with the flour and roll the pie dough
2. Press in on the bottom of the pie pan your air fryer has
3. In a bowl; mix butter with mushrooms, ham, onion, eggs, heavy cream, salt, pepper, thyme and nutmeg and whisk well.
4. Add this over pie crust, spread, sprinkle Swiss cheese all over and place pie pan in your air fryer.
5. Cook your quiche at 400°F, for 10 minutes. Slice and serve for breakfast

Mushroom Oatmeal Breakfast

(Prep + Cooking Time: 30 Minutes | **Servings:** 4)

Ingredients:

- 1 small yellow onion; chopped
- 1 cup steel cut oats
- 2 garlic cloves; minced
- 2 tablespoon butter
- 1/2 cup water
- 14-ounce canned chicken stock
- 3 thyme springs; chopped
- 2 tablespoon extra-virgin olive oil
- 1/2 cup gouda cheese; grated
- 8-ounce mushroom; sliced
- Salt and black pepper to the taste

Directions:

1. Heat up a pan that fits your air fryer with the butter over medium heat, add onions and garlic; stir and cook for 4 minutes
2. Add oats, water, salt, pepper, stock and thyme; stir, introduce in your air fryer and cook at 360°F, for 16 minutes. Meanwhile; heat up a pan with the olive oil over medium heat, add mushrooms, cook them for 3 minutes; add to oatmeal and cheese; stir, divide into bowls and serve for breakfast

Easy Onion Frittata

(Prep + Cooking Time: 30 Minutes | **Servings:** 6)

Ingredients:

- 10 eggs; whisked
- 1/2 cup sour cream
- 2 yellow onions; chopped
- 1 tablespoon olive oil
- 1-pound small potatoes; chopped
- 1-ounce cheddar cheese; grated
- Salt and black pepper to the taste

Directions:

1. In a large bowl; mix eggs with potatoes, onions, salt, pepper, cheese and sour cream and whisk well.
2. Grease your air fryer's pan with the oil, add eggs mix; place in air fryer and cook for 20 minutes at 320 degrees F. Slice frittata, divide among plates and serve for breakfast

French Beans and Egg Mix

(Prep + Cooking Time: 20 Minutes | **Servings:** 3)

Ingredients:

- 3-ounce French beans; trimmed and sliced diagonally
- 2 eggs; whisked
- 1 tablespoon olive oil
- 4 garlic cloves; minced
- 1/2 teaspoon soy sauce
- Salt and white pepper to the taste

Directions:

1. In a bowl; mix eggs with soy sauce, salt and pepper and whisk well
2. Heat up your air fryer at 320 degrees F; add oil and heat it up as well
3. Add garlic and brown for 1 minute.
4. Add French beans and egg mix; toss and cook for 10 minutes. Divide among plates and serve for breakfast.

Smoked Fried Tofu

(Prep + Cooking Time: 22 Minutes | **Servings:** 2)

Ingredients:

- 1 tofu block; pressed and cubed
- 1/4 cup cornstarch
- 1 tablespoon smoked paprika
- Salt and black pepper to the taste
- Cooking spray

Directions:

1. Grease your air fryer's basket with cooking spray and heat the fryer at 370 degrees F
2. In a bowl; mix tofu with salt, pepper, smoked paprika and cornstarch and toss well.
3. Add tofu to you air fryer's basket and cook for 12 minutes shaking the fryer every 4 minutes. Divide into bowls and serve for breakfast

Lunch Recipes

Cheering Chicken Sandwiches

(Prep + Cooking Time: 20 Minutes | Servings: 4)

Ingredients:

- 2 chicken breasts; skinless, boneless and cubed
- 1/2 cup Italian seasoning
- 1 red bell pepper; sliced
- 2 cups butter lettuce; torn
- 4 pita pockets
- 1/2 teaspoon thyme; dried
- 1 red onion; chopped.
- 1 cup cherry tomatoes; halved
- 1 tablespoon olive oil

Directions:

1. In your air fryer, mix chicken with onion, bell pepper, Italian seasoning and oil; toss and cook at 380°F, for 10 minutes. Transfer chicken mix to a bowl; add thyme, butter lettuce and cherry tomatoes, toss well; stuff pita pockets with this mix and serve for lunch

Zucchini and Tuna Tortillas

(Prep + Cooking Time: 20 Minutes | Servings: 4)

Ingredients:

- 1 cup zucchini; shredded.
- 1/3 cup mayonnaise
- 4 corn tortillas
- 4 tablespoon butter; soft
- 6-ounce canned tuna; drained
- 2 tablespoon mustard
- 1 cup cheddar cheese; grated

Directions:

1. Spread butter on tortillas; place them in your air fryer's basket and cook them at 400°F, for 3 minutes.
2. Meanwhile; in a bowl, mix tuna with zucchini, mayo and mustard and stir
3. Divide this mix on each tortilla, top with cheese, roll tortillas; place them in your air fryer's basket again and cook them at 400°F, for 4 minutes more. Serve for lunch

Turkish Style Koftas

(Prep + Cooking Time: 25 Minutes | Servings: 2)

Ingredients:

- 2 tablespoon feta cheese; crumbled
- 1/2-pound lean beef; minced
- 1 tablespoon cumin; ground
- 1 tablespoon mint; chopped
- 1 leek; chopped
- 1 tablespoon parsley; chopped
- 1 teaspoon garlic; minced
- Salt and black pepper to the taste

Directions:

1. In a bowl; mix beef with leek, cheese, cumin, mint, parsley, garlic, salt and pepper; stir well, shape your koftas and place them on sticks
2. Add koftas to your preheated air fryer at 360°F and cook them for 15 minutes. Serve them with a side salad for lunch

Dill and Scallops

(Prep + Cooking Time: 15 Minutes | **Servings:** 4)

Ingredients:
- 1-pound sea scallops; debearded
- 1 tablespoon lemon juice
- 1 teaspoon dill; chopped
- 2 teaspoon olive oil
- Salt and black pepper to the taste

Directions:
1. In your air fryer, mix scallops with dill, oil, salt, pepper and lemon juice; cover and cook at 360°F, for 5 minutes. Discard unopened ones, divide scallops and dill sauce on plates and serve for lunch

Egg Rolls

(Prep + Cooking Time: 25 Minutes | **Servings:** 4)

Ingredients:
- 1/2 cup mushrooms; chopped.
- 1/2 cup carrots; grated
- 1 eggs; whisked
- 2 green onions; chopped
- 2 tablespoon soy sauce
- 1/2 cup zucchini; grated
- 8 egg roll wrappers
- 1 tablespoon cornstarch

Directions:
1. In a bowl; mix carrots with mushrooms, zucchini, green onions and soy sauce and stir well
2. Arrange egg roll wrappers on a working surface; divide veggie mix on each and roll well
3. In a bowl; mix cornstarch with egg, whisk well and brush eggs rolls with this mix.
4. Seal edges, place all rolls in your preheated air fryer and cook them at 370°F, for 15 minutes. Arrange them on a platter and serve them for lunch

Fish and Kettle Chips

(Prep + Cooking Time: 22 Minutes | **Servings:** 2)

Ingredients:
- 2 medium cod fillets; skinless and boneless
- 3 cups kettle chips; cooked
- 1/4 cup buttermilk
- Salt and black pepper to the taste

Directions:
1. In a bowl mix fish with salt, pepper and buttermilk; toss and leave aside for 5 minutes
2. Put chips in your food processor, crush them and spread them on a plate.
3. Add fish and press well on all sides.
4. Transfer fish to your air fryer's basket and cook at 400°F, for 12 minutes. Serve hot for lunch

Succulent Turkey Cakes

(Prep + Cooking Time: 20 Minutes | **Servings:** 4)

Ingredients:
- 6 mushrooms; chopped
- 1 teaspoon garlic powder
- 1 teaspoon onion powder
- 1 ¼-pound turkey meat; ground
- Tomato sauce for serving
- Cooking spray
- Salt and black pepper to the taste

Directions:
1. In your blender, mix mushrooms with salt and pepper, pulse well and transfer to a bowl
2. Add turkey, onion powder, garlic powder, salt and pepper; stir and shape cakes out of this mix.
3. Spray them with cooking spray; transfer them to your air fryer and cook at 320°F, for 10 minutes. Serve them with tomato sauce on the side and a tasty side salad

Beef Meatballs

(Prep + Cooking Time: 25 Minutes | **Servings:** 4)

Ingredients:

- 1/2-pound Italian sausage; chopped.
- 1/2 cup cheddar cheese; grated
- 1/2-pound beef; ground
- 1/2 teaspoon garlic powder
- 1/2 teaspoon onion powder
- Mashed potatoes for serving
- Salt and black pepper to the taste

Directions:

1. In a bowl; mix beef with sausage, garlic powder, onion powder, salt, pepper and cheese; stir well and shape 16 meatballs out of this mix
2. Place meatballs in your air fryer and cook them at 370°F, for 15 minutes. Serve your meatballs with some mashed potatoes on the side

Special Prosciutto Sandwich

(Prep + Cooking Time: 15 Minutes | **Servings:** 1)

Ingredients:

- 2 bread slices
- 2 mozzarella slices
- 2 tomato slices
- 2 prosciutto slices
- 2 basil leaves
- 1 teaspoon olive oil
- A pinch of salt and black pepper

Directions:

1. Arrange mozzarella and prosciutto on a bread slice
2. Season with salt and pepper; place in your air fryer and cook at 400°F, for 5 minutes. Drizzle oil over prosciutto, add tomato and basil; cover with the other bread slice, cut sandwich in half and serve

Cheese and Macaroni

(Prep + Cooking Time: 40 Minutes | **Servings:** 3)

Ingredients:

- 1 ½ cups favorite macaroni
- 1 cup chicken stock
- 3/4 cup cheddar cheese; shredded.
- 1/2 cup heavy cream
- 1/2 cup mozzarella cheese; shredded.
- 1/4 cup parmesan; shredded.
- Salt and black pepper to the taste
- Cooking spray

Directions:

1. Spray a pan with cooking spray; add macaroni, heavy cream, stock, cheddar cheese, mozzarella and parmesan but also salt and pepper; toss well, place pan in your air fryer's basket and cook for 30 minutes. Divide among plates and serve for lunch

Delicious Fajitas

(Prep + Cooking Time: 20 Minutes | **Servings:** 4)

Ingredients:

- 1-pound chicken breasts; cut into strips
- 1 teaspoon garlic powder
- 1/4 teaspoon cumin; ground
- 4 tortillas; warmed up
- 1 tablespoon lime juice
- 1/2 teaspoon chili powder
- 1 green bell pepper; sliced
- 1 yellow onion; chopped
- 1/4 teaspoon coriander; ground
- 1 red bell pepper; sliced
- Salt and black pepper to the taste
- Cooking spray
- 1 cup lettuce leaves; torn for serving
- Salsa for serving
- Sour cream for serving

Directions:

1. In a bowl; mix chicken with garlic powder, cumin, chili, salt, pepper, coriander, lime juice, red bell pepper, green bell pepper and onion; toss, leave aside for 10 minutes, transfer to your air fryer and drizzle some cooking spray all over
2. Toss and cook at 400°F, for 10 minutes. Arrange tortillas on a working surface, divide chicken mix, also add salsa, sour cream and lettuce; wrap and serve for lunch

Fried Thai Salad

(Prep + Cooking Time: 15 Minutes | **Servings:** 4)

Ingredients:

- 12 big shrimp; cooked, peeled and deveined
- 1 cup carrots; grated
- 2 teaspoon red curry paste
- 1 cup red cabbage; shredded.
- A handful cilantro; chopped
- 1 small cucumber; chopped.
- Juice from 1 lime
- A pinch of salt and black pepper

Directions:

1. In a pan, mix cabbage with carrots, cucumber and shrimp; toss, introduce in your air fryer and cook at 360°F, for 5 minutes. Add salt, pepper, cilantro, lime juice and red curry paste; toss again, divide among plates and serve right away

Tasty Turkey Burgers

(Prep + Cooking Time: 18 Minutes | **Servings:** 4)

Ingredients:

- 1-pound turkey meat; ground
- 1 shallot; minced
- 1 teaspoon cumin; ground
- 1 teaspoon sweet paprika
- A drizzle of olive oil
- 1 small jalapeno pepper; minced
- 2 teaspoon lime juice
- Zest from 1 lime; grated
- Salt and black pepper to the taste
- Guacamole for serving

Directions:

1. In a bowl; mix turkey meat with salt, pepper, cumin, paprika, shallot, jalapeno, lime juice and zest; stir well, shape burgers from this mix, drizzle the oil over them; introduce in preheated air fryer and cook them at 370°F, for 8 minutes on each side. Divide among plates and serve with guacamole on top

Italian Style Eggplant Sandwich

(Prep + Cooking Time: 26 Minutes | Servings: 4)

Ingredients:

- 1 eggplant; sliced
- 2 teaspoon parsley; dried
- 1/2 cup breadcrumbs
- 1/2 cup mayonnaise
- 3/4 cup tomato sauce
- 2 cups mozzarella cheese; grated
- 1/2 teaspoon Italian seasoning
- 1/2 teaspoon garlic powder
- 1/2 teaspoon onion powder
- 2 tablespoon milk
- 4 bread slices
- Cooking spray
- Salt and black pepper to the taste

Directions:

1. Season eggplant slices with salt and pepper, leave aside for 10 minutes and then pat dry them well.
2. In a bowl; mix parsley with breadcrumbs, Italian seasoning, onion and garlic powder, salt and black pepper and stir
3. In another bowl; mix milk with mayo and whisk well
4. Brush eggplant slices with mayo mix, dip them in breadcrumbs, place them in your air fryer's basket, spray with cooking oil and cook them at 400°F, for 15 minutes; flipping them after 8 minutes.
5. Brush each bread slice with olive oil and arrange 2 on a working surface
6. Add mozzarella and parmesan on each, add baked eggplant slices; spread tomato sauce and basil and top with the other bread slices, greased side down. Divide sandwiches on plates; cut them in halves and serve for lunch.

Special Pancake

(Prep + Cooking Time: 20 Minutes | Servings: 2)

Ingredients:

- 1 cup small shrimp; peeled and deveined
- 1/2 cup flour
- 1/2 cup milk
- 1 tablespoon butter
- 3 eggs; whisked
- 1 cup salsa

Directions:

1. Preheat your air fryer at 400 degrees F; add fryer's pan, add 1 tablespoon butter and melt it
2. In a bowl; mix eggs with flour and milk, whisk well and pour into air fryer's pan, spread, cook at 350 degrees for 12 minutes and transfer to a plate. In a bowl; mix shrimp with salsa; stir and serve your pancake with this on the side

Stuffed Portobello Mushrooms

(Prep + Cooking Time: 30 Minutes | Servings: 4)

Ingredients:

- 4 big Portobello mushroom caps
- 1 tablespoon olive oil
- 1/4 cup ricotta cheese
- 5 tablespoon parmesan; grated
- 1/3 cup bread crumbs
- 1/4 teaspoon rosemary; chopped
- 1 cup spinach; torn

Directions:

1. Rub mushrooms caps with the oil; place them in your air fryer's basket and cook them at 350°F, for 2 minutes
2. Meanwhile; in a bowl, mix half of the parmesan with ricotta, spinach, rosemary and bread crumbs and stir well.
3. Stuff mushrooms with this mix; sprinkle the rest of the parmesan on top; place them in your air fryer's basket again and cook at 350°F, for 10 minutes. Divide them on plates and serve with a side salad for lunch

Steak and Cabbage

(Prep + Cooking Time: 20 Minutes | **Servings:** 4)

Ingredients:
- 1/2-pound sirloin steak; cut into strips
- 2 green onions; chopped
- 1 tablespoon peanut oil
- 2 cups green cabbage; chopped
- 1 yellow bell pepper; chopped
- 2 garlic cloves; minced
- 2 teaspoon cornstarch
- Salt and black pepper to the taste

Directions:
1. In a bowl; mix cabbage with salt, pepper and peanut oil; toss, transfer to air fryer's basket, cook at 370°F, for 4 minutes and transfer to a bowl
2. Add steak strips to your air fryer; also add green onions, bell pepper, garlic, salt and pepper, toss and cook for 5 minutes. Add over cabbage; toss, divide among plates and serve for lunch

Cheesy Ravioli and Marinara Sauce

(Prep + Cooking Time: 18 Minutes | **Servings:** 6)

Ingredients:
- 20-ounce cheese ravioli
- 1 tablespoon olive oil
- 1 cup buttermilk
- 10-ounce marinara sauce
- 1/4 cup parmesan; grated
- 2 cups bread crumbs

Directions:
1. Put buttermilk in a bowl and breadcrumbs in another bowl
2. Dip ravioli in buttermilk, then in breadcrumbs and place them in your air fryer on a baking sheet. Drizzle olive oil over them; cook at 400°F, for 5 minutes; divide them on plates, sprinkle parmesan on top and serve for lunch.

Asian Chicken

(Prep + Cooking Time: 40 Minutes | **Servings:** 4)

Ingredients:
- 2 chicken breasts; skinless, boneless and sliced
- 14-ounce pizza dough
- 1 ½ cups cheddar cheese; grated
- 1/2 cup jarred cheese sauce
- 1 teaspoon olive oil
- 1 yellow onion; sliced
- 1 tablespoon Worcestershire sauce
- Salt and black pepper to the taste

Directions:
1. Preheat your air fryer at 400 degrees F; add half of the oil and onions and fry them for 8 minutes, stirring once
2. Add chicken pieces, Worcestershire sauce, salt and pepper; toss, air fry for 8 minutes more, stirring once and transfer everything to a bowl
3. Roll pizza dough on a working surface and shape a rectangle.
4. Spread half of the cheese all over, add chicken and onion mix and top with cheese sauce
5. Roll your dough and shape into a "U"
6. Place your roll in your air fryer's basket, brush with the rest of the oil and cook at 370 degrees for 12 minutes, flipping the roll halfway. Slice your roll when it's warm and serve for lunch.

Summer Squash Fritters

(Prep + Cooking Time: 17 Minutes | **Servings:** 4)

Ingredients:

- 3-ounce cream cheese
- 1 egg; whisked
- 1 yellow summer squash; grated
- 2 tablespoon olive oil
- 1/2 teaspoon oregano; dried
- 1/3 cup carrot; grated
- 2/3 cup bread crumbs
- A pinch of salt and black pepper

Directions:

1. In a bowl; mix cream cheese with salt, pepper, oregano, egg, breadcrumbs, carrot and squash and stir well
2. Shape medium patties out of this mix and brush them with the oil.
3. Place squash patties in your air fryer and cook them at 400°F, for 7 minutes. Serve them for lunch

Chicken Pie Recipe

(Prep + Cooking Time: 29 Minutes | **Servings:** 4)

Ingredients:

- 2 chicken thighs; boneless, skinless and cubed
- 1 carrot; chopped
- 1 teaspoon Worcestershire sauce
- 1 tablespoon butter; melted
- 1 yellow onion; chopped
- 2 potatoes; chopped
- 2 mushrooms; chopped
- 1 teaspoon soy sauce
- 1 tablespoon flour
- 1 tablespoon milk
- 2 puff pastry sheets
- Salt and black pepper to the taste
- 1 teaspoon Italian seasoning
- 1/2 teaspoon garlic powder

Directions:

1. Heat up a pan over medium high heat, add potatoes, carrots and onion; stir and cook for 2 minutes.
2. Add chicken and mushrooms, salt, soy sauce, pepper, Italian seasoning, garlic powder, Worcestershire sauce, flour and milk; stir really well and take off heat
3. Place 1 puff pastry sheet on the bottom of your air fryer's pan and trim edge excess.
4. Add chicken mix, top with the other puff pastry sheet; trim excess as well and brush pie with butter.
5. Place in your air fryer and cook at 360°F, for 6 minutes. Leave pie to cool down; slice and serve for breakfast

Fresh Style Chicken

(Prep + Cooking Time: 32 Minutes | **Servings:** 4)

Ingredients:

- 2 chicken breasts; skinless, boneless and cubed
- 8 button mushrooms; sliced
- 1 red bell pepper; chopped
- 1 tablespoon olive oil
- 6 bread slices
- 1/2 teaspoon thyme; dried
- 10-ounce alfredo sauce
- 2 tablespoon butter; soft

Directions:

1. In your air fryer, mix chicken with mushrooms, bell pepper and oil; toss to coat well and cook at 350°F, for 15 minutes
2. Transfer chicken mix to a bowl; add thyme and alfredo sauce, toss, return to air fryer and cook at 350°F, for 4 minutes more.
3. Spread butter on bread slices; add it to the fryer, butter side up and cook for 4 minutes more. Arrange toasted bread slices on a platter; top each with chicken mix and serve for lunch

Chicken Wings

(Prep + Cooking Time: 55 Minutes **| Servings:** 4)

Ingredients:
- 3-pound chicken wings
- 1/2 cup butter
- 1 tablespoon old bay seasoning
- 3/4 cup potato starch
- 1 teaspoon lemon juice
- Lemon wedges for serving

Directions:
1. In a bowl; mix starch with old bay seasoning and chicken wings and toss well.
2. Place chicken wings in your air fryer's basket and cook them at 360°F, for 35 minutes shaking the fryer from time to time
3. Increase temperature to 400 degrees F; cook chicken wings for 10 minutes more and divide them on plates.
4. Heat up a pan over medium heat; add butter and melt it.
5. Add lemon juice; stir well, take off heat and drizzle over chicken wings. Serve them for lunch with lemon wedges on the side

Japanese Style Chicken

(Prep + Cooking Time: 18 Minutes **| Servings:** 2)

Ingredients:
- 2 chicken thighs; skinless and boneless
- 1/8 cup sake
- 3 garlic cloves; minced
- 1/4 cup soy sauce
- 1/4 cup mirin
- 2 tablespoon sugar
- 1/2 teaspoon sesame oil
- 1/8 cup water
- 2 ginger slices; chopped
- 1 tablespoon cornstarch mixed with 2 tablespoon water
- Sesame seeds for serving

Directions:
1. In a bowl; mix chicken thighs with ginger, garlic, soy sauce, mirin, sake, oil, water, sugar and cornstarch; toss well, transfer to preheated air fryer and cook at 360°F, for 8 minutes. Divide among plates; sprinkle sesame seeds on top and serve with a side salad for lunch

Chicken Zucchini Lunch

(Prep + Cooking Time: 30 Minutes **| Servings:** 4)

Ingredients:
- 1-pound chicken breasts; skinless, boneless and cubed
- 4 zucchinis; cut with a spiralizer
- 1 teaspoon olive oil

For the pesto:
- 2 cups kale; chopped
- 1 tablespoon lemon juice
- 2 cups basil
- 3/4 cup pine nuts

- 2 cups cherry tomatoes; halved
- 1/2 cup almonds; chopped
- 2 garlic cloves; minced
- Salt and black pepper to the taste

- 1/2 cup olive oil
- 1 garlic clove
- A pinch of salt

Directions:
1. In your food processor, mix basil with kale, lemon juice, garlic, pine nuts, oil and a pinch of salt, pulse really well and leave aside
2. Heat up a pan that fits your air fryer with the oil over medium heat, add garlic; stir and cook for 1 minute.
3. Add chicken, salt, pepper, stir, almonds, zucchini noodles, garlic, cherry tomatoes and the pesto you've made at the beginning, stir gently; introduce in preheated air fryer and cook at 360°F, for 17 minutes. Divide among plates and serve for lunch

Beef Cubes

(Prep + Cooking Time: 22 Minutes | **Servings:** 4)

Ingredients:

- 1-pound sirloin; cubed
- 1/2 teaspoon marjoram; dried
- 2 tablespoon olive oil
- 16-ounce jarred pasta sauce
- 1 ½ cups bread crumbs
- White rice; already cooked for serving

Directions:

1. In a bowl; mix beef cubes with pasta sauce and toss well
2. In another bowl; mix bread crumbs with marjoram and oil and stir well.
3. Dip beef cubes in this mix, place them in your air fryer and cook at 360°F, for 12 minutes. Divide among plates and serve with white rice on the side

Shrimp Croquettes

(Prep + Cooking Time: 18 Minutes | **Servings:** 4)

Ingredients:

- 2/3-pound shrimp; cooked; peeled; deveined and chopped.
- 1 ½ cups bread crumbs
- 3 green onions; chopped
- 1/2 teaspoon basil; dried
- 1 egg; whisked
- 2 tablespoon olive oil
- 2 tablespoon lemon juice
- Salt and black pepper to the taste

Directions:

1. In a bowl; mix half of the bread crumbs with egg and lemon juice and stir well
2. Add green onions, basil, salt, pepper and shrimp and stir really well.
3. In a separate bowl; mix the rest of the bread crumbs with the oil and toss well.
4. Shape round balls out of shrimp mix, dredge them in bread crumbs; place them in preheated air fryer and cook the for 8 minutes at 400 degrees F. Serve them with a dip for lunch

Different Pasta Salad

(Prep + Cooking Time: 22 Minutes | **Servings:** 6)

Ingredients:

- 1 zucchini; sliced in half and roughly chopped.
- 1/2 cup kalamata olive; pitted and halved
- 1 red onion; roughly chopped
- 4-ounce brown mushrooms; halved
- 1 teaspoon Italian seasoning
- 1/4 cup olive oil
- 1 orange bell pepper; roughly chopped.
- 1 green bell pepper; roughly chopped
- 1-pound penne rigate; already cooked
- 1 cup cherry tomatoes; halved
- 3 tablespoon balsamic vinegar
- 2 tablespoon basil; chopped
- Salt and black pepper to the taste

Directions:

1. In a bowl; mix zucchini with mushrooms, orange bell pepper, green bell pepper, red onion, salt, pepper, Italian seasoning and oil; toss well, transfer to preheated air fryer at 380°F and cook them for 12 minutes.
2. In a large salad bowl; mix pasta with cooked veggies, cherry tomatoes, olives, vinegar and basil; toss and serve for lunch

Chicken Corn Casserole

(Prep + Cooking Time: 40 Minutes | **Servings:** 6)

Ingredients:
- 1 cup clean chicken stock
- 6-ounce canned coconut milk
- 3 cups corn
- 3 handfuls spinach
- 3 green onions; chopped
- 2 teaspoon garlic powder
- 1 ½ cups green lentils
- 2-pound chicken breasts; skinless, boneless and cubed
- 1/3 cup cilantro; chopped
- Salt and black pepper to the taste

Directions:
1. In a pan that fits your air fryer; mix stock with coconut milk, salt, pepper, garlic powder, chicken and lentils. Add corn, green onions, cilantro and spinach; stir well, introduce in your air fryer and cook at 350°F, for 30 minutes

Tasty Stuffed Meatballs

(Prep + Cooking Time: 20 Minutes | **Servings:** 4)

Ingredients:
- 1/3 cup bread crumbs
- 20 cheddar cheese cubes
- 1/2 teaspoon marjoram; dried
- 3 tablespoon milk
- 1 tablespoon ketchup
- 1 egg
- 1-pound lean beef; ground
- 1 tablespoon olive oil
- Salt and black pepper to the taste

Directions:
1. In a bowl; mix bread crumbs with ketchup, milk, marjoram, salt, pepper and egg and whisk well
2. Add beef; stir and shape 20 meatballs out of this mix.
3. Shape each meatball around a cheese cube, drizzle the oil over them and rub.
4. Place all meatballs in your preheated air fryer and cook at 390°F, for 10 minutes. Serve them for lunch with a side salad

Chicken and Coconut Casserole

(Prep + Cooking Time: 35 Minutes | **Servings:** 4)

Ingredients:
- 1-pound chicken breast; skinless, boneless and cut into thin strips
- 4 lime leaves; torn
- 1 cup veggie stock
- 4 Thai chilies; chopped.
- 4 tablespoon fish sauce
- 6-ounce coconut milk
- 1/4 cup lime juice
- 1 lemongrass stalk; chopped
- 1-inch piece; grated
- 8-ounce mushrooms; chopped
- 1/4 cup cilantro; chopped
- Salt and black pepper to the taste

Directions:
1. Put stock into a pan that fits your air fryer; bring to a simmer over medium heat, add lemongrass, ginger and lime leaves; stir and cook for 10 minutes
2. Strain soup, return to pan, add chicken, mushrooms, milk, chilies, fish sauce, lime juice, cilantro, salt and pepper; stir, introduce in your air fryer and cook at 360°F, for 15 minutes. Divide into bowls and serve

Tasty Hot Dogs

(Prep + Cooking Time: 17 Minutes | Servings: 2)

Ingredients:
- 2 hot dog buns
- 2 hot dogs
- 1 tablespoon Dijon mustard
- 2 tablespoon cheddar cheese; grated

Directions:
1. Put hot dogs in preheated air fryer and cook them at 390°F, for 5 minutes
2. Divide hot dogs into hot dog buns, spread mustard and cheese; return everything to your air fryer and cook for 2 minutes more at 390 degrees F. Serve for lunch

Sweet Potato Casserole

(Prep + Cooking Time: 60 Minutes | Servings: 6)

Ingredients:
- 3 big sweet potatoes; pricked with a fork
- 1/4 teaspoon nutmeg; ground
- 1/3 cup coconut cream
- 1 cup chicken stock
- Salt and black pepper to the taste
- A pinch of cayenne pepper

Directions:
1. Place sweet potatoes in your air fryer; cook them at 350°F, for 40 minutes; cool them down, peel, roughly chop and transfer to a pan that fits your air fryer.
2. Add stock, salt, pepper, cayenne and coconut cream; toss, introduce in your air fryer and cook at 360°F, for 10 minutes more. Divide casserole into bowls and serve

Chicken and Quinoa Casserole

(Prep + Cooking Time: 40 Minutes | Servings: 8)

Ingredients:
- 1 cup quinoa; already cooked
- 3 cups chicken breast; cooked and shredded.
- 2 teaspoon chili powder
- 2 teaspoon cumin; ground
- 6 kale leaves; chopped.
- 1/2 cup green onions; chopped
- 1 cup clean tomato sauce
- 1 cup clean salsa
- 1 tablespoon garlic powder
- 3 cups mozzarella cheese; shredded.
- 14-ounce canned black beans
- 12-ounce corn
- 1/2 cup cilantro; chopped.
- Cooking spray
- 2 jalapeno peppers; chopped

Directions:
1. Spray a baking dish that fits your air fryer with cooking spray, add quinoa, chicken, black beans, corn, cilantro, kale, green onions, tomato sauce, salsa, chili powder, cumin, garlic powder, jalapenos and mozzarella; toss, introduce in your fryer and cook at 350°F, for 17 minutes. Slice and serve warm for lunch

Delicious Lentils Fritters

(Prep + Cooking Time: 20 Minutes | **Servings:** 2)

Ingredients:

- 1 cup yellow lentils; soaked in water for 1 hour and drained
- 1 hot chili pepper; chopped.
- 1-inch ginger piece; grated
- 1/2 teaspoon turmeric powder
- 1/2 cup cilantro; chopped
- 1 ½ cup spinach; chopped
- 4 garlic cloves; minced
- 3/4 cup red onion; chopped
- 1 teaspoon garam masala
- 1 teaspoon baking powder
- 2 teaspoon olive oil
- 1/3 cup water
- Salt and black pepper to the taste
- Mint chutney for serving

Directions:

1. In your blender; mix lentils with chili pepper, ginger, turmeric, garam masala, baking powder, salt, pepper, olive oil, water, cilantro, spinach, onion and garlic, blend well and shape medium balls out of this mix
2. Place them all in your preheated air fryer at 400°F and cook for 10 minutes. Serve your veggie fritters with a side salad for lunch

Chicken Salad

(Prep + Cooking Time: 30 Minutes | **Servings:** 4)

Ingredients:

- 1-pound chicken tenders; boneless
- 2 ears of corn; hulled
- 12 cherry tomatoes; sliced
- 1/2 iceberg lettuce head; cut into medium strips
- 1/2 romaine lettuce head; cut into medium strips
- 1 cup canned black beans; drained
- 1 cup cheddar cheese; shredded.
- 1/4 cup ranch dressing
- 3 tablespoon BBQ sauce
- 1 teaspoon sweet paprika
- 1 tablespoon brown sugar
- 1/2 teaspoon garlic powder
- 3 tablespoon cilantro; chopped
- 4 green onions; chopped.
- Olive oil as needed
- Salt and black pepper to the taste

Directions:

1. Put corn in your air fryer; drizzle some oil, toss, cook at 400°F, for 10 minutes; transfer to a plate and leave aside for now
2. Put chicken in your air fryer's basket, add salt, pepper, brown sugar, paprika and garlic powder; toss, drizzle some more oil, cook at 400°F, for 10 minutes; flipping them halfway, transfer tenders to a cutting board and chop them
3. Cur kernels off the cob, transfer corn to a bowl; add chicken, iceberg lettuce, romaine lettuce, black beans, cheese, cilantro, tomatoes, onions, BBQ sauce and ranch dressing; toss well and serve for lunch.

Chinese Style Pork

(**Prep + Cooking Time:** 22 Minutes | **Servings:** 4)

Ingredients:

- 2-pound pork; cut into medium cubes
- 3 tablespoon canola oil
- 2 eggs
- 1 cup cornstarch
- 1 teaspoon sesame oil
- A pinch of Chinese five spice
- Sweet tomato sauce for serving
- Salt and black pepper to the taste

Directions:

1. In a bowl; mix five spice with salt, pepper and cornstarch and stir
2. In another bowl; mix eggs with sesame oil and whisk well
3. Dredge pork cubes in cornstarch mix; then dip in eggs mix and place them in your air fryer which you've greased with the canola oil.
4. Cook at 340°F, for 12 minutes; shaking the fryer once. Serve pork for lunch with the sweet tomato sauce on the side

Lunch Pizzas

(**Prep + Cooking Time:** 17 Minutes | **Servings:** 4)

Ingredients:

- 3/4 cup pizza sauce
- 2 green onions; chopped
- 1 tablespoon olive oil
- 4-ounce jarred mushrooms; sliced
- 1/2 teaspoon basil; dried
- 2 cup mozzarella; grated
- 4 pitas
- 1 cup grape tomatoes; sliced

Directions:

1. Spread pizza sauce on each pita bread; sprinkle green onions and basil, divide mushrooms and top with cheese.
2. Arrange pita pizzas in your air fryer and cook them at 400°F, for 7 minutes. Top each pizza with tomato slices; divide among plates and serve

Creamy Chicken Stew Recipe

(**Prep + Cooking Time:** 35 Minutes | **Servings:** 4)

Ingredients:

- 6 chicken tenders
- 1 ½ cups canned cream of celery soup
- 2 potatoes; chopped
- 1 bay leaf
- 1 thyme spring; chopped
- 1 tablespoon milk
- 1 egg yolk
- 1/2 cup heavy cream
- Salt and black pepper to the taste

Directions:

1. In a bowl; mix chicken with cream of celery, potatoes, heavy cream, bay leaf, thyme, salt and pepper; toss, pour into your air fryer's pan and cook at 320°F, for 25 minutes. Leave your stew to cool down a bit; discard bay leaf, divide among plates and serve right away

Special Gnocchi

(Prep + Cooking Time: 27 Minutes | **Servings:** 4)

Ingredients:
- 16-ounce gnocchi
- 1/4 cup parmesan; grated
- 1 yellow onion; chopped
- 1 tablespoon olive oil
- 3 garlic cloves; minced
- 8-ounce spinach pesto

Directions:
1. Grease your air fryer's pan with olive oil, add gnocchi, onion and garlic, toss; put pan in your air fryer and cook at 400°F, for 10 minutes
2. Add pesto, toss and cook for 7 minutes more at 350 degrees F. Divide among plates and serve for lunch.

Succulent Turkey Breast

(Prep + Cooking Time: 57 Minutes | **Servings:** 4)

Ingredients:
- 1 big turkey breast
- 2 tablespoon mustard
- 1/4 cup maple syrup
- 1 tablespoon butter; soft
- 2 teaspoon olive oil
- 1/2 teaspoon smoked paprika
- 1 teaspoon thyme; dried
- 1/2 teaspoon sage; dried
- Salt and black pepper to the taste

Directions:
1. Brush turkey breast with the olive oil; season with salt, pepper, thyme, paprika and sage, rub, place in your air fryer's basket and fry at 350°F, for 25 minutes
2. Flip turkey; cook for 10 minutes more; flip one more time and cook for another 10 minutes.
3. Meanwhile; heat up a pan with the butter over medium heat, add mustard and maple syrup; stir well, cook for a couple of minutes and take off heat. Slice turkey breast, divide among plates and serve with the maple glaze drizzled on top.

Mouthwatering Chicken Kabobs

(Prep + Cooking Time: 30 Minutes | **Servings:** 2)

Ingredients:
- 2 chicken breasts; skinless, boneless and roughly cubed
- 3 orange bell peppers; cut into squares
- 6 mushrooms; halved
- 1/4 cup honey
- 1/3 cup soy sauce
- Cooking spray
- Salt and black pepper to the taste

Directions:
1. In a bowl; mix chicken with salt, pepper, honey, say sauce and some cooking spray and toss well
2. Thread chicken, bell peppers and mushrooms on skewers; place them in your air fryer and cook at 338°F, for 20 minutes. Divide among plates and serve for lunch

Cheese Burgers

Ingredients:

- 12-ounce lean beef; ground
- 2 teaspoon mustard
- 4 cheddar cheese slices
- 2 burger buns; halved
- 4 teaspoon ketchup
- 3 tablespoon yellow onion; chopped
- Salt and black pepper to the taste

Directions:

1. In a bowl; mix beef with onion, ketchup, mustard, salt and pepper; stir well and shape 4 patties out of this mix
2. Divide cheese on 2 patties and top with the other 2 patties
3. Place them in preheated air fryer at 370°F and fry them for 20 minutes. Divide cheeseburger on 2 bun halves; top with the other 2 serve for lunch.

Potato Salad

(**Prep + Cooking Time:** 35 Minutes | **Servings:** 4)

Ingredients:

- 2-pound red potatoes; halved
- 2 tablespoon olive oil
- 2 green onions; chopped
- 1 red bell pepper; chopped
- 1/3 cup lemon juice
- 3 tablespoon mustard
- Salt and black pepper to the taste

Directions:

1. On your air fryer's basket; mix potatoes with half of the olive oil, salt and pepper and cook at 350°F, for 25 minutes shaking the fryer once
2. In a bowl; mix onions with bell pepper and roasted potatoes and toss.
3. In a small bowl; mix lemon juice with the rest of the oil and mustard and whisk really well. Add this to potato salad; toss well and serve for lunch

Awesome Buttermilk Chicken

(**Prep + Cooking Time:** 28 Minutes | **Servings:** 4)

Ingredients:

- 1 ½-pound chicken thighs
- 2 cups buttermilk
- 2 cups white flour
- 1 tablespoon garlic powder
- 1 tablespoon baking powder
- 1 tablespoon sweet paprika
- A pinch of cayenne pepper
- Salt and black pepper to the taste

Directions:

1. In a bowl; mix chicken thighs with buttermilk, salt, pepper and cayenne; toss and leave aside for 6 hours
2. In a separate bowl; mix flour with paprika, baking powder and garlic powder and stir.
3. Drain chicken thighs, dredge them in flour mix; arrange them in your air fryer and cook at 360°F, for 8 minutes. Flip chicken pieces, cook them for 10 minutes more; arrange on a platter and serve for lunch

Corn Casserole Recipe

(**Prep + Cooking Time:** 25 Minutes | **Servings:** 4)

Ingredients:
- 2 cups corn
- 1/2 cup light cream
- 3 tablespoon flour
- 1 egg
- 1/4 cup milk
- 1/2 cup Swiss cheese; grated
- 2 tablespoon butter
- Salt and black pepper to the taste
- Cooking spray

Directions:
1. In a bowl; mix corn with flour, egg, milk, light cream, cheese, salt, pepper and butter and stir well
2. Grease your air fryer's pan with cooking spray, pour cream mix; spread and cook at 320°F, for 15 minutes. Serve warm for lunch

Air Fryer Bacon Pudding

(**Prep + Cooking Time:** 40 Minutes | **Servings:** 6)

Ingredients:
- 4 bacon strips; cooked and chopped.
- 1 tablespoon butter; soft
- 2 cups corn
- 3 eggs; whisked
- 1 teaspoon thyme; chopped
- 2 teaspoon garlic; minced
- 1/2 cup heavy cream
- 1 ½ cups milk
- 3 cups bread; cubed
- 4 tablespoon parmesan; grated
- 1 yellow onion; chopped.
- 1/4 cup celery; chopped
- 1/2 cup red bell pepper; chopped
- Cooking spray
- Salt and black pepper to the taste

Directions:
1. Grease your air fryer's pan with cooking spray
2. In a bowl; mix bacon with butter, corn, onion, bell pepper, celery, thyme, garlic, salt, pepper, milk, heavy cream, eggs and bread cubes; toss, pour into greased pan and sprinkle cheese all over
3. Add this to your preheated air fryer at 320 degrees and cook for 30 minutes. Divide among plates and serve warm for a quick lunch

Mouthwatering Bacon Sandwiches

(**Prep + Cooking Time:** 17 Minutes | **Servings:** 4)

Ingredients:
- 8 bacon slices; cooked and cut into thirds
- 1 red bell pepper; sliced
- 1 yellow bell pepper; sliced
- 3 pita pockets; halved
- 1/3 cup BBQ sauce
- 1 ¼ cup butter lettuce leaves; torn
- 2 tablespoon honey
- 2 tomatoes; sliced

Directions:
1. In a bowl, mix BBQ sauce with honey and whisk well
2. Brush bacon and all bell peppers with some of this mix; place them in your air fryer and cook at 350°F, for 4 minutes.
3. Shake fryer and cook them for 2 minutes more. Stuff pita pockets with bacon mix, also stuff with tomatoes and lettuce; spread the rest of the BBQ sauce and serve for lunch

Special Seafood Stew

(Prep + Cooking Time: 30 Minutes | Servings: 4)

Ingredients:

- 5-ounce white rice
- 3-ounce sea bass fillet; skinless, boneless and chopped.
- 2-ounce peas
- 7-ounce mussels
- 6 scallops
- 3.5-ounce clams
- 4 shrimp
- 4 crayfish
- 1 red bell pepper; chopped
- 14-ounce white wine
- 3-ounce water
- 2-ounce squid pieces
- 1 tablespoon olive oil
- Salt and black pepper to the taste

Directions:

1. In your air fryer's pan; mix sea bass with shrimp, mussels, scallops, crayfish, clams and squid
2. Add the oil, salt and pepper and toss to coat.
3. In a bowl; mix peas salt, pepper, bell pepper and rice and stir
4. Add this over seafood, also add wine and water, place pan in your air fryer and cook at 400°F, for 20 minutes; stirring halfway. Divide into bowls and serve for lunch

Zucchini Casseroles

(Prep + Cooking Time: 26 Minutes | Servings: 8)

Ingredients:

- 1 cup veggie stock
- 2 tablespoon olive oil
- 1/4 teaspoon thyme; dried
- 8 zucchinis; cut into medium wedges
- 2 yellow onions; chopped
- 1 cup coconut milk
- 1 tablespoon soy sauce
- 1/4 teaspoon rosemary; dried
- 4 tablespoon dill; chopped
- 1/2 teaspoon basil; chopped
- 2 sweet potatoes; peeled and cut into medium wedges
- Salt and black pepper to the taste

Directions:

1. Heat up a pan that fits your air fryer with the oil over medium heat; add onion, stir and cook for 2 minutes
2. Add zucchinis, thyme, rosemary, basil, potato, salt, pepper, stock, milk, soy sauce and dill; stir, introduce in your air fryer; cook at 360°F, for 14 minutes, divide among plates and serve right away

Tasty Hash Brown Toasts

(Prep + Cooking Time: 17 Minutes | Servings: 4)

Ingredients:

- 4 hash brown patties; frozen
- 3 tablespoon mozzarella; shredded.
- 2 tablespoon parmesan; grated
- 1 tablespoon olive oil
- 1 tablespoon balsamic vinegar
- 1 tablespoon basil; chopped
- 1/4 cup cherry tomatoes; chopped

Directions:

1. Put hash brown patties in your air fryer; drizzle the oil over them and cook them at 400°F, for 7 minutes
2. In a bowl; mix tomatoes with mozzarella, parmesan, vinegar and basil and stir well. Divide hash brown patties on plates; top each with tomatoes mix and serve for lunch

Asparagus and Salmon

(Prep + Cooking Time: 33 Minutes | Servings: 4)

Ingredients:
- 1-pound asparagus; trimmed
- 1 tablespoon olive oil
- 1 red bell pepper; cut into halves
- 4-ounce smoked salmon
- A pinch of sweet paprika
- A pinch of garlic powder
- A pinch of cayenne pepper
- Salt and black pepper to the taste

Directions:
1. Put asparagus spears and bell pepper on a lined baking sheet that fits your air fryer; add salt, pepper, garlic powder, paprika, olive oil, cayenne pepper, toss to coat, introduce in the fryer; cook at 390°F, for 8 minutes, flip and cook for 8 minutes more. Add salmon, cook for 5 minutes more; divide everything on plates and serve

Bacon Garlic Pizzas

(Prep + Cooking Time: 20 Minutes | Servings: 4)

Ingredients:
- 4 dinner rolls; frozen
- 8 bacon slices; cooked and chopped.
- 1/2 teaspoon oregano dried
- 1/2 teaspoon garlic powder
- 1 ¼ cups cheddar cheese; grated
- 4 garlic cloves minced
- 1 cup tomato sauce
- Cooking spray

Directions:
1. Place dinner rolls on a working surface and press them to obtain 4 ovals
2. Spray each oval with cooking spray; transfer them to your air fryer and cook them at 370°F, for 2 minutes.
3. Spread tomato sauce on each oval, divide garlic, sprinkle oregano and garlic powder and top with bacon and cheese
4. Return pizzas to your heated air fryer and cook them at 370°F, for 8 minutes more. Serve them warm for lunch.

Chicken Lunch Recipe

(Prep + Cooking Time: 30 Minutes | Servings: 6)

Ingredients:
- 1 cup chicken; shredded.
- 1 bunch kale; chopped
- 1/4 cup chicken stock
- 3 carrots; chopped
- 1 cup shiitake mushrooms; roughly sliced
- Salt and black pepper to the taste

Directions:
1. In a blender, mix stock with kale, pulse a few times and pour into a pan that fits your air fryer. Add chicken, mushrooms, carrots, salt and pepper to the taste; toss, introduce in your air fryer and cook at 350°F, for 18 minutes

Veggie Toasts

(Prep + Cooking Time: 25 Minutes | Servings: 4)

Ingredients:

- 1 red bell pepper; cut into thin strips
- 1 cup cremini mushrooms; sliced
- 4 bread slices
- 1 yellow squash; chopped
- 2 green onions; sliced
- 1 tablespoon olive oil
- 2 tablespoon butter; soft
- 1/2 cup goat cheese; crumbled

Directions:

1. In a bowl; mix red bell pepper with mushrooms, squash, green onions and oil, toss; transfer to your air fryer, cook them at 350°F, for 10 minutes; shaking the fryer once and transfer them to a bowl
2. Spread butter on bread slices; place them in air fryer and cook them at 350°F, for 5 minutes. Divide veggie mix on each bread slice, top with crumbled cheese and serve for lunch

Special Sausage

(Prep + Cooking Time: 20 Minutes | Servings: 4)

Ingredients:

- 1-pound sausages; sliced
- 1/3 cup ketchup
- 3 tablespoon brown sugar
- 2 tablespoon mustard
- 1 red bell pepper; cut into strips
- 1/2 cup yellow onion; chopped
- 1/2 cup chicken stock
- 2 tablespoon apple cider vinegar

Directions:

1. In a bowl; mix sugar with ketchup, mustard, stock and vinegar and whisk well
2. In your air fryer's pan; mix sausage slices with bell pepper, onion and sweet and sour mix; toss and cook at 350°F, for 10 minutes. Divide into bowls and serve for lunch

Meatballs Sandwich Delight

(Prep + Cooking Time: 32 Minutes | Servings: 4)

Ingredients:

- 3 baguettes; sliced more than halfway through
- 14-ounce beef; ground
- 1 tablespoon olive oil
- 1 egg; whisked
- 1 tablespoon bread crumbs
- 2 tablespoon cheddar cheese; grated
- 1 tablespoon oregano; chopped
- 1 teaspoon thyme; dried
- 1 teaspoon basil; dried
- 7-ounce tomato sauce
- 1 small onion; chopped
- Salt and black pepper to the taste

Directions:

1. In a bowl; combine meat with salt, pepper, onion, breadcrumbs, egg, cheese, oregano, thyme and basil; stir, shape medium meatballs and add them to your air fryer after you've greased it with the oil
2. Cook them at 375°F, for 12 minutes; flipping them halfway
3. Add tomato sauce, cook meatballs for 10 minutes more and arrange them on sliced baguettes. Serve them right away.

Meatballs, Tomato Sauce

(Prep + Cooking Time: 245 Minutes | **Servings:** 4)

Ingredients:

- 1-pound lean beef; ground
- 3 green onions; chopped.
- 1 tablespoon olive oil
- 16-ounce tomato sauce
- 2 tablespoon mustard
- 2 garlic cloves; minced
- 1 egg yolk
- 1/4 cup bread crumbs
- Salt and black pepper to the taste

Directions:

1. In a bowl; mix beef with onion, garlic, egg yolk, bread crumbs, salt and pepper; stir well and shape medium meatballs out of this mix
2. Grease meatballs with the oil, place them in your air fryer and cook them at 400°F, for 10 minutes.
3. In a bowl; mix tomato sauce with mustard, whisk, add over meatballs; toss them and cook at 400°F, for 5 minutes more. Divide meatballs and sauce on plates and serve for lunch

Amazing Beef Stew

(Prep + Cooking Time: 30 Minutes | **Servings:** 4)

Ingredients:

- 2-pound beef meat; cut into medium chunks
- 1-quart veggie stock
- 1/2 teaspoon smoked paprika
- 2 carrots; chopped
- 4 potatoes; chopped
- A handful thyme; chopped
- Salt and black pepper to the taste

Directions:

1. In a dish that fits your air fryer; mix beef with carrots, potatoes, stock, salt, pepper, paprika and thyme; stir, place in air fryer's basket and cook at 375°F, for 20 minutes. Divide into bowls and serve right away for lunch

Pork and Potatoes Recipe

(Prep + Cooking Time: 35 Minutes | **Servings:** 2)

Ingredients:

- 2-pound pork loin
- 2 red potatoes; cut into medium wedges
- 1/2 teaspoon red pepper flakes
- 1/2 teaspoon garlic powder
- 1 teaspoon parsley; dried
- A drizzle of balsamic vinegar
- Salt and black pepper to the taste

Directions:

1. In your air fryer's pan; mix pork with potatoes, salt, pepper, garlic powder, pepper flakes, parsley and vinegar; toss and cook at 390°F, for 25 minutes. Slice pork, divide it and potatoes on plates and serve for lunch

Fish & Seafood Recipes

Salmon & Blackberry Glaze

(Prep + Cooking Time: 43 Minutes **| Servings:** 4)

Ingredients:

- 4 medium salmon fillets; skinless
- 1 cup water
- 1-inch ginger piece; grated
- 12-ounce blackberries
- 1 tablespoon olive oil
- 1/4 cup sugar
- Juice from 1/2 lemon
- Salt and black pepper to the taste

Directions:

1. Heat up a pot with the water over medium high heat, add ginger, lemon juice and blackberries; stir, bring to a boil, cook for 4 - 5 minutes; take off heat, strain into a bowl, return to pan and combine with sugar.
2. Stir this mix, bring to a simmer over medium low heat and cook for 20 minutes
3. Leave blackberry sauce to cool down, brush salmon with it, season with salt and pepper, drizzle olive oil all over and rub fish well.
4. Place fish in your preheated air fryer at 350°F and cook for 10 minutes; flipping fish fillets once. Divide among plates, drizzle some of the remaining blackberry sauce all over and serve

Lemon Sole & Swiss Chard

(Prep + Cooking Time: 24 Minutes **| Servings:** 4)

Ingredients:

- 2 bunches Swiss chard; chopped
- 4 tablespoon butter
- 1/4 cup walnuts; chopped
- 1/4 cup parmesan; grated
- 4 tablespoon olive oil
- 1/4 cup lemon juice
- 3 tablespoon capers
- 2 garlic cloves; minced
- 1 teaspoon lemon zest; grated
- 4 white bread slices; quartered
- 4 sole fillets; boneless
- Salt and black pepper to the taste

Directions:

1. In your food processor, mix bread with walnuts, cheese and lemon zest and pulse well
2. Add half of the olive oil, pulse really well again and leave aside for now
3. Heat up a pan with the butter over medium heat, add lemon juice, salt, pepper and capers; stir well, add fish and toss it.
4. Transfer fish to your preheated air fryer's basket, top with bread mix you've made at the beginning and cook at 350°F, for 14 minutes
5. Meanwhile; heat up another pan with the rest of the oil, add garlic, Swiss chard, salt and pepper; stir gently, cook for 2 minutes and take off heat. Divide fish on plates and serve with sautéed chard on the side

Coconut Tilapia Recipe

(Prep + Cooking Time: 20 Minutes | **Servings:** 4)

Ingredients:

- 4 medium tilapia fillets
- 1/2 cup coconut milk
- 1/2 teaspoon garam masala
- 1 teaspoon ginger; grated
- 2 garlic cloves; chopped
- 1/2 cup cilantro; chopped
- Salt and black pepper to the taste
- Cooking spray
- 1/2 jalapeno; chopped.

Directions:

1. In your food processor, mix coconut milk with salt, pepper, cilantro, ginger, garlic, jalapeno and garam masala and pulse really well
2. Spray fish with cooking spray, spread coconut mix all over, rub well, transfer to your air fryer's basket and cook at 400°F, for 10 minutes. Divide among plates and serve hot

Asian Style Halibut

(Prep + Cooking Time: 40 Minutes | **Servings:** 3)

Ingredients:

- 1-pound halibut steaks
- 2/3 cup soy sauce
- 1/4 cup sugar
- 2 tablespoon lime juice
- 1/2 cup mirin
- 1/4 teaspoon red pepper flakes; crushed
- 1/4 cup orange juice
- 1/4 teaspoon ginger; grated
- 1 garlic clove; minced

Directions:

1. Put soy sauce in a pan; heat up over medium heat, add mirin, sugar, lime and orange juice, pepper flakes, ginger and garlic; stir well, bring to a boil and take off heat
2. Transfer half of the marinade to a bowl, add halibut, toss to coat and leave aside in the fridge for 30 minutes.
3. Transfer halibut to your air fryer and cook at 390°F, for 10 minutes; flipping once. Divide halibut steaks on plates; drizzle the rest of the marinade all over and serve hot

Special Tuna and Chimichurri Sauce

(Prep + Cooking Time: 18 Minutes | **Servings:** 4)

Ingredients:

- 1-pound sushi tuna steak
- 1 teaspoon red pepper flakes
- 1 teaspoon thyme; chopped
- 3 garlic cloves; minced
- 1/3 cup olive oil+ 2 tablespoon
- 1 small red onion; chopped.
- 1 jalapeno pepper; chopped
- 6-ounce baby arugula
- 3 tablespoon balsamic vinegar
- 2 tablespoon parsley; chopped
- 2 tablespoon basil; chopped
- 2 avocados; pitted, peeled and sliced
- 1/2 cup cilantro; chopped
- Salt and black pepper to the taste

Directions:

1. In a bowl; mix ⅓ cup oil with jalapeno, vinegar, onion, cilantro, basil, garlic, parsley, pepper flakes, thyme, salt and pepper; whisk well and leave aside for now.
2. Season tuna with salt and pepper, rub with the rest of the oil; place in your air fryer and cook at 360°F, for 3 minutes on each side
3. Mix arugula with half of the chimichuri mix you've made and toss to coat. Divide arugula on plates, slice tuna and also divide among plates; top with the rest of the chimichuri and serve

Shrimp and Cauliflower Recipe

(Prep + Cooking Time: 22 Minutes | **Servings:** 2)

Ingredients:

- 4 bacon slices; cooked and crumbled
- 1-pound shrimp; peeled and deveined
- 1 cauliflower head; riced
- 2 garlic cloves; minced
- 1/2 cup beef stock
- 1 tablespoon butter
- 1 tablespoon parsley; finely chopped.
- 1 tablespoon chives; chopped
- 1/4 cup heavy cream
- 8-ounce mushrooms; roughly chopped
- A pinch of red pepper flakes
- Salt and black pepper to the taste
- Cooking spray

Directions:

1. Season shrimp with salt and pepper, spray with cooking oil, place in your air fryer and cook at 360°F, for 7 minutes
2. Meanwhile; heat up a pan with the butter over medium heat, add mushrooms; stir and cook for 3 - 4 minutes.
3. Add garlic, cauliflower rice, pepper flakes, stock, cream, chives, parsley, salt and pepper; stir, cook for a few minutes and take off heat. Divide shrimp on plates, add cauliflower mix on the side, sprinkle bacon on top and serve.

Peas and Cod Fillets

(Prep + Cooking Time: 20 Minutes | **Servings:** 4)

Ingredients:

- 4 cod fillets; boneless
- 2 cups peas
- 4 tablespoon wine
- 2 garlic cloves; minced
- 1/2 teaspoon oregano; dried
- 1/2 teaspoon sweet paprika
- 2 tablespoon parsley; chopped
- Salt and pepper to the taste

Directions:

1. In your food processor mix garlic with parsley, salt, pepper, oregano, paprika and wine and blend well.
2. Rub fish with half of this mix, place in your air fryer and cook at 360°F, for 10 minutes
3. Meanwhile; put peas in a pot, add water to cover, add salt, bring to a boil over medium high heat, cook for 10 minutes; drain and divide among plates. Also divide fish on plates, spread the rest of the herb dressing all over and serve

Simple Squid and Guacamole

(Prep + Cooking Time: 16 Minutes | **Servings:** 2)

Ingredients:

- 2 medium squids; tentacles separated and tubes scored lengthwise
- 1 tablespoon olive oil
- Juice from 1 lime
- Salt and black pepper to the taste

For the guacamole:

- 1 tomato; chopped
- 1 tablespoon coriander; chopped
- 2 red chilies; chopped
- 1 red onion; chopped
- 2 avocados; pitted, peeled and chopped.
- Juice from 2 limes

Directions:

1. Season squid and squid tentacles with salt, pepper, drizzle the olive oil all over, put in your air fryer's basket and cook at 360°F, for 3 minutes on each side
2. Transfer squid to a bowl; drizzle lime juice all over and toss.
3. Meanwhile; put avocado in a bowl, mash with a fork, add coriander, chilies, tomato, onion and juice from 2 limes and toss. Divide squid on plates, top with guacamole and serve

Trout Fillet & Orange Sauce

(Prep + Cooking Time: 20 Minutes | **Servings:** 4)

Ingredients:
- 4 trout fillets; skinless and boneless
- 1 tablespoon olive oil
- 1 tablespoon ginger; minced
- 4 spring onions; chopped
- Salt and black pepper to the taste
- Juice and zest from 1 orange

Directions:
1. Season trout fillets with salt, pepper, rub them with the olive oil, place in a pan that fits your air fryer, add ginger, green onions, orange zest and juice; toss well, place in your air fryer and cook at 360°F, for 10 minutes. Divide fish and sauce on plates and serve right away

Tangy Saba Fish

(Prep + Cooking Time: 18 Minutes | **Servings:** 1)

Ingredients:
- 4 Saba fish fillet; boneless
- 2 tablespoon olive oil
- 2 tablespoon garlic; minced
- 3 red chili pepper; chopped
- 2 tablespoon lemon juice
- Salt and black pepper to the taste

Directions:
1. Season fish fillets with salt and pepper and put in a bowl.
2. Add lemon juice, oil, chili and garlic toss to coat, transfer fish to your air fryer and cook at 360°F, for 8 minutes; flipping halfway. Divide among plates and serve with some fries

Crusted Salmon Recipe

(Prep + Cooking Time: 20 Minutes | **Servings:** 4)

Ingredients:
- 4 salmon fillets
- 1 cup pistachios; chopped
- 1 tablespoon mustard
- 1 teaspoon dill; chopped
- 1/4 cup lemon juice
- 2 tablespoon honey
- Salt and black pepper to the taste

Directions:
1. In a bowl; mix pistachios with mustard, honey, lemon juice, salt, black pepper and dill; whisk and spread over salmon
2. Put in your air fryer and cook at 350°F, for 10 minutes. Divide among plates and serve with a side salad

Asian Style Salmon

(Prep + Cooking Time: 1 hour 15 Minutes | **Servings:** 2)

Ingredients:
- 2 medium salmon fillets
- 6 tablespoon honey
- 6 tablespoon light soy sauce
- 1 teaspoon water
- 3 teaspoon mirin

Directions:
1. In a bowl; mix soy sauce with honey, water and mirin, whisk well, add salmon, rub well and leave aside in the fridge for 1 hour
2. Transfer salmon to your air fryer and cook at 360°F, for 15 minutes; flipping them after 7 minutes
3. Meanwhile; put the soy marinade in a pan, heat up over medium heat; whisk well, cook for 2 minutes and take off heat. Divide salmon on plates, drizzle marinade all over and serve.

Shrimp and Crab Recipe

(Prep + Cooking Time: 35 Minutes | **Servings:** 4)

Ingredients:

- 1-pound shrimp; peeled and deveined
- 1/2 cup yellow onion; chopped
- 1 cup green bell pepper; chopped.
- 1 cup celery; chopped
- 2 tablespoon breadcrumbs
- 1 tablespoon butter; melted
- 1 teaspoon sweet paprika
- 1 cup crabmeat; flaked
- 1 cup mayonnaise
- 1 teaspoon Worcestershire sauce
- Salt and black pepper to the taste

Directions:

1. In a bowl; mix shrimp with crab meat, bell pepper, onion, mayo, celery, salt, pepper and Worcestershire sauce; toss well and transfer to a pan that fits your air fryer
2. Sprinkle bread crumbs and paprika, add melted butter, place in your air fryer and cook at 320°F, for 25 minutes; shaking halfway. Divide among plates and serve right away.

Tabasco Shrimp Recipe

(Prep + Cooking Time: 20 Minutes | **Servings:** 4)

Ingredients:

- 1-pound shrimp; peeled and deveined
- 1/2 teaspoon parsley; dried
- 2 tablespoon water
- 1 teaspoon oregano; dried
- 1/2 teaspoon smoked paprika
- 1 teaspoon red pepper flakes
- 2 tablespoon olive oil
- 1 teaspoon Tabasco sauce
- Salt and black pepper to the taste

Directions:

1. In a bowl; mix oil with water, Tabasco sauce, pepper flakes, oregano, parsley, salt, pepper, paprika and shrimp and toss well to coat
2. Transfer shrimp to your preheated air fryer at 370°F and cook for 10 minutes shaking the fryer once. Divide shrimp on plates and serve with a side salad.

Flavored Fried Salmon

(Prep + Cooking Time: 1 hour 8 Minutes | **Servings:** 2)

Ingredients:

- 2 salmon fillets
- 2 tablespoon lemon juice
- 1/3 cup brown sugar
- 1/2 teaspoon garlic powder
- 1/3 cup water
- 1/3 cup soy sauce
- 3 scallions; chopped
- 2 tablespoon olive oil
- Salt and black pepper to the taste

Directions:

1. In a bowl; mix sugar with water, soy sauce, garlic powder, salt, pepper, oil and lemon juice, whisk well, add salmon fillets; toss to coat and leave aside in the fridge for 1 hour
2. Transfer salmon fillets to the fryer's basket and cook at 360°F, for 8 minutes flipping them halfway. Divide salmon on plates; sprinkle scallions on top and serve right away

Vinaigrette and Cod

(Prep + Cooking Time: 25 Minutes | **Servings:** 4)

Ingredients:
- 4 cod fillets; skinless and boneless
- 8 black olives; pitted and roughly chopped
- 12 cherry tomatoes; halved
- 2 tablespoon olive oil
- 1 bunch basil; chopped
- 2 tablespoon lemon juice
- Salt and black pepper to the taste
- Cooking spray

Directions:
1. Season cod with salt and pepper to the taste; place in your air fryer's basket and cook at 360°F, for 10 minutes; flipping after 5 minutes.
2. Meanwhile; heat up a pan with the oil over medium heat, add tomatoes, olives and lemon juice; stir, bring to a simmer, add basil, salt and pepper; stir well and take off heat. Divide fish on plates and serve with the vinaigrette drizzled on top

Halibut and Sun Dried Tomatoes

(Prep + Cooking Time: 20 Minutes | **Servings:** 2)

Ingredients:
- 2 medium halibut fillets
- 2 garlic cloves; minced
- 9 black olives; pitted and sliced
- 4 rosemary springs; chopped
- 1/2 teaspoon red pepper flakes; crushed
- 2 teaspoon olive oil
- 6 sun dried tomatoes; chopped
- 2 small red onions; sliced
- 1 fennel bulb; sliced
- Salt and black pepper to the taste

Directions:
1. Season fish with salt, pepper, rub with garlic and oil and put in a heat proof dish that fits your air fryer.
2. Add onion slices, sun dried tomatoes, fennel, olives, rosemary and sprinkle pepper flakes, transfer to your air fryer and cook at 380°F, for 10 minutes. Divide fish and veggies on plates and serve

Salmon with Mash and Capers

(Prep + Cooking Time: 30 Minutes | **Servings:** 4)

Ingredients:
- 4 salmon fillets; skinless and boneless
- 1 tablespoon capers; drained
- Juice from 1 lemon

For the potato mash:
- 1-pound potatoes; chopped.
- 2 tablespoon olive oil
- 2 teaspoon olive oil
- Salt and black pepper to the taste

- 1/2 cup milk
- 1 tablespoon dill; dried

Directions:
1. Put potatoes in a pot, add water to cover, add some salt, bring to a boil over medium high heat, cook for 15 minutes; drain, transfer to a bowl; mash with a potato masher, add 2 tablespoon oil, dill, salt, pepper and milk, whisk well and leave aside for now
2. Season salmon with salt and pepper, drizzle 2 teaspoon oil over them, rub, transfer to your air fryer's basket, add capers on top, cook at 360°F and cook for 8 minutes. Divide salmon and capers on plates; add mashed potatoes on the side, drizzle lemon juice all over and serve.

Cod with Pearl Onions Recipe

(Prep + Cooking Time: 25 Minutes | Servings: 2)

Ingredients:

- 14-ounce pearl onions
- 1 tablespoon parsley; dried
- 1 teaspoon thyme; dried
- 8-ounce mushrooms; sliced
- 2 medium cod fillets
- Black pepper to the taste

Directions:

1. Put fish in a heat proof dish that fits your air fryer; add onions, parsley, mushrooms, thyme and black pepper; toss well, put in your air fryer and cook at 350°F and cook for 15 minutes. Divide everything on plates and serve

Mouthwatering Cod Steaks with Plum Sauce

(Prep + Cooking Time: 30 Minutes | Servings: 2)

Ingredients:

- 2 big cod steaks
- 1/2 teaspoon garlic powder
- 1 tablespoon plum sauce
- 1/2 teaspoon ginger powder
- 1/4 teaspoon turmeric powder
- Salt and black pepper to the taste
- Cooking spray

Directions:

1. Season cod steaks with salt and pepper, spray them with cooking oil, add garlic powder, ginger powder and turmeric powder and rub well.
2. Place cod steaks in your air fryer and cook at 360°F, for 15 minutes; flipping them after 7 minutes.
3. Heat up a pan over medium heat, add plum sauce; stir and cook for 2 minutes. Divide cod steaks on plates, drizzle plum sauce all over and serve

Cod Fillets with Grapes and Fennel Salad

(Prep + Cooking Time: 25 Minutes | Servings: 2)

Ingredients:

- 2 black cod fillets; boneless
- 1 cup grapes; halved
- 1/2 cup pecans
- 1 tablespoon olive oil
- 1 fennel bulb; thinly sliced
- Salt and black pepper to the taste

Directions:

1. Drizzle half of the oil over fish fillets; season with salt and pepper, rub well, place fillets in your air fryer's basket; cook for 10 minutes at 400°F and transfer to a plate.
2. In a bowl; mix pecans with grapes, fennel, the rest of the oil, salt and pepper; toss to coat, add to a pan that fits your air fryer and cook at 400°F, for 5 minutes. Divide cod on plates; add fennel and grapes mix on the side and serve

Tasty Catfish

(Prep + Cooking Time: 30 Minutes | Servings: 4)

Ingredients:

- 4 cat fish fillets
- 1 tablespoon lemon juice
- 1 tablespoon olive oil
- 1 tablespoon parsley; chopped
- A pinch of sweet paprika
- Salt and black pepper to the taste

Directions:

1. Season catfish fillets with salt, pepper, paprika, drizzle oil, rub well, place in your air fryer's basket and cook at 400°F, for 20 minutes; flipping the fish after 10 minutes. Divide fish on plates, drizzle lemon juice all over, sprinkle parsley and serve

East Trout and Butter Sauce

(Prep + Cooking Time: 20 Minutes **| Servings:** 4)

Ingredients:
- 4 trout fillets; boneless
- 6 tablespoon butter
- 2 tablespoon olive oil
- 3 teaspoon lemon zest; grated
- 3 tablespoon chives; chopped
- 2 teaspoon lemon juice
- Salt and black pepper to the taste

Directions:
1. Season trout with salt and pepper, drizzle the olive oil, rub, transfer to your air fryer and cook at 360°F, for 10 minutes; flipping once
2. Meanwhile; heat up a pan with the butter over medium heat, add salt, pepper, chives, lemon juice and zest, whisk well; cook for 1 - 2 minutes and take off heat. Divide fish fillets on plates, drizzle butter sauce all over and serve

Salmon and Orange Marmalade Recipe

(Prep + Cooking Time: 25 Minutes **| Servings:** 4)

Ingredients:
- 1-pound wild salmon; skinless, boneless and cubed
- 2 lemons; sliced
- 1/4 cup balsamic vinegar
- 1/4 cup orange juice
- 1/3 cup orange marmalade
- A pinch of salt and black pepper

Directions:
1. Heat up a pot with the vinegar over medium heat; add marmalade and orange juice; stir, bring to a simmer, cook for 1 minute and take off heat
2. Thread salmon cubes and lemon slices on skewers, season with salt and black pepper, brush them with half of the orange marmalade mix, arrange in your air fryer's basket and cook at 360°F, for 3 minutes on each side. Brush skewers with the rest of the vinegar mix; divide among plates and serve right away with a side salad

Mouthwatering Salmon and Avocado Salsa

(Prep + Cooking Time: 40 Minutes **| Servings:** 4)

Ingredients:
- 4 salmon fillets
- 1 tablespoon olive oil
- 1/2 teaspoon chili powder
- 1 teaspoon garlic powder
- 1 teaspoon cumin; ground
- 1 teaspoon sweet paprika
- Salt and black pepper to the taste

For the salsa:
- 1 small red onion; chopped
- 2 tablespoon cilantro; chopped
- 1 avocado; pitted, peeled and chopped
- Juice from 2 limes
- Salt and black pepper to the taste

Directions:
1. In a bowl; mix salt, pepper, chili powder, onion powder, paprika and cumin; stir, rub salmon with this mix, drizzle the oil, rub again, transfer to your air fryer and cook at 350°F, for 5 minutes on each side
2. Meanwhile; in a bowl, mix avocado with red onion, salt, pepper, cilantro and lime juice and stir. Divide fillets on plates, top with avocado salsa and serve

Salmon and Lemon Relish Recipe

(Prep + Cooking Time: 40 Minutes | Servings: 2)

Ingredients:
- 2 salmon fillets; boneless
- 1 tablespoon olive oil

- Salt and black pepper to the taste

For the relish:
- 1 Meyer lemon; cut in wedges and then sliced
- 1 tablespoon lemon juice

- 1 shallot; chopped.
- 1/4 cup olive oil
- 2 tablespoon parsley; chopped

Directions:
1. Season salmon with salt and pepper, rub with 1 tablespoon oil, place in your air fryer's basket and cook at 320°F, for 20 minutes; flipping the fish halfway
2. Meanwhile; in a bowl, mix shallot with the lemon juice, a pinch of salt and black pepper; stir and leave aside for 10 minutes.
3. In a separate bowl; mix marinated shallot with lemon slices, salt, pepper, parsley and 1/4 cup oil and whisk well. Divide salmon on plates, top with lemon relish and serve

Salmon Thyme and Parsley

(Prep + Cooking Time: 25 Minutes | Servings: 4)

Ingredients:
- 4 salmon fillets; boneless
- 1 yellow onion; chopped
- 3 tomatoes; sliced
- 4 thyme springs

- 4 parsley springs
- 3 tablespoon extra virgin olive oil
- Juice from 1 lemon
- Salt and black pepper to the taste

Directions:
1. Drizzle 1 tablespoon oil in a pan that fits your air fryer; add a layer of tomatoes, salt and pepper, drizzle 1 more tablespoon oil, add fish, season them with salt and pepper, drizzle the rest of the oil, add thyme and parsley springs, onions, lemon juice, salt and pepper, place in your air fryer's basket
2. Cook at 360°F, for 12 minutes shaking once. Divide everything on plates and serve right away

Air Fried Cod

(Prep + Cooking Time: 22 Minutes | Servings: 4)

Ingredients:
- 2 cod fish; 7-ounce each
- 1 teaspoon dark soy sauce
- 4 tablespoon light soy sauce
- 1 tablespoon sugar
- 4 ginger slices
- 3 spring onions; chopped

- 2 tablespoon coriander; chopped
- 1 cup water
- 3 tablespoon olive oil
- A drizzle of sesame oil
- Salt and black pepper to the taste

Directions:
1. Season fish with salt, pepper, drizzle sesame oil, rub well and leave aside for 10 minutes
2. Add fish to your air fryer and cook at 356°F, for 12 minutes.
3. Meanwhile; heat up a pot with the water over medium heat, add dark and light soy sauce and sugar; stir, bring to a simmer and take off heat
4. Heat up a pan with the olive oil over medium heat, add ginger and green onions; stir, cook for a few minutes and take off heat. Divide fish on plates, top with ginger and green onions, drizzle soy sauce mix, sprinkle coriander and serve right away.

Tilapia & Chives Sauce

(Prep + Cooking Time: 18 Minutes | **Servings:** 4)

Ingredients:

- 4 medium tilapia fillets
- 2 tablespoon chives; chopped
- 2 teaspoon honey
- 1/4 cup Greek yogurt
- Juice from 1 lemon
- Cooking spray
- Salt and black pepper to the taste

Directions:

1. Season fish with salt and pepper, spray with cooking spray, place in preheated air fryer 350°F and cook for 8 minutes; flipping halfway
2. Meanwhile; in a bowl, mix yogurt with honey, salt, pepper, chives and lemon juice and whisk really well. Divide air fryer fish on plates, drizzle yogurt sauce all over and serve right away

Red Snapper Recipe

(Prep + Cooking Time: 45 Minutes | **Servings:** 4)

Ingredients:

- 1 big red snapper; cleaned and scored
- 1 red bell pepper; chopped
- 2 tablespoon white wine
- 2 tablespoon parsley; chopped
- 3 garlic cloves; minced
- 1 jalapeno; chopped
- 1/4-pound okra; chopped.
- 1 tablespoon butter
- 2 tablespoon olive oil
- Salt and black pepper to the taste

Directions:

1. In a bowl; mix jalapeno, wine with garlic; stir well and rub snapper with this mix
2. Season fish with salt and pepper and leave it aside for 30 minutes.
3. Meanwhile; heat up a pan with 1 tablespoon butter over medium heat, add bell pepper and okra; stir and cook for 5 minutes.
4. Stuff red snapper's belly with this mix; also add parsley and rub with the olive oil
5. Place in preheated air fryer and cook at 400°F, for 15 minutes; flipping the fish halfway. Divide among plates and serve.

Oriental Fish Recipe

(Prep + Cooking Time: 22 Minutes | **Servings:** 4)

Ingredients:

- 2-pound red snapper fillets; boneless
- 1 tablespoon lemon juice
- 1 yellow onion; chopped
- 1 tablespoon tamarind paste
- 1 tablespoon oriental sesame oil
- 3 garlic cloves; minced
- 2 tablespoon water
- 1/2 teaspoon cumin; ground
- 1 tablespoon ginger; grated
- 3 tablespoon mint; chopped
- Salt and black pepper to the taste

Directions:

1. In your food processor, mix garlic with onion, salt, pepper, tamarind paste, sesame oil, ginger, water and cumin, pulse well and rub fish with this mix.
2. Place fish in your preheated air fryer at 320°F and cook for 12 minutes; flipping fish halfway. Divide fish on plates, drizzle lemon juice all over, sprinkle mint and serve right away

Special Swordfish and Mango Salsa

(Prep + Cooking Time: 16 Minutes | Servings: 2)

Ingredients:
- 2 medium swordfish steaks
- 2 teaspoon avocado oil
- 1 avocado; pitted, peeled and chopped
- 1 orange; peeled and sliced
- 1/2 tablespoon balsamic vinegar
- 1 tablespoon cilantro; chopped
- 1 mango; chopped
- A pinch of cumin
- A pinch of onion powder
- A pinch of garlic powder
- Salt and black pepper to the taste

Directions:
1. Season fish steaks with salt, pepper, garlic powder, onion powder and cumin and rub with half of the oil; place in your air fryer and cook at 360°F, for 6 minutes; flipping halfway
2. Meanwhile; in a bowl, mix avocado with mango, cilantro, balsamic vinegar, salt, pepper and the rest of the oil and stir well. Divide fish on plates; top with mango salsa and serve with orange slices on the side

Salmon & Chives Vinaigrette

(Prep + Cooking Time: 22 Minutes | Servings: 4)

Ingredients:
- 4 salmon fillets; boneless
- 2 tablespoon chives; chopped
- 1/3 cup maple syrup
- 2 tablespoon dill; chopped.
- 1 tablespoon olive oil
- 3 tablespoon balsamic vinegar
- Salt and black pepper to the taste

Directions:
1. Season fish with salt and pepper, rub with the oil, place in your air fryer and cook at 350°F, for 8 minutes; flipping once
2. Heat up a small pot with the vinegar over medium heat, add maple syrup, chives and dill; stir and cook for 3 minutes. Divide fish on plates and serve with chives vinaigrette on top.

Chinese Style Cod

(Prep + Cooking Time: 20 Minutes | Servings: 2)

Ingredients:
- 2 medium cod fillets; boneless
- 1 teaspoon peanuts; crushed
- 1 tablespoon light soy sauce
- 1/2 teaspoon ginger; grated
- 2 teaspoon garlic powder

Directions:
1. Put fish fillets in a heat proof dish that fits your air fryer, add garlic powder, soy sauce and ginger; toss well, put in your air fryer and cook at 350°F, for 10 minutes. Divide fish on plates, sprinkle peanuts on top and serve

Italian Barramundi Fillets

(Prep + Cooking Time: 18 Minutes | **Servings:** 4)

Ingredients:
- 2 barramundi fillets; boneless
- 1 tablespoon olive oil+ 2 teaspoon
- 2 tablespoon parsley; chopped
- 1 tablespoon lemon zest
- 2 tablespoon lemon zest
- 2 teaspoon Italian seasoning
- 1/4 cup green olives; pitted and chopped
- 1/4 cup cherry tomatoes; chopped
- 1/4 cup black olives; chopped
- Salt and black pepper to the taste

Directions:
1. Rub fish with salt, pepper, Italian seasoning and 2 teaspoon olive oil, transfer to your air fryer and cook at 360°F, for 8 minutes; flipping them halfway
2. In a bowl; mix tomatoes with black olives, green olives, salt, pepper, lemon zest and lemon juice, parsley and 1 tablespoon olive oil and toss well. Divide fish on plates; add tomato salsa on top and serve

Salmon and Greek Yogurt Sauce

(Prep + Cooking Time: 30 Minutes | **Servings:** 2)

Ingredients:
- 2 medium salmon fillets
- 1 tablespoon basil; chopped
- 6 lemon slices
- 1/2 teaspoon mint; chopped.
- 1/2 teaspoon cilantro; chopped
- 1 cup Greek yogurt
- 2 teaspoon curry powder
- A pinch of cayenne pepper
- 1 garlic clove; minced
- Sea salt and black pepper to the taste

Directions:
1. Place each salmon fillet on a parchment paper piece, make 3 splits in each and stuff them with basil
2. Season with salt and pepper, top each fillet with 3 lemon slices, fold parchment, seal edges, introduce in the oven at 400°F and bake for 20 minutes
3. Meanwhile; in a bowl, mix yogurt with cayenne pepper, salt to the taste, garlic, curry, mint and cilantro and whisk well. Transfer fish to plates, drizzle the yogurt sauce you've just prepared on top and serve right away!

Marinated Salmon Recipe

(Prep + Cooking Time: 1 hour 20 Minutes | **Servings:** 6)

Ingredients:
- 1 whole salmon
- 1 tablespoon dill; chopped
- 1 lemon; sliced
- 1 tablespoon tarragon; chopped
- 1 tablespoon garlic; minced
- Juice from 2 lemons
- A pinch of salt and black pepper

Directions:
1. In a large fish, mix fish with salt, pepper and lemon juice; toss well and keep in the fridge for 1 hour
2. Stuff salmon with garlic and lemon slices, place in your air fryer's basket and cook at 320°F, for 25 minutes. Divide among plates and serve with a tasty coleslaw on the side

Stuffed Calamari Recipe

(Prep + Cooking Time: 35 Minutes | **Servings:** 4)

Ingredients:

- 4 big calamari; tentacles separated and chopped and tubes reserved
- 2 tablespoon parsley; chopped.
- 5-ounce kale; chopped
- 2 garlic cloves; minced
- 1 red bell pepper; chopped
- 1 tablespoon olive oil
- 2-ounce canned tomato puree
- 1 yellow onion; chopped
- Salt and black pepper to the taste

Directions:

1. Heat up a pan with the oil over medium heat; add onion and garlic; stir and cook for 2 minutes.
2. Add bell pepper, tomato puree, calamari tentacles, kale, salt and pepper; stir, cook for 10 minutes and take off heat. stir and cook for 3 minutes
3. Stuff calamari tubes with this mix, secure with toothpicks, put in your air fryer and cook at 360°F, for 20 minutes. Divide calamari on plates; sprinkle parsley all over and serve

Creamy-Shrimp and Veggies

(Prep + Cooking Time: 40 Minutes | **Servings:** 4)

Ingredients:

- 8-ounce mushrooms; chopped
- 1 asparagus bunch; cut into medium pieces
- 1-pound shrimp; peeled and deveined
- 1 teaspoon red pepper flakes; crushed
- 1 yellow onion; chopped
- 2 garlic cloves; minced
- 1 cup heavy cream
- 1/4 cup butter; melted
- 1 cup parmesan cheese; grated
- 1 spaghetti squash; cut into halves
- 2 tablespoon olive oil
- 2 teaspoon Italian seasoning
- Salt and black pepper to the taste

Directions:

1. Place squash halves in you air fryer's basket; cook at 390°F, for 17 minutes; transfer to a cutting board, scoop insides and transfer to a bowl
2. Put water in a pot, add some salt, bring to a boil over medium heat, add asparagus, steam for a couple of minutes; transfer to a bowl filled with ice water, drain and leave aside as well.
3. Heat up a pan that fits your air fryer with the oil over medium heat, add onions and mushrooms; stir and cook for 7 minutes
4. Add pepper flakes, Italian seasoning, salt, pepper, squash, asparagus, shrimp, melted butter, cream, parmesan and garlic; toss and cook in your air fryer at 360°F, for 6 minutes. Divide everything on plates and serve

Roasted Cod & Prosciutto

(Prep + Cooking Time: 20 Minutes | **Servings:** 4)

Ingredients:

- 4 medium cod filets
- 1 tablespoon parsley; chopped
- 1/4 cup butter; melted
- 1 teaspoon Dijon mustard
- 1 shallot; chopped
- 2 garlic cloves; minced
- 2 tablespoon lemon juice
- 3 tablespoon prosciutto; chopped.
- Salt and black pepper to the taste

Directions:

1. In a bowl; mix mustard with butter, garlic, parsley, shallot, lemon juice, prosciutto, salt and pepper and whisk well
2. Season fish with salt and pepper; spread prosciutto mix all over, put in your air fryer and cook at 390°F, for 10 minutes. Divide among plates and serve

Chili Salmon Recipe

(Prep + Cooking Time: 25 Minutes **| Servings:** 12)

Ingredients:

- 1¼ cups coconut; shredded.
- 1-pound salmon; cubed
- 1/3 cup flour
- 4 red chilies; chopped
- 3 garlic cloves; minced
- 1 egg
- 2 tablespoon olive oil
- 1/4 cup water
- 1/4 cup balsamic vinegar
- A pinch of salt and black pepper
- 1/2 cup honey

Directions:

1. In a bowl; mix flour with a pinch of salt and stir.
2. In another bowl; mix egg with black pepper and whisk
3. Put coconut in a third bowl
4. Dip salmon cubes in flour, egg and coconut, put them in your air fryer's basket, cook at 370°F, for 8 minutes; shaking halfway and divide among plates.
5. Heat up a pan with the water over medium high heat, add chilies, cloves, vinegar and honey; stir very well, bring to a boil, simmer for a couple of minutes; drizzle over salmon and serve

Buttery Shrimp Skewers

(Prep + Cooking Time: 16 Minutes **| Servings:** 2)

Ingredients:

- 8 shrimps; peeled and deveined
- 1 tablespoon butter; melted
- 4 garlic cloves; minced
- 8 green bell pepper slices
- 1 tablespoon rosemary; chopped
- Salt and black pepper to the taste

Directions:

1. In a bowl; mix shrimp with garlic, butter, salt, pepper, rosemary and bell pepper slices; toss to coat and leave aside for 10 minutes
2. Arrange 2 shrimp and 2 bell pepper slices on a skewer and repeat with the rest of the shrimp and bell pepper pieces
3. Place them all in your air fryer's basket and cook at 360°F, for 6 minutes. Divide among plates and serve right away.

Stuffed Salmon Delight

(Prep + Cooking Time: 30 Minutes **| Servings:** 2)

Ingredients:

- 2 salmon fillets; skinless and boneless
- 5-ounce tiger shrimp; peeled, deveined and chopped
- 6 mushrooms; chopped.
- 3 green onions; chopped
- 2 cups spinach; torn
- 1 tablespoon olive oil
- 1/4 cup macadamia nuts; toasted and chopped
- Salt and black pepper to the taste

Directions:

1. Heat up a pan with half of the oil over medium high heat, add mushrooms, onions, salt and pepper; stir and cook for 4 minutes
2. Add macadamia nuts, spinach and shrimp; stir, cook for 3 minutes and take off heat.
3. Make an incision lengthwise in each salmon fillet, season with salt and pepper, divide spinach and shrimp mix into incisions and rub with the rest of the olive oil
4. Place in your air fryer's basket and cook at 360°F and cook for 10 minutes; flipping halfway. Divide stuffed salmon on plates and serve

Fried Branzino

(Prep + Cooking Time: 20 Minutes | **Servings:** 4)

Ingredients:
- 4 medium branzino fillets; boneless
- 1/2 cup parsley; chopped
- A pinch of red pepper flakes; crushed
- Zest from 1 lemon; grated
- Zest from 1 orange; grated
- 2 tablespoon olive oil
- Juice from 1/2 lemon
- Juice from 1/2 orange
- Salt and black pepper to the taste

Directions:
1. In a large bowl; mix fish fillets with lemon zest, orange zest, lemon juice, orange juice, salt, pepper, oil and pepper flakes; toss really well, transfer fillets to your preheated air fryer at 350°F and bake for 10 minutes; flipping fillets once. Divide fish on plates, sprinkle with parsley and serve right away

Creamy Salmon Recipe

(Prep + Cooking Time: 20 Minutes | **Servings:** 4)

Ingredients:
- 4 salmon fillets; boneless
- 1/2 cup coconut cream
- 1 tablespoon olive oil
- 1/3 cup cheddar cheese; grated
- 1 ½ teaspoon mustard
- Salt and black pepper to the taste

Directions:
1. Season salmon with salt and pepper, drizzle the oil and rub well
2. In a bowl; mix coconut cream with cheddar, mustard, salt and pepper and stir well.
3. Transfer salmon to a pan that fits your air fryer; add coconut cream mix, introduce in your air fryer and cook at 320°F, for 10 minutes. Divide among plates and serve

Black Cod & Plum Sauce

(Prep + Cooking Time: 25 Minutes | **Servings:** 2)

Ingredients:
- 2 medium black cod fillets; skinless and boneless
- 1 red plum; pitted and chopped
- 2 teaspoon raw honey
- 2 teaspoon whole wheat flour
- 4 teaspoon lemon juice
- 1/2 teaspoon smoked paprika
- 1 teaspoon olive oil
- 2 teaspoon parsley
- 1/4 teaspoon black peppercorns; crushed
- 1 egg white
- 1/2 cup red quinoa; already cooked
- 1/4 cup water

Directions:
1. In a bowl; mix 1 teaspoon lemon juice with egg white, flour and 1/4 teaspoon paprika and whisk well.
2. Put quinoa in a bowl and mix it with ⅓ of egg white mix
3. Put the fish into the bowl with the remaining egg white mix and toss to coat.
4. Dip fish in quinoa mix; coat well and leave aside for 10 minutes.
5. Heat up a pan with 1 teaspoon oil over medium heat; add peppercorns, honey and plum; stir, bring to a simmer and cook for 1 minute
6. Add the rest of the lemon juice, the rest of the paprika and the water; stir well and simmer for 5 minutes.
7. Add parsley; stir, take sauce off heat and leave aside for now.
8. Put fish in your air fryer and cook at 380°F, for 10 minute. Arrange fish on plates, drizzle plum sauce on top and serve

Catfish Fillets Recipe

(Prep + Cooking Time: 22 Minutes | **Servings:** 4)

Ingredients:
- 2 catfish fillets
- 1 teaspoon mustard
- 1 tablespoon balsamic vinegar
- 1 tablespoon parsley; chopped
- 4-ounce Worcestershire sauce
- 1/2 teaspoon jerk seasoning
- 3/4 cup catsup
- 1/2 teaspoon garlic; minced
- 2-ounce butter
- Salt and black pepper to the taste

Directions:
1. Heat up a pan with the butter over medium heat, add Worcestershire sauce, garlic, jerk seasoning, mustard, catsup, vinegar, salt and pepper; stir well, take off heat and add fish fillets
2. Toss well, leave aside for 10 minutes; drain fillets, transfer them to your preheated air fryer's basket at 350°F and cook for 8 minutes; flipping fillets halfway. Divide among plates, sprinkle parsley on top and serve right away

Salmon and Avocado Salad Recipe

(Prep + Cooking Time: 30 Minutes | **Servings:** 4)

Ingredients:
- 2 medium salmon fillets
- 1/4 cup melted butter
- 5 cilantro springs; chopped
- 2 tablespoon white wine vinegar
- 4-ounce mushrooms; sliced
- 1 avocado; pitted, peeled and cubed
- 12 cherry tomatoes; halved
- 2 tablespoon olive oil
- 8-ounce lettuce leaves; torn
- 1 jalapeno pepper; chopped
- 1-ounce feta cheese; crumbled
- Sea salt and black pepper to the taste

Directions:
1. Place salmon on a lined baking sheet, brush with 2 tablespoon melted butter, season with salt and pepper; broil for 15 minutes over medium heat and then keep warm
2. Meanwhile; heat up a pan with the rest of the butter over medium heat, add mushrooms; stir and cook for a few minutes
3. Put tomatoes in a bowl, add salt, pepper and 1 tablespoon olive oil and toss to coat
4. In a salad bowl; mix salmon with mushrooms, lettuce, avocado, tomatoes, jalapeno and cilantro. Add the rest of the oil, vinegar, salt and pepper, sprinkle cheese on top and serve

Special Salmon Recipe

(Prep + Cooking Time: 35 Minutes | **Servings:** 4)

Ingredients:
- 1-pound medium beets; sliced
- 1 ½-pound salmon fillets; skinless and boneless
- 1 tablespoon fresh tarragon; chopped
- 3 tablespoon shallots; chopped
- 1 tablespoon grated lemon zest
- 1/4 cup lemon juice
- 4 cups mixed baby greens
- 6 tablespoon olive oil
- 1 tablespoon chives; chopped
- 1 tablespoon parsley; chopped.
- Salt and pepper to the taste

Directions:
1. In a bowl; mix beets with 1/2 tablespoon oil and toss to coat.
2. Season them with salt and pepper, arrange them on a baking sheet; introduce in the oven at 450°F and bake for 20 minutes
3. Take beets out of the oven, add salmon on top, brush it with the rest if the oil and season with salt and pepper
4. In a bowl; mix chives with parsley and tarragon and sprinkle 1 tablespoon of this mix over salmon.

5. Introduce in the oven again and bake for 15 minutes.
6. Meanwhile; in a boil with shallots with lemon peel, salt, pepper and lemon juice and the rest of the herbs mixture and stir gently
7. Combine 2 tablespoon of shallots dressing with mixed greens and toss gently. Take salmon out of the oven, arrange on plates, add beets and greens on the side, drizzle the rest of the shallot dressing on top and serve right away.

Tasty Pollock Recipe

(Prep + Cooking Time: 25 Minutes | **Servings:** 6)

Ingredients:

- 4 Pollock fillets; boneless
- 1/4 cup parmesan; grated
- 2 tablespoon butter; melted
- Salt and black pepper to the taste
- 1/2 cup sour cream
- Cooking spray

Directions:

1. In a bowl, mix sour cream with butter, parmesan, salt and pepper and whisk well
2. Spray fish with cooking spray and season with salt and pepper.
3. Spread sour cream mix on one side of each Pollock fillet, arrange them in your preheated air fryer at 320°F and cook them for 15 minutes. Divide Pollock fillets on plates and serve with a tasty side salad

Hawaiian Salmon Recipe

(Prep + Cooking Time: 20 Minutes | **Servings:** 2)

Ingredients:

- 20-ounce canned pineapple pieces and juice
- 2 teaspoon garlic powder
- 1 teaspoon onion powder
- 1 tablespoon balsamic vinegar
- 2 medium salmon fillets; boneless
- 1/2 teaspoon ginger; grated
- Salt and black pepper to the taste

Directions:

1. Season salmon with garlic powder, onion powder, salt and black pepper, rub well, transfer to a heat proof dish that fits your air fryer, add ginger and pineapple chunks and toss them really gently
2. Drizzle the vinegar all over, put in your air fryer and cook at 350°F, for 10 minutes. Divide everything on plates and serve

Salmon and Avocado Sauce Recipe

(Prep + Cooking Time: 20 Minutes | **Servings:** 4)

Ingredients:

- 4 salmon fillets; boneless
- 1 avocado; pitted, peeled and chopped
- 1 tablespoon lime juice
- 1 tablespoon lime zest; grated
- 1 teaspoon onion powder
- 1 teaspoon garlic powder
- 1/4 cup cilantro; chopped
- 1/3 cup coconut milk
- Salt and black pepper to the taste

Directions:

1. Season salmon fillets with salt, black pepper and lime zest, rub well, put in your air fryer, cook at 350°F, for 9 minutes; flipping once and divide among plates
2. In your food processor, mix avocado with cilantro, garlic powder, onion powder, lime juice, salt, pepper and coconut milk; blend well, drizzle over salmon and serve right away

Spanish Salmon Recipe

(Prep + Cooking Time: 25 Minutes | **Servings:** 6)

Ingredients:
- 2 cups bread croutons
- 3/4 cup green olives; pitted
- 3 red bell peppers; cut into medium wedges
- 1/2 teaspoon smoked paprika
- 3 red onions; cut into medium wedges
- 5 tablespoon olive oil
- 6 medium salmon fillets; skinless and boneless
- 2 tablespoon parsley; chopped
- Salt and black pepper to the taste

Directions:
1. In a heat proof dish that fits your air fryer, mix bread croutons with onion wedges, bell pepper ones, olives, salt, pepper, paprika and 3 tablespoon olive oil; toss well, place in your air fryer and cook at 356°F, for 7 minutes
2. Rub salmon with the rest of the oil; add over veggies and cook at 360°F, for 8 minutes. Divide fish and veggie mix on plates, sprinkle parsley all over and serve

Fish and Couscous Recipe

(Prep + Cooking Time: 25 Minutes | **Servings:** 4)

Ingredients:
- 2½-pound sea bass; gutted
- 5 teaspoon fennel seeds
- 2 small fennel bulbs; cored and sliced
- 1/4 cup almonds; toasted and sliced
- 3/4 cup whole wheat couscous; cooked
- 2 red onions; chopped
- Cooking spray
- Salt and black pepper to the taste

Directions:
1. Season fish with salt and pepper, spray with cooking spray; place in your air fryer and cook at 350°F, for 10 minutes
2. Meanwhile; spray a pan with some cooking oil and heat it up over medium heat
3. Add fennel seeds to this pan; stir and toast them for 1 minute
4. Add onion, salt, pepper, fennel bulbs, almonds and couscous; stir, cook for 2 - 3 minutes and divide among plates. Add fish next to couscous mix and serve right away.

Mustard Salmon Recipe

(Prep + Cooking Time: 20 Minutes | **Servings:** 1)

Ingredients:
- 1 big salmon fillet; boneless
- 1 tablespoon coconut oil
- 1 tablespoon maple extract
- 2 tablespoon mustard
- Salt and black pepper to the taste

Directions:
1. In a bowl; mix maple extract with mustard, whisk well, season salmon with salt and pepper and brush salmon with this mix
2. Spray some cooking spray over fish; place in your air fryer and cook at 370°F, for 10 minutes; flipping halfway. Serve with a tasty side salad

Snapper Fillets and Veggies Recipe

(Prep + Cooking Time: 24 Minutes | Servings: 2)

Ingredients:

- 2 red snapper fillets; boneless
- 1/2 cup green bell pepper; chopped
- 1/2 cup leeks; chopped
- 1 teaspoon tarragon; dried
- 1 tablespoon olive oil
- 1/2 cup red bell pepper; chopped.
- A splash of white wine
- Salt and black pepper to the taste

Directions:

1. In a heat proof dish that fits your air fryer; mix fish fillets with salt, pepper, oil, green bell pepper, red bell pepper, leeks, tarragon and wine; toss well everything, introduce in preheated air fryer at 350°F and cook for 14 minutes; flipping fish fillets halfway. Divide fish and veggies on plates and serve warm

Delightful French Cod

(Prep + Cooking Time: 32 Minutes | Servings: 4)

Ingredients:

- 2-pound cod; boneless
- 14-ounce canned tomatoes; stewed
- 2 tablespoon olive oil
- 1 yellow onion; chopped
- 1/2 cup white wine
- 2 garlic cloves; minced
- 3 tablespoon parsley; chopped
- Salt and black pepper to the taste
- 2 tablespoon butter

Directions:

1. Heat up a pan with the oil over medium heat, add garlic and onion; stir and cook for 5 minutes
2. Add wine; stir and cook for 1 minute more
3. Add tomatoes; stir, bring to a boil, cook for 2 minutes; add parsley; stir again and take off heat
4. Pour this mix into a heat proof dish that fits your air fryer, add fish, season it with salt and pepper and cook in your fryer at 350°F, for 14 minutes. Divide fish and tomatoes mix on plates and serve.

Honey Sea Bass Recipe

(Prep + Cooking Time: 20 Minutes | Servings: 2)

Ingredients:

- 2 sea bass fillets
- Zest from 1/2 orange; grated
- 2-ounce watercress
- 2 tablespoon mustard
- 2 teaspoon honey
- 2 tablespoon olive oil
- 1/2-pound canned lentils; drained
- Juice from 1/2 orange
- A small bunch of dill; chopped
- A small bunch of parsley; chopped
- A pinch of salt and black pepper

Directions:

1. Season fish fillets with salt and pepper, add orange zest and juice, rub with 1 tablespoon oil, with honey and mustard, rub, transfer to your air fryer and cook at 350°F, for 10 minutes; flipping halfway
2. Meanwhile; put lentils in a small pot, warm it up over medium heat, add the rest of the oil, watercress, dill and parsley; stir well and divide among plates. Add fish fillets and serve right away

Flavored Jamaican Salmon Recipe

(Prep + Cooking Time: 20 Minutes | **Servings:** 4)

Ingredients:

- 4 cups baby arugula
- 2 cups radish; julienned
- 2 teaspoon sriracha sauce
- 1/4 cup pepitas; toasted
- 2 teaspoon olive oil
- 4 teaspoon apple cider vinegar
- 3 teaspoon avocado oil
- 4 teaspoon sugar
- 3 scallions; chopped
- 2 cups cabbage; shredded.
- 1 ½ teaspoon Jamaican jerk seasoning
- 4 medium salmon fillets; boneless
- Salt and black pepper to the taste

Directions:

1. In a bowl; mix sriracha with sugar, whisk and transfer 2 teaspoon to another bowl
2. Combine 2 teaspoon sriracha mix with the avocado oil, olive oil, vinegar, salt and pepper and whisk well.
3. Sprinkle jerk seasoning over salmon, rub with sriracha and sugar mix and season with salt and pepper.
4. Transfer to your air fryer and cook at 360°F, for 10 minutes; flipping once
5. In a bowl; mix radishes with cabbage, arugula, salt, pepper, sriracha and vinegar mix and toss well. Divide salmon and radish mix on plates, sprinkle pepitas and scallions on top and serve

Meat Recipes

Pork with Couscous Recipe

(Prep + Cooking Time: 45 Minutes | **Servings:** 6)

Ingredients:

- 2 ½-pound pork loin; boneless and trimmed
- 2 ¼ teaspoon sage; dried
- 3/4 cup chicken stock
- 1/4 teaspoon marjoram; dried
- 1/4 teaspoon rosemary; dried
- 1 teaspoon basil; dried
- 2 tablespoon olive oil
- 2 cups couscous; cooked
- 1/2 tablespoon sweet paprika
- 1/2 tablespoon garlic powder
- 1 teaspoon oregano; dried
- Salt and black pepper to the taste

Directions:

1. In a bowl; mix oil with stock, paprika, garlic powder, sage, rosemary, thyme, marjoram, oregano, salt and pepper to the taste, whisk well, add pork loin, toss well and leave aside for 1 hour
2. Transfer everything to a pan that fits your air fryer and cook at 370°F, for 35 minutes. Divide among plates and serve with couscous on the side

Lemony Lamb Leg Recipe

(Prep + Cooking Time: 1 hour 10 Minutes | **Servings:** 6)

Ingredients:

- 4-pound lamb leg
- 2 tablespoon olive oil
- 2 tablespoon parsley; chopped
- 2 tablespoon oregano; chopped
- 1 tablespoon lemon rind; grated
- 3 garlic cloves; minced
- 2 springs rosemary; chopped.
- 2 tablespoon lemon juice
- 2-pound baby potatoes
- 1 cup beef stock
- Salt and black pepper to the taste

Directions:

1. Make small cuts all over lamb, insert rosemary springs and season with salt and pepper
2. In a bowl; mix 1 tablespoon oil with oregano, parsley, garlic, lemon juice and rind; stir and rub lamb with this mix.
3. Heat up a pan that fits your air fryer with the rest of the oil over medium high heat, add potatoes; stir and cook for 3 minutes.
4. Add lamb and stock; stir, introduce in your air fryer and cook at 360°F, for 1 hour. Divide everything on plates and serve

Fennel Flavored Pork Roast Recipe

(Prep + Cooking Time: 1 hour 10 Minutes | **Servings:** 10)

Ingredients:

- 5 ½-pound pork loin roast; trimmed
- 3 garlic cloves; minced
- 2 tablespoon rosemary; chopped
- 1 teaspoon fennel; ground
- 1 tablespoon fennel seeds
- 2 teaspoon red pepper; crushed
- 1/4 cup olive oil
- Salt and black pepper to the taste

Directions:

1. In your food processor mix garlic with fennel seeds, fennel, rosemary, red pepper, some black pepper and the olive oil and blend until you obtain a paste
2. Spread 2 tablespoon garlic paste on pork loin, rub well, season with salt and pepper, introduce in your preheated air fryer and cook at 350°F, for 30 minutes
3. Reduce heat to 300°F and cook for 15 minutes more. Slice pork, divide among plates and serve.

Beef Fillets with Garlic Mayo Recipe

(Prep + Cooking Time: 50 Minutes **| Servings:** 8)

Ingredients:

- 3-pound beef fillet
- 1 cup mayonnaise
- 2 tablespoon mustard
- 1/4 cup tarragon; chopped
- 1/3 cup sour cream
- 2 tablespoon chives; chopped
- 2 tablespoon mustard
- 2 garlic cloves; minced
- Salt and black pepper to the taste

Directions:

1. Season beef with salt and pepper to the taste, place in your air fryer, cook at 370°F, for 20 minutes; transfer to a plate and leave aside for a few minutes
2. In a bowl; mix garlic with sour cream, chives, mayo, some salt and pepper, whisk and leave aside.
3. In another bowl, mix mustard with Dijon mustard and tarragon, whisk, add beef, toss, return to your air fryer and cook at 350°F, for 20 minutes more. Divide beef on plates, spread garlic mayo on top and serve

Beef and Cabbage Mix Recipe

(Prep + Cooking Time: 50 Minutes **| Servings:** 6)

Ingredients:

- 2 ½-pound beef brisket
- 1 cabbage head; cut into medium wedges
- 3 turnips; cut into quarters
- 1 cup beef stock
- 3 garlic cloves; chopped
- 4 carrots; chopped
- 2 bay leaves
- Salt and black pepper to the taste

Directions:

1. Put beef brisket and stock in a large pan that fits your air fryer, season beef with salt and pepper, add garlic and bay leaves, carrots, cabbage, potatoes and turnips, toss, introduce in your air fryer and cook at 360°F and cook for 40 minutes. Divide among plates and serve

Lamb and Lemon Sauce Recipe

(Prep + Cooking Time: 40 Minutes **| Servings:** 4)

Ingredients:

- 2 lamb shanks
- 2 garlic cloves; minced
- 1/2 teaspoon oregano; dried
- 4 tablespoon olive oil
- Juice from 1/2 lemon
- Zest from 1/2 lemon
- Salt and black pepper to the taste

Directions:

1. Season lamb with salt, pepper, rub with garlic, put in your air fryer and cook at 350°F, for 30 minutes
2. Meanwhile; in a bowl, mix lemon juice with lemon zest, some salt and pepper, the olive oil and oregano and whisk very well. Shred lamb, discard bone, divide among plates, drizzle the lemon dressing all over and serve.

Simple Braised Pork Recipe

(Prep + Cooking Time: 1 hour 20 Minutes | **Servings:** 4)

Ingredients:

- 2-pound pork loin roast; boneless and cubed
- 2 cups chicken stock
- 4 tablespoon butter; melted
- 1/2 cup dry white wine
- 2 garlic cloves; minced
- 1 teaspoon thyme; chopped
- 1 thyme spring
- 1/2-pound red grapes
- 1 bay leaf
- 1/2 yellow onion; chopped.
- 2 tablespoon white flour
- Salt and black pepper to the taste

Directions:

1. Season pork cubes with salt and pepper, rub with 2 tablespoon melted butter, put in your air fryer and cook at 370°F, for 8 minutes
2. Meanwhile; heat up a pan that fits your air fryer with 2 tablespoon butter over medium high heat, add garlic and onion; stir and cook for 2 minutes.
3. Add wine, stock, salt, pepper, thyme, flour and bay leaf; stir well, bring to a simmer and take off heat.
4. Add pork cubes and grapes, toss, introduce in your air fryer and cook at 360°F, for 30 minutes more.
5. Divide everything on plates and serve

Chinese Steak and Broccoli Recipe

(Prep + Cooking Time: 57 Minutes | **Servings:** 4)

Ingredients:

- 3/4-pound round steak; cut into strips
- 1-pound broccoli florets
- 1 tablespoon olive oil
- 1 garlic clove; minced
- 2 teaspoon sesame oil
- 1 teaspoon sugar
- 1/3 cup sherry
- 1/3 cup oyster sauce
- 1 teaspoon soy sauce

Directions:

1. In a bowl; mix sesame oil with oyster sauce, soy sauce, sherry and sugar; stir well, add beef, toss and leave aside for 30 minutes
2. Transfer beef to a pan that fits your air fryer, also add broccoli, garlic and oil, toss everything and cook at 380°F, for 12 minutes. Divide among plates and serve

Provencal Pork Recipe

(Prep + Cooking Time: 25 Minutes | **Servings:** 2)

Ingredients:

- 7-ounce pork tenderloin
- 1/2 tablespoon mustard
- 1 tablespoon olive oil
- 1 red onion; sliced
- 1 yellow bell pepper; cut into strips
- 2 teaspoon Provencal herbs
- 1 green bell pepper; cut into strips
- Salt and black pepper to the taste

Directions:

1. In a baking dish that fits your air fryer, mix yellow bell pepper with green bell pepper, onion, salt, pepper, Provencal herbs and half of the oil and toss well
2. Season pork with salt, pepper, mustard and the rest of the oil, toss well and add to veggies. Introduce everything in your air fryer,
3. Cook at 370°F, for 15 minutes; divide among plates and serve

Greek Beef Meatballs Salad Recipe

(Prep + Cooking Time: 20 Minutes | **Servings:** 6)

Ingredients:
- 17-ounce beef; ground
- 1 yellow onion; grated
- 5 bread slices; cubed
- 2 garlic cloves; minced
- 1/4 cup mint; chopped
- 2 ½ teaspoon oregano; dried
- 7-ounce cherry tomatoes; halved
- 1 cup baby spinach
- 1 ½ tablespoon lemon juice
- 7-ounce Greek yogurt
- 1/4 cup milk
- 1 egg; whisked
- 1/4 cup parsley; chopped.
- Salt and black pepper to the taste
- 1 tablespoon olive oil
- Cooking spray

Directions:
1. Put torn bread in a bowl; add milk, soak for a few minutes; squeeze and transfer to another bowl.
2. Add beef, egg, salt, pepper, oregano, mint, parsley, garlic and onion; stir and shape medium meatballs out of this mix
3. Spray them with cooking spray, place them in your air fryer and cook at 370°F, for 10 minutes.
4. In a salad bowl, mix spinach with cucumber and tomato. Add meatballs, the oil, some salt, pepper, lemon juice and yogurt, toss and serve

Marinated Pork Chops and Onions

(Prep + Cooking Time: 24 hours 25 Minutes | **Servings:** 6)

Ingredients:
- 2 pork chops
- 2 yellow onions; sliced
- 2 garlic cloves; minced
- 2 teaspoon mustard
- 1 teaspoon sweet paprika
- 1/2 teaspoon oregano; dried
- 1/2 teaspoon thyme; dried
- 1/4 cup olive oil
- A pinch of cayenne pepper
- Salt and black pepper to the taste

Directions:
1. In a bowl; mix oil with garlic, mustard, paprika, black pepper, oregano, thyme and cayenne and whisk well.
2. Combine onions with meat and mustard mix, toss to coat, cover and keep in the fridge for 1 day
3. Transfer meat and onions mix to a pan that fits your air fryer and cook at 360°F, for 25 minutes.
4. Divide everything on plates and serve

Simple Fried Pork Shoulder Recipe

(Prep + Cooking Time: 1 hour and 50 minutes | **Servings:** 6)

Ingredients:
- 4-pound pork shoulder
- 3 tablespoon garlic; minced
- 3 tablespoon olive oil
- Salt and black pepper to the taste

Directions:
1. In a bowl; mix olive oil with salt, pepper and oil, whisk well and brush pork shoulder with this mix.
2. Place in preheated air fryer and cook at 390°F, for 10 minutes
3. Reduce heat to 300°F and roast pork for 1 hour and 10 minutes. Slice pork shoulder, divide among plates and serve with a side salad

Short Ribs and Sauce Recipe

(Prep + Cooking Time: 46 Minutes | Servings: 4)

Ingredients:
- 2 green onions; chopped
- 1 teaspoon vegetable oil
- 3 garlic cloves; minced
- 3 ginger slices
- 4-pound short ribs
- 1/2 cup water
- 1/2 cup soy sauce
- 1/4 cup rice wine
- 1/4 cup pear juice
- 2 teaspoon sesame oil

Directions:
1. Heat up a pan that fits your air fryer with the oil over medium heat, add green onions, ginger and garlic; stir and cook for 1 minute
2. Add ribs, water, wine, soy sauce, sesame oil and pear juice; stir, introduce in your air fryer and cook at 350°F, for 35 minutes. Divide ribs and sauce on plates and serve

Beef and Green Onions Marinade

(Prep + Cooking Time: 30 Minutes | Servings: 4)

Ingredients:
- 1 cup green onion; chopped
- 5 garlic cloves; minced
- 1 teaspoon black pepper
- 1/4 cup brown sugar
- 1 cup soy sauce
- 1/2 cup water
- 1/4 cup sesame seeds
- 1-pound lean beef

Directions:
1. In a bowl; mix onion with soy sauce, water, sugar, garlic, sesame seeds and pepper, whisk, add meat, toss and leave aside for 10 minutes
2. Drain beef, transfer to your preheated air fryer and cook at 390°F, for 20 minutes. Slice, divide among plates and serve with a side salad

Lamb Roast and Potatoes Recipe

(Prep + Cooking Time: 55 Minutes | Servings: 6)

Ingredients:
- 4-pound lamb roast
- 6 potatoes; halved
- 1/2 cup lamb stock
- 4 bay leaves
- 3 garlic cloves; minced
- 1 spring rosemary
- Salt and black pepper to the taste

Directions:
1. Put potatoes in a dish that fits your air fryer, add lamb, garlic, rosemary spring, salt, pepper, bay leaves and stock, toss, introduce in your air fryer and cook at 360°F, for 45 minutes. Slice lamb, divide among plates and serve with potatoes and cooking juices

Lamb and Creamy Brussels Sprouts

(Prep + Cooking Time: 1 hour and 20 minutes | Servings: 4)

Ingredients:
- 2-pound leg of lamb; scored
- 1 ½-pound Brussels sprouts; trimmed
- 1 tablespoon butter; melted
- 1/2 cup sour cream
- 1 garlic clove; minced
- 2 tablespoon olive oil
- 1 tablespoon rosemary; chopped
- 1 tablespoon lemon thyme; chopped.
- Salt and black pepper to the taste

Directions:

1. Season leg of lamb with salt, pepper, thyme and rosemary, brush with oil, place in your air fryer's basket, cook at 300°F, for 1 hour, transfer to a plate and keep warm
2. In a pan that fits your air fryer, mix Brussels sprouts with salt, pepper, garlic, butter and sour cream, toss, put in your air fryer and cook at 400°F, for 10 minutes. Divide lamb on plates, add Brussels sprouts on the side and serve

Marinated Lamb and Veggies

(Prep + Cooking Time: 40 Minutes | **Servings:** 4)

Ingredients:

- 1 carrot; chopped
- 1 onion; sliced
- 8-ounce lamb loin; sliced

- 1/2 tablespoon olive oil
- 3-ounce bean sprouts

For the marinade:

- 1 garlic clove; minced
- 1/2 apple; grated
- 1 tablespoon ginger; grated
- 1 small yellow onion; grated

- 2 tablespoon orange juice
- 5 tablespoon soy sauce
- 1 tablespoon sugar
- Salt and black pepper to the taste

Directions:

1. In a bowl; mix 1 grated onion with the apple, garlic, 1 tablespoon ginger, soy sauce, orange juice, sugar and black pepper, whisk well, add lamb and leave aside for 10 minutes
2. Heat up a pan that fits your air fryer with the olive oil over medium high heat, add 1 sliced onion, carrot and bean sprouts; stir and cook for 3 minutes.
3. Add lamb and the marinade, transfer pan to your preheated air fryer and cook at 360°F, for 25 minutes. Divide everything into bowls and serve

Lamb Ribs Recipe

(Prep + Cooking Time: 55 Minutes | **Servings:** 8)

Ingredients:

- 8 lamb ribs
- 2 cups veggie stock
- 1 tablespoon rosemary; chopped
- 2 tablespoon extra-virgin olive oil

- 4 garlic cloves; minced
- 2 carrots; chopped
- 3 tablespoon white flour
- Salt and black pepper to the taste

Directions:

1. Season lamb ribs with salt and pepper, rub with oil and garlic, put in preheated air fryer and cook at 360°F, for 10 minutes
2. In a heat proof dish that fits your fryer, mix stock with flour and whisk well.
3. Add rosemary, carrots and lamb ribs, place in your air fryer and cook at 350°F, for 30 minutes. Divide lamb mix on plates and serve hot

Creamy Pork Recipe

(Prep + Cooking Time: 32 Minutes **| Servings:** 6)

Ingredients:

- 2-pound pork meat; boneless and cubed
- 1 garlic clove; minced
- 3 cups chicken stock
- 2 tablespoon white flour
- 1 ½ cups sour cream
- 2 yellow onions; chopped
- 2 tablespoon dill; chopped.
- 2 tablespoon sweet paprika
- 1 tablespoon olive oil
- Salt and black pepper to the taste

Directions:

1. In a pan that fits your air fryer, mix pork with salt, pepper and oil, toss, introduce in your air fryer and cook at 360°F, for 7 minutes
2. Add onion, garlic, stock, paprika, flour, sour cream and dill, toss and cook at 370°F, for 15 minutes more. Divide everything on plates and serve right away

Beef Kabobs Recipe

(Prep + Cooking Time: 20 Minutes **| Servings:** 4)

Ingredients:

- 2 red bell peppers; chopped
- 2-pound sirloin steak; cut into medium pieces
- 1 red onion; chopped
- 1 zucchini; sliced
- Juice form 1 lime
- 2 tablespoon chili powder
- 2 tablespoon hot sauce
- 1/2 tablespoon cumin; ground
- 1/4 cup olive oil
- 1/4 cup salsa
- Salt and black pepper to the taste

Directions:

1. In a bowl; mix salsa with lime juice, oil, hot sauce, chili powder, cumin, salt and black pepper and whisk well.
2. Divide meat bell peppers, zucchini and onion on skewers, brush kabobs with the salsa mix you made earlier, put them in your preheated air fryer and cook them for 10 minutes at 370°F, flipping kabobs halfway. Divide among plates and serve with a side salad

Crispy Lamb Recipe

(Prep + Cooking Time: 40 Minutes **| Servings:** 4)

Ingredients:

- 1 tablespoon bread crumbs
- 1 tablespoon olive oil
- 1 egg;
- 1 tablespoon rosemary; chopped
- 1 garlic clove; minced
- 28-ounce rack of lamb
- 2 tablespoon macadamia nuts; toasted and crushed
- Salt and black pepper to the taste

Directions:

1. In a bowl; mix oil with garlic and stir well
2. Season lamb with salt, pepper and brush with the oil.
3. In another bowl, mix nuts with breadcrumbs and rosemary
4. Put the egg in a separate bowl and whisk well.
5. Dip lamb in egg, then in macadamia mix, place them in your air fryer's basket, cook at 360°F and cook for 25 minutes; increase heat to 400°F and cook for 5 minutes more. Divide among plates and serve right away

Short Ribs and Beer Sauce Recipe

(Prep + Cooking Time: 60 Minutes **| Servings:** 6)

Ingredients:
- 4-pound short ribs; cut into small pieces
- 1 yellow onion; chopped.
- 1 cup chicken stock
- 1/4 cup tomato paste
- 1 cup dark beer
- 1 Portobello mushroom; dried
- 1 bay leaf
- 6 thyme springs; chopped
- Salt and black pepper to the taste

Directions:
1. Heat up a pan that fits your air fryer over medium heat, add tomato paste, onion, stock, beer, mushroom, bay leaves and thyme and bring to a simmer.
2. Add ribs, introduce in your air fryer and cook at 350°F, for 40 minutes. Divide everything on plates and serve

Beef Steaks with Snow Peas & Mushrooms

(Prep + Cooking Time: 32 Minutes **| Servings:** 2)

Ingredients:
- 7-ounce snow peas
- 2 tablespoon soy sauce
- 1 yellow onion; cut into rings
- 1 teaspoon olive oil
- 2 beef steaks; cut into strips
- 8-ounce white mushrooms; halved
- Salt and black pepper to the taste

Directions:
1. In a bowl; mix olive oil with soy sauce, whisk, add beef strips and toss
2. In another bowl, mix snow peas, onion and mushrooms with salt, pepper and the oil, toss well, put in a pan that fits your air fryer and cook at 350°F, for 16 minutes.
3. Add beef strips to the pan as well and cook at 400°F, for 6 minutes more
4. Divide everything on plates and serve

Rib Eye Steak Recipe

(Prep + Cooking Time: 30 Minutes **| Servings:** 4)

Ingredients:
- 2-pound rib eye steak
- 1 tablespoon olive oil

For the rub:
- 3 tablespoon sweet paprika
- 2 tablespoon onion powder
- 2 tablespoon oregano; dried
- 2 tablespoon garlic powder
- Salt and black pepper to the taste

- 1 tablespoon brown sugar
- 1 tablespoon cumin; ground
- 1 tablespoon rosemary; dried

Directions:
1. In a bowl; mix paprika with onion and garlic powder, sugar, oregano, rosemary, salt, pepper and cumin; stir and rub steak with this mix
2. Season steak with salt and pepper, rub again with the oil, put in your air fryer and cook at 400°F, for 20 minutes; flipping them halfway. Transfer steak to a cutting board, slice and serve with a side salad

Asian Pork Recipe

(Prep + Cooking Time: 45 Minutes | **Servings:** 4)

Ingredients:
- 1 teaspoon ginger powder
- 1 shallot; chopped
- 1 teaspoon coriander; ground
- 14-ounce pork chops; cubed
- 2 teaspoon chili paste
- 2 garlic cloves; minced
- 2 tablespoon olive oil
- 3-ounce peanuts; ground
- 3 tablespoon soy sauce
- 7-ounce coconut milk
- Salt and black pepper to the taste

Directions:
1. In a bowl; mix ginger with 1 teaspoon chili paste, half of the garlic, half of the soy sauce and half of the oil, whisk, add meat, toss and leave aside for 10 minutes.
2. Transfer meat to your air fryer's basket and cook at 400°F, for 12 minutes; turning halfway
3. Meanwhile; heat up a pan with the rest of the oil over medium high heat, add shallot, the rest of the garlic, coriander, coconut milk, the rest of the peanuts, the rest of the chili paste and the rest of the soy sauce; stir and cook for 5 minutes. Divide pork on plates, spread coconut mix on top and serve

Burgundy Beef Mix Recipe

(Prep + Cooking Time: 1 hour 10 Minutes | **Servings:** 7)

Ingredients:
- 2-pound beef chuck roast; cubed
- 15-ounce canned tomatoes; chopped
- 1/2 teaspoon mustard powder
- 3 tablespoon almond flour
- 1 tablespoon thyme; chopped
- 4 carrots; chopped
- 1/2-pound mushrooms; sliced
- 2 celery ribs; chopped
- 2 yellow onions; chopped
- 1 cup water
- 1 cup beef stock
- Salt and black pepper to the taste

Directions:
1. Heat up a heat proof pot that fits your air fryer over medium high heat, add beef; stir and brown them for a couple of minutes
2. Add tomatoes, mushrooms, onions, carrots, celery, salt, pepper mustard, stock and thyme and stir.
3. In a bowl mix water with flour; stir well, add this to the pot, toss, introduce in your air fryer and cook at 300°F, for 1 hour. Divide into bowls and serve

Lamb Shanks and Carrots Recipe

(Prep + Cooking Time: 55 Minutes | **Servings:** 4)

Ingredients:
- 4 lamb shanks
- 2 tablespoon olive oil
- 4-ounce red wine
- 6 carrots; roughly chopped.
- 2 garlic cloves; minced
- 2 tablespoon tomato paste
- 1 yellow onion; finely chopped
- 1 teaspoon oregano; dried
- 1 tomato; roughly chopped.
- 2 tablespoon water
- Salt and black pepper to the taste

Directions:
1. Season lamb with salt and pepper, rub with oil, put in your air fryer and cook at 360°F, for 10 minutes.
2. In a pan that fits your air fryer, mix onion with carrots, garlic, tomato paste, tomato, oregano, wine and water and toss
3. Add lamb, toss, introduce in your air fryer and cook at 370°F, for 35 minutes. Divide everything on plates and serve

Sirloin Steaks and Pico De Gallo Recipe

(Prep + Cooking Time: 20 Minutes | **Servings:** 4)

Ingredients:

- 2 tablespoon chili powder
- 4 medium sirloin steaks
- 1 teaspoon cumin; ground
- 1/2 tablespoon sweet paprika
- 1 teaspoon onion powder
- 1 teaspoon garlic powder
- Salt and black pepper to the taste

For the Pico de gallo:

- 1 small red onion; chopped
- 2 garlic cloves; minced
- 2 tablespoon lime juice
- 1/4 cup cilantro; chopped
- 1 small green bell pepper; chopped
- 1 jalapeno; chopped.
- 2 tomatoes; chopped
- 1/4 teaspoon cumin; ground

Directions:

1. In a bowl; mix chili powder with a pinch of salt, black pepper, onion powder, garlic powder, paprika and 1 teaspoon cumin; stir well, season steaks with this mix, put them in your air fryer and cook at 360°F, for 10 minutes
2. In a bowl; mix red onion with tomatoes, garlic, lime juice, bell pepper, jalapeno, cilantro, black pepper to the taste and 1/4 teaspoon cumin and toss. Top steaks with this mix and serve right away.

Lamb and Spinach Mix Recipe

(Prep + Cooking Time: 45 Minutes | **Servings:** 6)

Ingredients:

- 1-pound lamb meat; cubed
- 2 teaspoon cumin powder
- 2 tablespoon ginger; grated
- 2 garlic cloves; minced
- 2 teaspoon cardamom; ground
- 1/2 teaspoon chili powder
- 1 teaspoon turmeric
- 2 teaspoon coriander; ground
- 1-pound spinach
- 1 red onion; chopped
- 1 teaspoon garam masala
- 14-ounce canned tomatoes; chopped

Directions:

1. In a heat proof dish that fits your air fryer, mix lamb with spinach, tomatoes, ginger, garlic, onion, cardamom, cloves, cumin, garam masala, chili, turmeric and coriander; stir, introduce in preheated air fryer and cook at 360°F, for 35 minutes Divide into bowls and serve

Pork Chops and Sage Sauce Recipe

(Prep + Cooking Time: 25 Minutes | **Servings:** 2)

Ingredients:

- 2 pork chops
- 1 shallot; sliced
- 1 handful sage; chopped
- 1 tablespoon olive oil
- 2 tablespoon butter
- 1 teaspoon lemon juice
- Salt and black pepper to the taste

Directions:

1. Season pork chops with salt and pepper, rub with the oil, put in your air fryer and cook at 370°F, for 10 minutes; flipping them halfway.
2. Meanwhile; heat up a pan with the butter over medium heat, add shallot; stir and cook for 2 minutes.
3. Add sage and lemon juice; stir well, cook for a few more minutes and take off heat.
4. Divide pork chops on plates, drizzle sage sauce all over and serve.

Fryer Lamb Shanks Recipe

(Prep + Cooking Time: 55 Minutes | **Servings:** 4)

Ingredients:
- 4 lamb shanks
- 1 yellow onion; chopped
- 2 ½ cups chicken stock
- 4 teaspoon coriander seeds; crushed
- 2 tablespoon white flour
- 1 tablespoon olive oil
- 2 teaspoon honey
- 5-ounce dry sherry
- 4 bay leaves
- Salt and pepper to the taste

Directions:
1. Season lamb shanks with salt and pepper, rub with half of the oil, put in your air fryer and cook at 360°F, for 10 minutes
2. Heat up a pan that fits your air fryer with the rest of the oil over medium high heat, add onion and coriander; stir and cook for 5 minutes.
3. Add flour, sherry, stock, honey and bay leaves, salt and pepper; stir, bring to a simmer, add lamb, introduce everything in your air fryer and cook at 360°F, for 30 minutes. Divide everything on plates and serve

Beef Brisket and Onion Sauce Recipe

(Prep + Cooking Time: 2 hours 10 Minutes | **Servings:** 6)

Ingredients:
- 1-pound yellow onion; chopped
- 1/2-pound celery; chopped.
- 1-pound carrot; chopped
- 4-pound beef brisket
- 8 earl grey tea bags
- Salt and black pepper to the taste
- 4 cups water

For the sauce:
- 16-ounce canned tomatoes; chopped
- 8 earl grey tea bags
- 1/2-pound celery; chopped
- 1-ounce garlic; minced
- 1-pound sweet onion; chopped
- 1 cup brown sugar
- 4-ounce vegetable oil
- 1 cup white vinegar

Directions:
1. Put the water in a heat proof dish that fits your air fryer, add 1-pound onion, 1-pound carrot, 1/2-pound celery, salt and pepper; stir and bring to a simmer over medium high heat
2. Add beef brisket and 8 tea bags; stir, transfer to your air fryer and cook at 300°F, for 1 hour and 30 minutes.
3. Meanwhile; heat up a pan with the vegetable oil over medium high heat, add 1-pound onion; stir and sauté for 10 minutes.
4. Add garlic, 1/2-pound celery, tomatoes, sugar, vinegar, salt, pepper and 8 tea bags; stir, bring to a simmer, cook for 10 minutes and discard tea bags. Transfer beef brisket to a cutting board, slice, divide among plates, drizzle onion sauce all over and serve

Garlic and Bell Pepper Beef Recipe

(Prep + Cooking Time: 60 Minutes | **Servings:** 4)

Ingredients:
- 11-ounce steak fillets; sliced
- 2 tablespoon fish sauce
- 2 teaspoon corn flour
- 1/2 cup beef stock
- 4 garlic cloves; minced
- 2 tablespoon olive oil
- 1 tablespoon sugar
- 1 red bell pepper; cut into strips
- Black pepper to the taste
- 4 green onions; sliced

Directions:

1. In a pan that fits your air fryer mix beef with oil, garlic, black pepper and bell pepper; stir, cover and keep in the fridge for 30 minutes
2. Put the pan in your preheated air fryer and cook at 360°F, for 14 minutes
3. In a bowl; mix sugar with fish sauce; stir well, pour over beef and cook at 360°F, for 7 minutes more.
4. Add stock mixed with corn flour and green onions, toss and cook at 370°F, for 7 minutes more. Divide everything on plates and serve.

Mediterranean Steaks and Scallops

(Prep + Cooking Time: 24 Minutes | Servings: 2)

Ingredients:

- 2 beef steaks
- 10 sea scallops
- 1 shallot; chopped
- 2 tablespoon lemon juice
- 2 tablespoon parsley; chopped
- 1 teaspoon lemon zest
- 1/4 cup butter
- 1/4 cup veggie stock
- 4 garlic cloves; minced
- 2 tablespoon basil; chopped
- Salt and black pepper to the taste

Directions:

1. Season steaks with salt and pepper, put them in your air fryer, cook at 360°F, for 10 minutes and transfer to a pan that fits the fryer
2. Add shallot, garlic, butter, stock, basil, lemon juice, parsley, lemon zest and scallops, toss everything gently and cook at 360°F, for 4 minutes more. Divide steaks and scallops on plates and serve

Beef Medallions Mix Recipe

(Prep + Cooking Time: 2 hours 10 Minutes | Servings: 4)

Ingredients:

- 4 beef medallions
- 2 teaspoon chili powder
- 1 cup tomatoes; crushed
- 1 tablespoon hot pepper
- 2 tablespoon lime juice
- 2 teaspoon onion powder
- 2 tablespoon soy sauce
- Salt and black pepper to the taste

Directions:

1. In a bowl; mix tomatoes with hot pepper, soy sauce, chili powder, onion powder, a pinch of salt, black pepper and lime juice and whisk well.
2. Arrange beef medallions in a dish, pour sauce over them, toss and leave them aside for 2 hours.
3. Discard tomato marinade, put beef in your preheated air fryer and cook at 360°F, for 10 minutes. Divide steaks on plates and serve with a side salad.

Beef Roast and Wine Sauce

(Prep + Cooking Time: 55 Minutes | Servings: 6)

Ingredients:

- 3-pound beef roast
- 17-ounce beef stock
- 1/2 teaspoon smoked paprika
- 1 yellow onion; chopped
- 4 garlic cloves; minced
- 3 carrots; chopped
- 5 potatoes; chopped
- 3-ounce red wine
- 1/2 teaspoon chicken salt
- Salt and black pepper to the taste

Directions:

1. In a bowl; mix salt, pepper, chicken salt and paprika; stir, rub beef with this mix and put it in a big pan that fits your air fryer
2. Add onion, garlic, stock, wine, potatoes and carrots, introduce in your air fryer and cook at 360°F, for 45 minutes. Divide everything on plates and serve

Pork Chops and Green Beans

(Prep + Cooking Time: 25 Minutes | **Servings:** 4)

Ingredients:

- 4 pork chops; bone in
- 3 garlic cloves; minced
- 2 tablespoon parsley; chopped
- 1 tablespoon sage; chopped
- 2 tablespoon olive oil
- 16-ounce green beans
- Salt and black pepper to the taste

Directions:

1. In a pan that fits your air fryer, mix pork chops with olive oil, sage, salt, pepper, green beans, garlic and parsley, toss, introduce in your air fryer and cook at 360°F, for 15 minutes.
2. Divide everything on plates and serve

Stuffed Pork Steaks Recipe

(Prep + Cooking Time: 30 Minutes | **Servings:** 4)

Ingredients:

- 4 pork loin steaks
- 2 pickles; chopped
- 4 ham slices
- 6 Swiss cheese slices
- 2 tablespoon mustard
- Zest from 2 limes; grated
- Zest from 1 orange; grated
- Juice from 1 orange
- Juice from 2 limes
- 4 teaspoon garlic; minced
- 3/4 cup olive oil
- 1 cup cilantro; chopped.
- 1 cup mint; chopped
- 1 teaspoon oregano; dried
- 2 teaspoon cumin; ground
- Salt and black pepper to the taste

Directions:

1. In your food processor, mix lime zest and juice with orange zest and juice, garlic, oil, cilantro, mint, oregano, cumin, salt and pepper and blend well
2. Season steaks with salt and pepper, place them into a bowl, add marinade and toss to coat.
3. Place steaks on a working surface, divide pickles, cheese, mustard and ham on them, roll and secure with toothpicks
4. Put stuffed pork steaks in your air fryer and cook at 340°F, for 20 minutes. Divide among plates and serve with a side salad.

Beef Curry Recipe

(Prep + Cooking Time: 55 Minutes | **Servings:** 4)

Ingredients:

- 2-pound beef steak; cubed
- 10-ounce canned coconut milk
- 2 tablespoon tomato sauce
- 2 tablespoon olive oil
- 3 potatoes; cubed
- 2 yellow onions; chopped
- 2 garlic cloves; minced
- 1 tablespoon wine mustard
- 2 ½ tablespoon curry powder
- Salt and black pepper to the taste

Directions:

1. Heat up a pan that fits your air fryer with the oil over medium high heat, add onions and garlic; stir and cook for 4 minutes
2. Add potatoes and mustard; stir and cook for 1 minute
3. Add beef, curry powder, salt, pepper, coconut milk and tomato sauce; stir, transfer to your air fryer and cook at 360°F, for 40 minutes. Divide into bowls and serve.

Oriental Fried Lamb Recipe

(Prep + Cooking Time: 52 Minutes | **Servings:** 8)

Ingredients:

- 2 ½-pound lamb shoulder; chopped
- 3 tablespoon honey
- 3-ounce almonds; peeled and chopped
- 9-ounce plumps; pitted
- 1 teaspoon cumin powder
- 1 teaspoon turmeric powder
- 1 teaspoon ginger powder
- 8-ounce veggie stock
- 2 yellow onions; chopped
- 2 garlic cloves; minced
- 1 teaspoon cinnamon powder
- 3 tablespoon olive oil
- Salt and black pepper to the tastes

Directions:

1. In a bowl; mix cinnamon powder with ginger, cumin, turmeric, garlic, olive oil and lamb, toss to coat, place in your preheated air fryer and cook at 350°F, for 8 minutes
2. Transfer meat to a dish that fits your air fryer, add onions, stock, honey and plums; stir, introduce in your air fryer and cook at 350°F, for 35 minutes. Divide everything on plates and serve with almond sprinkled on top.

Roasted Pork Belly and Apple Sauce

(Prep + Cooking Time: 50 Minutes | **Servings:** 6)

Ingredients:

- 2-pound pork belly; scored
- A drizzle of olive oil
- 2 tablespoon sugar
- 1 tablespoon lemon juice
- 1-quart water
- 17-ounce apples; cored and cut into wedges
- Salt and black pepper to the taste

Directions:

1. In your blender, mix water with apples, lemon juice and sugar, pulse well, transfer to a bowl, add meat, toss well, drain, put in your air fryer and cook at 400°F, for 40 minutes
2. Pour the sauce in a pot, heat up over medium heat and simmer for 15 minutes. Slice pork belly, divide among plates, drizzle the sauce all over and serve.

Ham and Veggie Air Fried Mix

(Prep + Cooking Time: 30 Minutes | **Servings:** 6)

Ingredients:

- 1/4 cup butter
- 3 cups milk
- 1/2 teaspoon thyme; dried
- 2 cups ham; chopped
- 1/4 cup flour
- 6-ounce sweet peas
- 4-ounce mushrooms; halved
- 1 cup baby carrots

Directions:

1. Heat up a large pan that fits your air fryer with the butter over medium heat, melt it, add flour and whisk well
2. Add milk and, well again and take off heat
3. Add thyme, ham, peas, mushrooms and baby carrots, toss, put in your air fryer and cook at 360°F, for 20 minutes. Divide everything on plates and serve

Garlic Lamb Chops Recipe

(Prep + Cooking Time: 20 Minutes | **Servings:** 4)

Ingredients:
- 8 lamb chops
- 1 tablespoon oregano; chopped.
- 1 tablespoon coriander; chopped
- 3 tablespoon olive oil
- 4 garlic cloves; minced
- Salt and black pepper to the taste

Directions:
1. In a bowl; mix oregano with salt, pepper, oil, garlic and lamb chops and toss to coat
2. Transfer lamb chops to your air fryer and cook at 400°F, for 10 minutes. Divide lamb chops on plates and serve with a side salad.

Tasty Ham and Greens Recipe

(Prep + Cooking Time: 26 Minutes | **Servings:** 8)

Ingredients:
- 16-ounce collard greens; chopped
- 3 cups chicken stock
- 14-ounce canned black eyed peas; drained
- 4 cups ham; chopped
- 2 tablespoon olive oil
- 2 tablespoon flour
- 5-ounce onion; chopped
- 1/2 teaspoon red pepper; crushed

Directions:
1. Drizzle the oil in a pan that fits your air fryer, add ham, stock and flour and whisk
2. Also add onion, black eyed peas, red pepper and collard greens, introduce in your air fryer and cook at 390°F, for 16 minutes. Divide everything on plates and serve

Coffee Flavored Steaks Recipe

(Prep + Cooking Time: 25 Minutes | **Servings:** 4)

Ingredients:
- 1/4 teaspoon; coriander, ground
- 1/2 tablespoon sweet paprika
- 2 tablespoon chili powder
- 2 teaspoon garlic powder
- 1 ½ tablespoon coffee; ground
- 4 rib eye steaks
- 2 teaspoon onion powder
- 1/4 teaspoon ginger; ground
- A pinch of cayenne pepper
- Black pepper to the taste

Directions:
1. In a bowl; mix coffee with paprika, chili powder, garlic powder, onion powder, ginger, coriander, cayenne and black pepper; stir, rub steaks with this mix, put in preheated air fryer and cook at 360°F, for 15 minutes. Divide steaks on plates and serve with a side salad

Balsamic Beef Recipe

(Prep + Cooking Time: 1 hour 10 Minutes | **Servings:** 6)

Ingredients:
- 1/2 cup balsamic vinegar
- 1 cup beef stock
- 1 medium beef roast
- 1 tablespoon Worcestershire sauce
- 1 tablespoon honey
- 1 tablespoon soy sauce
- 4 garlic cloves; minced

Directions:
1. In a heat proof dish that fits your air fryer, mix roast with roast with Worcestershire sauce, vinegar, stock, honey, soy sauce and garlic, toss well, introduce in your air fryer and cook at 370°F, for 1 hour
2. Slice roast, divide among plates, drizzle the sauce all over and serve

Fried Sausage and Mushrooms

(**Prep + Cooking Time:** 50 Minutes | **Servings:** 6)

Ingredients:

- 2-pound Portobello mushrooms; sliced
- 2-pound pork sausage; sliced
- 3 red bell peppers; chopped
- 2 sweet onions; chopped.
- 1 tablespoon brown sugar
- 1 teaspoon olive oil
- Salt and black pepper to the taste

Directions:

1. In a baking dish that fits your air fryer, mix sausage slices with oil, salt, pepper, bell pepper, mushrooms, onion and sugar, toss, introduce in your air fryer and cook at 300°F, for 40 minutes. Divide among plates and serve right away

Lamb and Green Pesto Recipe

(**Prep + Cooking Time:** 1 hour 45 Minutes | **Servings:** 4)

Ingredients:

- 2-pound lamb riblets
- 1/2 onion; chopped.
- 5 garlic cloves; minced
- Juice from 1 orange
- 1 cup parsley
- 1 cup mint
- 1 small yellow onion; roughly chopped
- 1/3 cup pistachios; chopped
- 1 teaspoon lemon zest; grated
- 5 tablespoon olive oil
- Salt and black pepper to the taste

Directions:

1. In your food processor, mix parsley with mint, onion, pistachios, lemon zest, salt, pepper and oil and blend very well
2. Rub lamb with this mix, place in a bowl; cover and leave in the fridge for 1 hour
3. Transfer lamb to a baking dish that fits your air fryer, also add garlic, drizzle orange juice and cook in your air fryer at 300°F, for 45 minutes.

Beef Patties and Mushroom Sauce

(**Prep + Cooking Time:** 35 Minutes | **Servings:** 6)

Ingredients:

- 2-pound beef; ground
- 1/2 teaspoon garlic powder
- 1 tablespoon parsley; chopped
- 1 tablespoon onion flakes
- 1 tablespoon soy sauce
- 1/4 cup beef stock
- 3/4 cup flour
- Salt and black pepper to the taste

For the sauce:

- 1 cup yellow onion; chopped.
- 2 cups mushrooms; sliced
- 2 tablespoon bacon fat
- 2 tablespoon butter
- 1/2 teaspoon soy sauce
- 1/4 cup sour cream
- 1/2 cup beef stock
- Salt and black pepper to the taste

Directions:

1. In a bowl; mix beef with salt, pepper, garlic powder, 1 tablespoon soy sauce, 1/4 cup beef stock, flour, parsley and onion flakes; stir well, shape 6 patties, place them in your air fryer and cook at 350°F, for 14 minutes.
2. Meanwhile; heat up a pan with the butter and the bacon fat over medium heat, add mushrooms; stir and cook for 4 minutes
3. Add onions; stir and cook for 4 minutes more
4. Add 1/2 teaspoon soy sauce, sour cream and 1/2 cup stock; stir well, bring to a simmer and take off heat. Divide beef patties on plates and serve with mushroom sauce on top.

Filet Mignon and Mushrooms Sauce

(Prep + Cooking Time: 35 Minutes | **Servings:** 4)

Ingredients:

- 12 mushrooms; sliced
- 2 tablespoon parsley; chopped
- 1 shallot; chopped
- 4 fillet mignons
- 2 garlic cloves; minced
- 1/4 cup Dijon mustard
- 1/4 cup wine
- 1¼ cup coconut cream
- 2 tablespoon olive oil
- Salt and black pepper to the taste

Directions:

1. Heat up a pan with the oil over medium high heat, add garlic and shallots; stir and cook for 3 minutes.
2. Add mushrooms; stir and cook for 4 minutes more
3. Add wine; stir and cook until it evaporates.
4. Add coconut cream, mustard, parsley, a pinch of salt and black pepper to the taste; stir, cook for 6 minutes more and take off heat
5. Season fillets with salt and pepper, put them in your air fryer and cook at 360°F, for 10 minutes. Divide fillets on plates and serve with the mushroom sauce on top.

Lamb Racks and Fennel Mix Recipe

(Prep + Cooking Time: 26 Minutes | **Servings:** 4)

Ingredients:

- 12-ounce lamb racks
- 1/8 cup apple cider vinegar
- 1 tablespoon brown sugar
- 4 figs; cut into halves
- 2 fennel bulbs; sliced
- 2 tablespoon olive oil
- Salt and black pepper to the taste

Directions:

1. In a bowl; mix fennel with figs, vinegar, sugar and oil, toss to coat well, transfer to a baking dish that fits your air fryer, introduce in your air fryer and cook at 350°F, for 6 minutes
2. Season lamb with salt and pepper, add to the baking dish with the fennel mix and air fry for 10 minutes more. Divide everything on plates and serve.

Ham and Cauliflower Mix Recipe

(Prep + Cooking Time: 4 hours 10 Minutes | **Servings:** 6)

Ingredients:

- 8-ounce cheddar cheese; grated
- 16-ounce cauliflower florets
- 14-ounce chicken stock
- 1/2 teaspoon garlic powder
- 4 cups ham; cubed
- 4 garlic cloves; minced
- 1/4 cup heavy cream
- 1/2 teaspoon onion powder
- Salt and black pepper to the taste

Directions:

1. In a pot that fits your air fryer, mix ham with stock, cheese, cauliflower, garlic powder, onion powder, salt, pepper, garlic and heavy cream; stir, put in your air fryer and cook at 300°F, for 1 hour. Divide into bowls and serve

Pork Chops and Roasted Peppers

(Prep + Cooking Time: 26 Minutes | **Servings:** 4)

Ingredients:

- 4 pork chops; bone in
- 3 tablespoon lemon juice
- 3 garlic cloves; minced
- 3 tablespoon olive oil
- 1 tablespoon smoked paprika
- 2 roasted bell peppers; chopped.
- 2 tablespoon thyme; chopped
- Salt and black pepper to the taste

Directions:

1. In a pan that fits your air fryer, mix pork chops with oil, lemon juice, smoked paprika, thyme, garlic, bell peppers, salt and pepper, toss well, introduce in your air fryer and cook at 400°F, for 16 minutes
2. Divide pork chops and peppers mix on plates and serve right away

Mustard Marinated Beef Recipe

(Prep + Cooking Time: 55 Minutes | **Servings:** 6)

Ingredients:

- 3-pound beef roast
- 1 ¾ cup beef stock
- 6 bacon strips
- 3/4 cup red wine
- 3 garlic cloves; minced
- 2 tablespoon butter
- 1 tablespoon horseradish
- 1 tablespoon mustard
- Salt and black pepper to the taste

Directions:

1. In a bowl; mix butter with mustard, garlic, salt, pepper and horseradish, whisk and rub beef with this mix.
2. Arrange bacon strips on a cutting board, place beef on top, fold bacon around beef, transfer to your air fryer's basket, cook at 400°F, for 15 minutes and transfer to a pan that fits your fryer
3. Add stock and wine to beef, introduce pan in your air fryer and cook at 360°F, for 30 minutes more.
4. Carve beef, divide among plates and serve with a side salad

Beef Stuffed Squash Recipe

(Prep + Cooking Time: 50 Minutes | **Servings:** 2)

Ingredients:

- 1 spaghetti squash; pricked
- 28-ounce canned tomatoes; chopped
- 1 teaspoon oregano; dried
- 1/4 teaspoon cayenne pepper
- 1/2 teaspoon thyme; dried
- 1-pound beef; ground
- Salt and black pepper to the taste
- 3 garlic cloves; minced
- 1 yellow onion; chopped
- 1 Portobello mushroom; sliced
- 1 green bell pepper; chopped

Directions:

1. Put spaghetti squash in your air fryer, cook at 350°F, for 20 minutes; transfer to a cutting board, and cut into halves and discard seeds
2. Heat up a pan over medium high heat, add meat, garlic, onion and mushroom; stir and cook until meat browns.
3. Add salt, pepper, thyme, oregano, cayenne, tomatoes and green pepper; stir and cook for 10 minutes.
4. Stuff squash with this beef mix, introduce in the fryer and cook at 360°F, for 10 minutes. Divide among plates and serve

Beef Casserole Recipe

(Prep + Cooking Time: 65 Minutes | **Servings:** 12)

Ingredients:
- 28-ounce canned tomatoes; chopped.
- 1 tablespoon olive oil
- 2-pound beef; ground
- 16-ounce tomato sauce
- 2 teaspoon mustard
- 2 tablespoon parsley; chopped
- 2 cups eggplant; chopped.
- 2 teaspoon gluten free Worcestershire sauce
- 2 cups mozzarella; grated
- 1 teaspoon oregano; dried
- Salt and black pepper to the taste

Directions:
1. In a bowl; mix eggplant with salt, pepper and oil and toss to coat
2. In another bowl, mix beef with salt, pepper, mustard and Worcestershire sauce; stir well and spread on the bottom of a pan that fits your air fryer.
3. Add eggplant mix, tomatoes, tomato sauce, parsley, oregano and sprinkle mozzarella at the end
4. Introduce in your air fryer and cook at 360°F, for 35 minutes Divide among plates and serve hot

Creamy Lamb Recipe

(Prep + Cooking Time: 1 day 1 hour | **Servings:** 8)

Ingredients:
- 5-pound leg of lamb
- 2 cups low fat buttermilk
- 2 tablespoon mustard
- 1 cup white wine
- 1 tablespoon cornstarch mixed with 1 tablespoon water
- 1/2 cup sour cream
- 1/2 cup butter
- 2 tablespoon basil; chopped
- 2 tablespoon tomato paste
- 2 garlic cloves; minced
- Salt and black pepper to the taste

Directions:
1. Put lamb roast in a big dish, add buttermilk, toss to coat, cover and keep in the fridge for 24 hours.
2. Pat dry lamb and put in a pan that fits your air fryer
3. In a bowl; mix butter with tomato paste, mustard, basil, rosemary, salt, pepper and garlic, whisk well, spread over lamb, introduce everything in your air fryer and cook at 300°F, for 1 hour
4. Slice lamb, divide among plates, leave aside for now and heat up cooking juices from the pan on your stove. Add wine, cornstarch mix, salt, pepper and sour cream; stir, take off heat, drizzle this sauce over lamb and serve.

Mexican Beef Mix Recipe

(Prep + Cooking Time: 1 hour and 20 minutes | **Servings:** 8)

Ingredients:
- 2 yellow onions; chopped
- 2 tablespoon olive oil
- 2 tablespoon cilantro; chopped.
- 4 jalapenos; chopped
- 14-ounce canned tomatoes; chopped.
- 1/2 cup water
- 1 ½ teaspoon cumin; ground
- 6 garlic cloves; minced
- 2-pound beef roast; cubed
- 2 green bell peppers; chopped
- 1 habanero pepper; chopped.
- 1/2 cup black olives; pitted and chopped
- 1 teaspoon oregano; dried
- Salt and black pepper to the taste

Directions:
1. In a pan that fits your air fryer, combine beef with oil, green bell peppers, onions, jalapenos, habanero pepper, tomatoes, garlic, water, cilantro, oregano, cumin, salt and pepper; stir, put in your air fryer and cook at 300°F, for 1 hour and 10 minutes. Add olives; stir, divide into bowls and serve

Pork Chops and Mushrooms Mix

(Prep + Cooking Time: 50 Minutes | **Servings:** 3)

Ingredients:
- 3 pork chops; boneless
- 8-ounce mushrooms; sliced
- 1 teaspoon garlic powder
- 1 yellow onion; chopped.
- 1 teaspoon nutmeg
- 1 tablespoon balsamic vinegar
- 1 cup mayonnaise
- 1/2 cup olive oil

Directions:
1. Heat up a pan that fits your air fryer with the oil over medium heat, add mushrooms and onions; stir and cook for 4 minutes
2. Add pork chops, nutmeg and garlic powder and brown on both sides.
3. Introduce pan your air fryer at 330°F and cook for 30 minutes. Add vinegar and mayo; stir, divide everything on plates and serve

Sausage and Kale Recipe

(Prep + Cooking Time: 30 Minutes | **Servings:** 4)

Ingredients:
- 5-pound kale; chopped
- 1 teaspoon garlic; minced
- 1/2 cup red bell pepper; chopped
- 1 cup yellow onion; chopped
- 1 ½-pound Italian pork sausage; sliced
- 1/4 cup red hot chili pepper; chopped.
- 1 cup water
- Salt and black pepper to the taste

Directions:
1. In a pan that fits your air fryer, mix sausage with onion, bell pepper, salt, pepper, kale, garlic, water and chili pepper, toss, introduce in preheated air fryer and cook at 300°F, for 20 minutes. Divide everything on plates and serve

Poultry Recipes

Chinese Stuffed Chicken

(Prep + Cooking Time: 45 Minutes | **Servings:** 8)

Ingredients:

- 1 whole chicken
- 1 yam; cubed
- 1 teaspoon soy sauce
- 3 teaspoon sesame oil
- 10 wolfberries
- 2 red chilies; chopped
- 4 ginger slices
- Salt and white pepper to the taste

Directions:

1. Season chicken with salt, pepper, rub with soy sauce and sesame oil and stuff with wolfberries, yam cubes, chilies and ginger
2. Place in your air fryer, cook at 400°F, for 20 minutes and then at 360°F, for 15 minutes. Carve chicken, divide among plates and serve

Chicken and Lentils Casserole

(Prep + Cooking Time: 1 hour 10 Minutes | **Servings:** 8)

Ingredients:

- 2-pound chicken breasts; skinless, boneless and chopped
- 1 ½ cups green lentils
- 3 cups chicken stock
- 3 teaspoon cumin; ground
- 2 cups Cheddar cheese; shredded.
- 2 tablespoon jalapeno pepper; chopped.
- 1 tablespoon garlic powder
- 1 cup cilantro; chopped
- 5 garlic cloves; minced
- 1 yellow onion; chopped
- 2 red bell peppers; chopped
- 14-ounce canned tomatoes; chopped
- 2 cups corn
- Cooking spray
- Salt and cayenne pepper to the taste

Directions:

1. Put the stock in a pot, add some salt, add lentils; stir, bring to a boil over medium heat, cover and simmer for 35 minutes
2. Meanwhile; spray chicken pieces with some cooking spray, season with salt, cayenne pepper and 1 teaspoon cumin, put them in your air fryer's basket and cook them at 370 degrees for 6 minutes. flipping half way.
3. Transfer chicken to a heat proof dish that fits your air fryer, add bell peppers, garlic, tomatoes, onion, salt, cayenne and 1 teaspoon cumin.
4. Drain lentils and add them to the chicken mix as well
5. Add jalapeno pepper, garlic powder, the rest of the cumin, corn, half of the cheese and half of the cilantro, introduce in your air fryer and cook at 320°F, for 25 minutes
6. Sprinkle the rest of the cheese and the remaining cilantro, divide chicken casserole on plates and serve.

Creamy Chicken, Peas and Rice

(Prep + Cooking Time: 40 Minutes | **Servings:** 4)

Ingredients:

- 1-pound chicken breasts; skinless, boneless and cut into quarters
- 1 cup white rice; already cooked
- 1 ½ cups parmesan; grated
- 1 tablespoon olive oil
- 3 garlic cloves; minced
- 1 cup chicken stock
- 1/4 cup parsley; chopped.
- 2 cups peas; frozen
- 1 yellow onion; chopped
- 1/2 cup white wine
- 1/4 cup heavy cream
- Salt and black pepper to the taste

Directions:

1. Season chicken breasts with salt and pepper, drizzle half of the oil over them, rub well, put in your air fryer's basket and cook them at 360°F, for 6 minutes
2. Heat up a pan with the rest of the oil over medium high heat, add garlic, onion, wine, stock, salt, pepper and heavy cream; stir, bring to a simmer and cook for 9 minutes.
3. Transfer chicken breasts to a heat proof dish that fits your air fryer, add peas, rice and cream mix over them, toss, sprinkle parmesan and parsley all over, place in your air fryer and cook at 420°F, for 10 minutes. Divide among plates and serve hot

Mexican Chicken Recipe

(Prep + Cooking Time: 30 Minutes | Servings: 4)

Ingredients:

- 16-ounce salsa verde
- 1½ cup Monterey Jack cheese; grated
- 1/4 cup cilantro; chopped
- 1 teaspoon garlic powder
- 1 tablespoon olive oil
- 1-pound chicken breast; boneless and skinless
- Salt and black pepper to the taste

Directions:

1. Pour salsa verde in a baking dish that fits your air fryer, season chicken with salt, pepper, garlic powder, brush with olive oil and place it over your salsa verde
2. Introduce in your air fryer and cook at 380°F, for 20 minutes.
3. Sprinkle cheese on top and cook for 2 minutes more. Divide among plates and serve hot

Chicken and Creamy Veggie Mix

(Prep + Cooking Time: 40 Minutes | Servings: 6)

Ingredients:

- 29-ounce chicken stock
- 3/4 cup red peppers; chopped
- 1 bay leaf
- 8-ounce mushrooms; chopped
- 17-ounce asparagus; trimmed
- 2 cups whipping cream
- 40-ounce chicken pieces; boneless and skinless
- 3 tablespoon butter; melted
- 1/2 cup yellow onion; chopped
- 3 teaspoon thyme; chopped.
- Salt and black pepper to the taste

Directions:

1. Heat up a pan with the butter over medium heat, add onion and peppers; stir and cook for 3 minutes.
2. Add stock, bay leaf, salt and pepper, bring to a boil and simmer for 10 minutes
3. Add asparagus, mushrooms, chicken, cream, thyme, salt and pepper to the taste; stir, introduce in your air fryer and cook at 360°F, for 15 minutes. Divide chicken and veggie mix on plates and serve

Chicken Parmesan Recipe

(Prep + Cooking Time: 25 Minutes | Servings: 4)

Ingredients:

- 1 ½-pound chicken cutlets; skinless and boneless
- 2 cups panko bread crumbs
- 1 cup mozzarella; grated
- 2 cups tomato sauce
- 1/4 cup parmesan; grated
- 1/2 teaspoon garlic powder
- 2 cups white flour
- 1 egg; whisked
- 3 tablespoon basil; chopped
- Salt and black pepper to the taste

Directions:

1. In a bowl, mix panko with parmesan and garlic powder and stir
2. Put flour in a second bowl and the egg in a third.
3. Season chicken with salt and pepper, dip in flour, then in egg mix and in panko

4. Put chicken pieces in your air fryer and cook them at 360°F, for 3 minutes on each side.
5. Transfer chicken to a baking dish that fits your air fryer, add tomato sauce and top with mozzarella, introduce in your air fryer and cook at 375°F, for 7 minutes. Divide among plates, sprinkle basil on top and serve

Chicken Wings and Mint Sauce

(Prep + Cooking Time: 36 Minutes | Servings: 6)

Ingredients:
- 18 chicken wings; halved
- 1 tablespoon turmeric powder
- 1 tablespoon ginger; grated
- 1 tablespoon coriander; ground
- 1 tablespoon sweet paprika
- 1 tablespoon cumin; ground
- 2 tablespoon olive oil
- Salt and black pepper to the taste

For the mint sauce:
- 3/4 cup cilantro
- 1 small ginger piece; chopped
- 1 tablespoon olive oil
- 1 Serrano pepper; chopped
- Juice from 1/2 lime
- 1 cup mint leaves
- 1 tablespoon water
- Salt and black pepper to the taste

Directions:
1. In a bowl, mix 1 tablespoon ginger with cumin, coriander, paprika, turmeric, salt, pepper, cayenne and 2 tablespoon oil and stir well
2. Add chicken wings pieces to this mix; toss to coat well and keep in the fridge for 10 minutes.
3. Transfer chicken to your air fryer's basket and cook at 370°F, for 16 minutes; flipping them halfway.
4. In your blender, mix mint with cilantro, 1 small ginger pieces, juice from 1/2 lime, 1 tablespoon olive oil, salt, pepper, water and Serrano pepper and blend very well. Divide chicken wings on plates, drizzle mint sauce all over and serve

Chicken Breasts and Tomatoes Sauce

(Prep + Cooking Time: 30 Minutes | Servings: 4)

Ingredients:
- 4 chicken breasts; skinless and boneless
- 1/4 teaspoon garlic powder
- 14-ounce canned tomatoes; chopped
- Salt and black pepper to the taste
- 1 red onion; chopped
- 1/4 cup balsamic vinegar
- 1/4 cup parmesan; grated
- Cooking spray

Directions:
1. Spray a baking dish that fits your air fryer with cooking oil, add chicken, season with salt, pepper, balsamic vinegar, garlic powder, tomatoes and cheese; toss, introduce in your air fryer and cook at 400°F, for 20 minutes. Divide among plates and serve hot

Chicken and Asparagus Recipe

(Prep + Cooking Time: 30 Minutes | Servings: 4)

Ingredients:
- 8 chicken wings; halved
- 1 tablespoon rosemary; chopped
- 1 teaspoon cumin; ground
- 8 asparagus spears
- Salt and black pepper to the taste

Directions:
1. Pat dry chicken wings, season with salt, pepper, cumin and rosemary, put them in your air fryer's basket and cook at 360°F, for 20 minutes
2. Meanwhile; heat up a pan over medium heat, add asparagus, add water to cover, steam for a few minutes; transfer to a bowl filled with ice water, drain and arrange on plates. Add chicken wings on the side and serve.

Easy Duck Breasts Recipe

(Prep + Cooking Time: 25 Minutes **| Servings:** 4)

Ingredients:

- 4 duck breasts; skinless and boneless
- 1/2 teaspoon lemon pepper
- 4 garlic heads; peeled, tops cut off and quartered
- 2 tablespoon lemon juice
- 1 ½ tablespoon olive oil
- Salt and black pepper to the taste

Directions:

1. In a bowl, mix duck breasts with garlic, lemon juice, salt, pepper, lemon pepper and olive oil and toss everything
2. Transfer duck and garlic to your air fryer and cook at 350°F, for 15 minutes. Divide duck breasts and garlic on plates and serve.

Chicken and Cauliflower Rice Mix

(Prep + Cooking Time: 30 Minutes **| Servings:** 6)

Ingredients:

- 3-pound chicken thighs; boneless and skinless
- 3 bacon slices; chopped
- 4 tablespoon olive oil
- 1 tablespoon garlic powder
- 1 tablespoon Italian seasoning
- 24-ounce cauliflower rice
- 3 carrots; chopped
- 2 bay leaves
- 1/4 cup red wine vinegar
- 4 garlic cloves; minced
- 1 teaspoon turmeric powder
- 1 cup beef stock
- Salt and black pepper to the taste

Directions:

1. Heat up a pan that fits your air fryer over medium high heat, add bacon, carrots, onion and garlic; stir and cook for 8 minutes
2. Add chicken, oil, vinegar, turmeric, garlic powder, Italian seasoning and bay leaves; stir, introduce in your air fryer and cook at 360°F, for 12 minutes. Add cauliflower rice and stock; stir, cook for 6 minutes more, divide among plates and serve

Chicken and Green Onions Sauce

(Prep + Cooking Time: 26 Minutes **| Servings:** 4)

Ingredients:

- 10 green onions; roughly chopped.
- 1 teaspoon Chinese five spice
- 10 chicken drumsticks
- 1 cup coconut milk
- 1 teaspoon butter; melted
- 1-inch piece ginger root; chopped
- 4 garlic cloves; minced
- 2 tablespoon fish sauce
- 3 tablespoon soy sauce
- 1/4 cup cilantro; chopped
- 1 tablespoon lime juice
- Salt and black pepper to the taste

Directions:

1. In your food processor, mix green onions with ginger, garlic, soy sauce, fish sauce, five spice, salt, pepper, butter and coconut milk and pulse well
2. In a bowl, mix chicken with green onions mix; toss well, transfer everything to a pan that fits your air fryer and cook at 370°F, for 16 minutes; shaking the fryer once. Divide among plates, sprinkle cilantro on top, drizzle lime juice and serve with a side salad

Cider Glazed Chicken Recipe

(Prep + Cooking Time: 24 Minutes | **Servings:** 4)

Ingredients:

- 6 chicken thighs; bone in and skin on
- 1 tablespoon olive oil
- 1 tablespoon rosemary; chopped.
- 2/3 cup apple cider
- 1 sweet potato; cubed
- 2 apples; cored and sliced
- 1 tablespoon mustard
- 2 tablespoon honey
- 1 tablespoon butter
- Salt and black pepper to the taste

Directions:

1. Heat up a pan that fits your air fryer with half of the oil over medium high heat, add cider, honey, butter and mustard, whisk well, bring to a simmer, take off heat, add chicken and toss really well
2. In a bowl, mix potato cubes with rosemary, apples, salt, pepper and the rest of the oil; toss well and add to chicken mix
3. Place pan in your air fryer and cook at 390°F, for 14 minutes. Divide everything on plates and serve.

Chinese Chicken Wings Recipe

(Prep + Cooking Time: 2 hours 15 Minutes | **Servings:** 6)

Ingredients:

- 16 chicken wings
- 1/4 teaspoon white pepper
- 3 tablespoon lime juice
- 2 tablespoon honey
- 2 tablespoon soy sauce
- Salt and black pepper to the taste

Directions:

1. In a bowl, mix honey with soy sauce, salt, black and white pepper and lime juice, whisk well, add chicken pieces, toss to coat and keep in the fridge for 2 hours
2. Transfer chicken to your air fryer, cook at 370°F, for 6 minutes on each side, increase heat to 400°F and cook for 3 minutes more. Serve hot.

Chicken Thighs and Baby Potatoes

(Prep + Cooking Time: 40 Minutes | **Servings:** 4)

Ingredients:

- 8 chicken thighs
- 1-pound baby potatoes; halved
- 2 tablespoon olive oil
- 2 teaspoon rosemary; dried
- 2 garlic cloves; minced
- 1 red onion; chopped
- 2 teaspoon thyme; chopped
- 2 teaspoon oregano; dried
- 1/2 teaspoon sweet paprika
- Salt and black pepper to the taste

Directions:

1. In a bowl, mix chicken thighs with potatoes, salt, pepper, thyme, paprika, onion, rosemary, garlic, oregano and oil
2. Toss to coat, spread everything in a heat proof dish that fits your air fryer and cook at 400°F, for 30 minutes; shaking halfway. Divide among plates and serve

Herbed Chicken Recipe

(Prep + Cooking Time: 70 Minutes **| Servings:** 4)

Ingredients:
- 1 whole chicken
- 1 teaspoon rosemary; dried
- 1 tablespoon lemon juice
- 1 teaspoon garlic powder
- 1 teaspoon onion powder
- 1/2 teaspoon thyme; dried
- 2 tablespoon olive oil
- Salt and black pepper to the taste

Directions:
1. Season chicken with salt and pepper, rub with thyme, rosemary, garlic powder and onion powder, rub with lemon juice and olive oil and leave aside for 30 minutes
2. Put chicken in your air fryer and cook at 360°F, for 20 minutes on each side. Leave chicken aside to cool down, carve and serve

Chicken and Creamy Mushrooms

(Prep + Cooking Time: 40 Minutes **| Servings:** 8)

Ingredients:
- 8 chicken thighs
- 1/2 teaspoon thyme; dried
- 1/2 teaspoon oregano; dried
- 3 garlic cloves; minced
- 3 tablespoon butter; melted
- 1 cup chicken stock
- 1/4 cup heavy cream
- 1 tablespoon mustard
- 1/4 cup parmesan; grated
- 8-ounce cremini mushrooms; halved
- 1/2 teaspoon basil; dried
- Salt and black pepper to the taste

Directions:
1. Rub chicken pieces with 2 tablespoon butter, season with salt and pepper, put in your air fryer's basket, cook at 370°F, for 5 minutes and leave aside in a bowl for now
2. Meanwhile; heat up a pan with the rest of the butter over medium high heat, add mushrooms and garlic; stir and cook for 5 minutes
3. Add salt, pepper, stock, oregano, thyme and basil; stir well and transfer to a heat proof dish that fits your air fryer.
4. Add chicken, toss everything, put in your air fryer and cook at 370°F, for 20 minutes. Add mustard, parmesan and heavy cream, toss everything again, cook for 5 minutes more, divide among plates and serve.

Cheese Crusted Chicken Recipe

(Prep + Cooking Time: 25 Minutes **| Servings:** 4)

Ingredients:
- 4 bacon slices; cooked and crumbled
- 4 chicken breasts; skinless and boneless
- 1 cup asiago cheese; shredded.
- 1/4 teaspoon garlic powder
- 1 tablespoon water
- 1/2 cup avocado oil
- 1 egg; whisked
- 1 cup parmesan cheese; grated
- Salt and black pepper to the taste

Directions:
1. In a bowl, mix parmesan with garlic, salt and pepper and stir
2. In another bowl, mix egg with water and whisk well
3. Season chicken with salt and pepper and dip each pieces into egg and then into cheese mix.
4. Add chicken to your air fryer and cook at 320°F, for 15 minutes. Divide chicken on plates, sprinkle bacon and asiago cheese on top and serve

Fried Japanese Duck Breasts

(Prep + Cooking Time: 30 Minutes | **Servings:** 6)

Ingredients:

- 20-ounce chicken stock
- 6 duck breasts; boneless
- 4 ginger slices
- 4 tablespoon hoisin sauce
- 1 teaspoon sesame oil
- 4 tablespoon soy sauce
- 1½ teaspoon five spice powder
- 2 tablespoon honey
- Salt and black pepper to the taste

Directions:

1. In a bowl, mix five spice powder with soy sauce, salt, pepper and honey, whisk, add duck breasts, toss to coat and leave aside for now
2. Heat up a pan with the stock over medium high heat, hoisin sauce, ginger and sesame oil; stir well, cook for 2 - 3 minutes more, take off heat and leave aside.
3. Put duck breasts in your air fryer and cook them at 400°F, for 15 minutes. Divide among plates, drizzle hoisin and ginger sauce all over them and serve

Quick Creamy Chicken Casserole

(Prep + Cooking Time: 22 Minutes | **Servings:** 4)

Ingredients:

- 10-ounce spinach; chopped
- 2 cup chicken breasts; skinless, boneless and cubed
- 1 cup bread crumbs
- 1/2 cup parmesan; grated
- 1/2 cup heavy cream
- 4 tablespoon butter
- 3 tablespoon flour
- 1 ½ cups milk
- Salt and black pepper to the taste

Directions:

1. Heat up a pan with the butter over medium heat, add flour and stir well
2. Add milk, heavy cream and parmesan; stir well, cook for 1 - 2 minutes more and take off heat.
3. In a pan that fits your air fryer, spread chicken and spinach
4. Add salt and pepper and toss.
5. Add cream mix and spread, sprinkle bread crumbs on top, introduce in your air fryer and cook at 350 for 12 minutes. Divide chicken and spinach mix on plates and serve

Chicken Cacciatore Recipe

(Prep + Cooking Time: 30 Minutes | **Servings:** 4)

Ingredients:

- 8 chicken drumsticks; bone-in
- 1 yellow onion; chopped
- 28-ounce canned tomatoes and juice; crushed
- 1 teaspoon oregano; dried
- 1/2 cup black olives; pitted and sliced
- 1 bay leaf
- 1 teaspoon garlic powder
- Salt and black pepper to the taste

Directions:

1. In a heat proof dish that fits your air fryer, mix chicken with salt, pepper, garlic powder, bay leaf, onion, tomatoes and juice, oregano and olives; toss, introduce in your preheated air fryer and cook at 365°F, for 20 minutes. Divide among plates and serve

Duck and Veggies Recipe

(Prep + Cooking Time: 30 Minutes | **Servings:** 8)

Ingredients:

- 1 duck; chopped in medium pieces
- 1 cup chicken stock
- 3 cucumbers; chopped.
- 3 tablespoon white wine
- 2 carrots; chopped
- 1 small ginger piece; grated
- Salt and black pepper to the taste

Directions:

1. In a pan that fits your air fryer, mix duck pieces with cucumbers, wine, carrots, ginger, stock, salt and pepper; toss, introduce in your air fryer and cook at 370°F, for 20 minutes. Divide everything on plates and serve

Italian Chicken Recipe

(Prep + Cooking Time: 26 Minutes | **Servings:** 4)

Ingredients:

- 5 chicken thighs
- 1 tablespoon olive oil
- 1 tablespoon thyme; chopped
- 1/2 cup heavy cream
- 3/4 cup chicken stock
- 1 teaspoon red pepper flakes; crushed
- 2 tablespoon basil; chopped
- 1/4 cup parmesan; grated
- 1/2 cup sun dried tomatoes
- 2 garlic cloves; minced
- Salt and black pepper to the taste

Directions:

1. Season chicken with salt and pepper, rub with half of the oil, place in your preheated air fryer at 350°F and cook for 4 minutes
2. Meanwhile; heat up a pan with the rest of the oil over medium high heat, add thyme garlic, pepper flakes, sun dried tomatoes, heavy cream, stock, parmesan, salt and pepper; stir, bring to a simmer, take off heat and transfer to a dish that fits your air fryer
3. Add chicken thighs on top, introduce in your air fryer and cook at 320°F, for 12 minutes. Divide among plates and serve with basil sprinkled on top.

Duck and Plum Sauce

(Prep + Cooking Time: 42 Minutes | **Servings:** 2)

Ingredients:

- 9-ounce red plumps; stoned; cut into small wedges
- 1 tablespoon butter; melted
- 1-star anise
- 1 tablespoon olive oil
- 1 shallot; chopped
- 2 tablespoon sugar
- 2 tablespoon red wine
- 2 duck breasts
- 1 cup beef stock

Directions:

1. Heat up a pan with the olive oil over medium heat, add shallot; stir and cook for 5 minutes;
2. Add sugar and plums; stir and cook until sugar dissolves
3. Add stock and wine; stir, cook for 15 minutes; take off heat and keep warm for now
4. Score duck breasts, season with salt and pepper, rub with melted butter, transfer to a heat proof dish that fits your air fryer, add star anise and plum sauce, introduce in your air fryer and cook at 360°F, for 12 minutes. Divide everything on plates and serve.

Duck Breasts Recipe

(Prep + Cooking Time: 50 Minutes **| Servings:** 6)

Ingredients:
- 6 duck breasts; halved
- 2 cups chicken stock
- 1/2 cup white wine
- 1/4 cup parsley; chopped
- 3 tablespoon flour
- 6 tablespoon butter; melted
- 2 cups mushrooms; chopped.
- Salt and black pepper to the taste

Directions:
1. Season duck breasts with salt and pepper, place them in a bowl, add melted butter; toss and transfer to another bowl.
2. Combine melted butter with flour, wine, salt, pepper and chicken stock and stir well
3. Arrange duck breasts in a baking dish that fits your air fryer, pour the sauce over them, add parsley and mushrooms, introduce in your air fryer and cook at 350°F, for 40 minutes. Divide among plates and serve

Chinese Duck Legs Recipe

(Prep + Cooking Time: 46 Minutes **| Servings:** 2)

Ingredients:
- 2 duck legs
- 2 dried chilies; chopped
- 4 ginger slices
- 1 tablespoon oyster sauce
- 1 tablespoon soy sauce
- 1 teaspoon sesame oil
- 1 tablespoon olive oil
- 2-star anise
- 1 bunch spring onions; chopped
- 14-ounce water
- 1 tablespoon rice wine

Directions:
1. Heat up a pan with the oil over medium high heat, add chili, star anise, sesame oil, rice wine, ginger, oyster sauce, soy sauce and water; stir and cook for 6 minutes
2. Add spring onions and duck legs, toss to coat, transfer to a pan that fits your air fryer, put in your air fryer and cook at 370°F, for 30 minutes. Divide among plates and serve

Honey Duck Breasts Recipe

(Prep + Cooking Time: 32 Minutes **| Servings:** 2)

Ingredients:
- 1 smoked duck breast; halved
- 1 tablespoon mustard
- 1 teaspoon honey
- 1 teaspoon tomato paste
- 1/2 teaspoon apple vinegar

Directions:
1. In a bowl, mix honey with tomato paste, mustard and vinegar, whisk well, add duck breast pieces, toss to coat well, transfer to your air fryer and cook at 370°F, for 15 minutes
2. Take duck breast out of the fryer, add to honey mix, toss again, return to air fryer and cook at 370°F, for 6 minutes more. Divide among plates and serve with a side salad

Veggie Stuffed Chicken Breasts

(Prep + Cooking Time: 25 Minutes | **Servings:** 4)

Ingredients:

- 4 chicken breasts; skinless and boneless
- 3 tomatoes; chopped
- 1 red onion; chopped
- 1 zucchini; chopped
- 1 teaspoon Italian seasoning
- 2 tablespoon olive oil
- 2 yellow bell peppers; chopped
- 1 cup mozzarella; shredded.
- Salt and black pepper to the taste

Directions:

1. Mix a slit on each chicken breast creating a pocket, season with salt and pepper and rub them with olive oil.
2. In a bowl, mix zucchini with Italian seasoning, bell peppers, tomatoes and onion and stir
3. Stuff chicken breasts with this mix, sprinkle mozzarella over them, place them in your air fryer's basket and cook at 350°F, for 15 minutes. Divide among plates and serve

Turkey Quarters and Veggies

(Prep + Cooking Time: 44 Minutes | **Servings:** 4)

Ingredients:

- 1/2 teaspoon rosemary; dried
- 3 garlic cloves; minced
- 2-pound turkey quarters
- 1 celery stalk; chopped
- 1 cup chicken stock
- 2 tablespoon olive oil
- 1/2 teaspoon sage; dried
- 1/2 teaspoon thyme; dried
- 1 yellow onion; chopped
- 1 carrot; chopped
- 2 bay leaves
- Salt and black pepper to the taste

Directions:

1. Rub turkey quarters with salt, pepper, half of the oil, thyme, sage, rosemary and thyme, put in your air fryer and cook at 360°F, for 20 minutes
2. In a pan that fits your air fryer, mix onion with carrot, garlic, celery, the rest of the oil, stock, bay leaves, salt and pepper and toss.
3. Add turkey, introduce everything in your air fryer and cook at 360°F, for 14 minutes more. Divide everything on plates and serve

Chicken Breasts and BBQ Chili Sauce

(Prep + Cooking Time: 30 Minutes | **Servings:** 6)

Ingredients:

- 6 chicken breasts; skinless and boneless
- 2 cups chili sauce
- 1 teaspoon garlic powder
- 1/2 teaspoon liquid smoke
- 1 teaspoon chili powder
- 1 teaspoon mustard powder
- 2 cups ketchup
- 1 cup pear jelly
- 1/4 cup honey
- 1 teaspoon sweet paprika
- Salt and black pepper to the taste

Directions:

1. Season chicken breasts with salt and pepper, put in preheated air fryer and cook at 350°F, for 10 minutes
2. Meanwhile; heat up a pan with the chili sauce over medium heat, add ketchup, pear jelly, honey, liquid smoke, chili powder, mustard powder, sweet paprika, salt, pepper and the garlic powder; stir, bring to a simmer and cook for 10 minutes. Add air fried chicken breasts; toss well, divide among plates and serve

Duck Breast with Fig Sauce

(Prep + Cooking Time: 30 Minutes **| Servings:** 4)

Ingredients:

- 2 duck breasts; skin on, halved
- 1 tablespoon white flour
- 1 tablespoon olive oil
- 1/4 teaspoon sweet paprika
- 1 cup beef stock
- 3 tablespoon butter; melted
- 1 shallot; chopped
- 1/2 teaspoon thyme; chopped
- 1/2 cup port wine
- 1/2 teaspoon garlic powder
- 4 tablespoon fig preserves
- Salt and black pepper to the taste

Directions:

1. Season duck breasts with salt and pepper, drizzle half of the melted butter, rub well, put in your air fryer's basket and cook at 350°F, for 5 minutes on each side
2. Meanwhile; heat up a pan with the olive oil and the rest of the butter over medium high heat, add shallot; stir and cook for 2 minutes
3. Add thyme, garlic powder, paprika, stock, salt, pepper, wine and figs; stir and cook for 7 - 8 minutes.
4. Add flour; stir well, cook until sauce thickens a bit and take off heat.
5. Divide duck breasts on plates, drizzle figs sauce all over and serve

Pepperoni Chicken Recipe

(Prep + Cooking Time: 32 Minutes **| Servings:** 6)

Ingredients:

- 4 medium chicken breasts; skinless and boneless
- 6-ounce mozzarella; sliced
- 1 teaspoon garlic powder
- 2-ounce pepperoni; sliced
- 14-ounce tomato paste
- 1 tablespoon olive oil
- 1 teaspoon oregano; dried
- Salt and black pepper to the taste

Directions:

1. In a bowl, mix chicken with salt, pepper, garlic powder and oregano and toss
2. Put chicken in your air fryer, cook at 350°F, for 6 minutes and transfer to a pan that fits your air fryer
3. Add mozzarella slices on top, spread tomato paste, top with pepperoni slices, introduce in your air fryer and cook at 350°F, for 15 minutes more. Divide among plates and serve.

Lemony Chicken

(Prep + Cooking Time: 40 Minutes **| Servings:** 6)

Ingredients:

- 1 whole chicken; cut into medium pieces
- Juice from 2 lemons
- 1 tablespoon olive oil
- Zest from 2 lemons; grated
- Salt and black pepper to the taste

Directions:

1. Season chicken with salt, pepper, rub with oil and lemon zest, drizzle lemon juice, put in your air fryer and cook at 350°F, for 30 minutes; flipping chicken pieces halfway. Divide among plates and serve with a side salad

Fall Fried Chicken

(Prep + Cooking Time: 30 Minutes **| Servings:** 8)

Ingredients:

- 3-pound chicken breasts; skinless and boneless
- 10 white mushrooms; halved
- 1 tablespoon olive oil
- 1 red bell pepper; chopped
- 1 green bell pepper
- 1 yellow onion; chopped.
- 1 garlic clove; minced
- 2 tablespoon mozzarella cheese; shredded.
- Salt and black pepper to the taste
- Cooking spray

Directions:

1. Season chicken with salt and pepper, rub with garlic, spray with cooking spray, place in your preheated air fryer and cook at 390°F, for 12 minutes
2. Meanwhile; heat up a pan with the oil over medium heat, add onion; stir and sauté for 2 minutes.
3. Add mushrooms, garlic and bell peppers; stir and cook for 8 minutes.
4. Divide chicken on plates, add mushroom mix on the side, sprinkle cheese while chicken is still hot and serve right away

Tea Glazed Chicken Recipe

(Prep + Cooking Time: 40 Minutes **| Servings:** 6)

Ingredients:

- 6 chicken legs
- 6 black tea bags
- 1/2 cup pineapple preserves
- 1/2 cup apricot preserves
- 1 cup hot water
- 1 tablespoon soy sauce
- 1/4 teaspoon red pepper flakes
- 1 tablespoon olive oil
- 1 onion; chopped
- Salt and black pepper to the taste

Directions:

1. Put the hot water in a bowl, add tea bags, leave aside covered for 10 minutes; discard bags at the end and transfer tea to another bowl
2. Add soy sauce, pepper flakes, apricot and pineapple preserves, whisk really well and take off heat.
3. Season chicken with salt and pepper, rub with oil, put in your air fryer and cook at 350°F, for 5 minutes.
4. Spread onion on the bottom of a baking dish that fits your air fryer, add chicken pieces, drizzle the tea glaze on top, introduce in your air fryer and cook at 320°F, for 25 minutes. Divide everything on plates and serve

Duck Breasts and Mango Mix

(Prep + Cooking Time: 1 hour 10 Minutes **| Servings:** 4)

Ingredients:

- 4 duck breasts
- 1½ tablespoon lemongrass; chopped
- 3 tablespoon lemon juice

For the mango mix:

- 1 mango; peeled and chopped
- 1 red onion; chopped
- 1 teaspoon ginger; grated
- 1 ½ tablespoon lemon juice
- 3 garlic cloves; minced
- 2 tablespoon olive oil
- Salt and black pepper to the taste

- 1 tablespoon coriander; chopped
- 3/4 teaspoon sugar
- 1 tablespoon sweet chili sauce

Directions:

1. In a bowl, mix duck breasts with salt, pepper, lemongrass, 3 tablespoon lemon juice, olive oil and garlic; toss well, keep in the fridge for 1 hour, transfer to your air fryer and cook at 360°F, for 10 minutes; flipping once

2. Meanwhile; in a bowl, mix mango with coriander, onion, chili sauce, lemon juice, ginger and sugar and toss well
3. Divide duck on plates, add mango mix on the side and serve.

Chicken & Parsley Sauce

(Prep + Cooking Time: 55 Minutes | **Servings:** 6)

Ingredients:
- 12 chicken thighs
- 1/2 cup olive oil
- 1/4 cup red wine
- 4 garlic cloves
- 1 cup parsley; chopped.
- 1 teaspoon oregano; dried
- A pinch of salt
- A drizzle of maple syrup

Directions:
1. In your food processor, mix parsley with oregano, garlic, salt, oil, wine and maple syrup and pulse really well.
2. In a bowl, mix chicken with parsley sauce; toss well and keep in the fridge for 30 minutes
3. Drain chicken, transfer to your air fryer's basket and cook at 380°F, for 25 minutes; flipping chicken once. Divide chicken on plates, drizzle parsley sauce all over and serve

Chicken Thighs and Apple

(Prep + Cooking Time: 12 hours 30 Minutes | **Servings:** 4)

Ingredients:
- 8 chicken thighs; bone in and skin on
- 1 tablespoon apple cider vinegar
- 3/4 cup apple juice
- 1/2 cup maple syrup
- 3 tablespoon onion; chopped
- 1 tablespoon ginger; grated
- 1/2 teaspoon thyme; dried
- 3 apples; cored and cut into quarters
- Salt and black pepper to the taste

Directions:
1. In a bowl, mix chicken with salt, pepper, vinegar, onion, ginger, thyme, apple juice and maple syrup; toss well, cover and keep in the fridge for 12 hours
2. Transfer this whole mix to a baking dish that fits your air fryer, add apple pieces, place in your air fryer and cook at 350°F, for 30 minutes. Divide among plates and serve warm.

Chicken Thighs Recipe

(Prep + Cooking Time: 30 Minutes | **Servings:** 6)

Ingredients:
- 2 ½-pound chicken thighs
- 5 green onions; chopped
- 2 tablespoon sesame oil
- 1/4 teaspoon sugar
- 1 tablespoon sherry wine
- 1/2 teaspoon white vinegar
- 1 tablespoon soy sauce
- Salt and black pepper to the taste

Directions:
1. Season chicken with salt and pepper, rub with half of the sesame oil, add to your air fryer and cook at 360°F, for 20 minutes.
2. Meanwhile; heat up a pan with the rest of the oil over medium high heat, add green onions, sherry wine, vinegar, soy sauce and sugar; toss, cover and cook for 10 minutes. Shred chicken using 2 forks divide among plates, drizzle sauce all over and serve

Chicken & Simple Coconut Sauce

(Prep + Cooking Time: 22 Minutes | **Servings:** 6)

Ingredients:

- 3 ½-pound chicken breasts
- 1 cup chicken stock
- 1 ¼ cups yellow onion; chopped
- 1 tablespoon lime juice
- 1/4 cup coconut milk
- 2 teaspoon sweet paprika
- 1 teaspoon red pepper flakes
- 2 tablespoon green onions; chopped
- 1 tablespoon olive oil
- Salt and black pepper to the taste

Directions:

1. Heat up a pan that fits your air fryer with the oil over medium high heat, add onions; stir and cook for 4 minutes
2. Add stock, coconut milk, pepper flakes, paprika, lime juice, salt and pepper and stir well
3. Add chicken to the pan, add more salt and pepper; toss, introduce in your air fryer and cook at 360°F, for 12 minutes. Divide chicken and sauce on plates and serve.

Chicken Tenders & Flavored Sauce

(Prep + Cooking Time: 20 Minutes | **Servings:** 6)

Ingredients:

- 2-pound chicken tenders
- 2 tablespoon cornstarch
- 1 teaspoon chili powder
- 1/2 cup chicken stock
- 2 cups heavy cream
- 2 tablespoon water
- 2 teaspoon garlic powder
- 1 teaspoon onion powder
- 1 teaspoon sweet paprika
- 2 tablespoon butter
- 2 tablespoon olive oil
- 2 tablespoon parsley; chopped
- Salt and black pepper to the taste

Directions:

1. In a bowl, mix garlic powder with onion powder, chili, salt, pepper and paprika; stir, add chicken and toss.
2. Rub chicken tenders with oil, place in your air fryer and cook at 360°F, for 10 minutes
3. Meanwhile; heat up a pan with the butter over medium high heat, add cornstarch, stock, cream, water and parsley; stir, cover and cook for 10 minutes. Divide chicken on plates, drizzle sauce all over and serve

Coconut Creamy Chicken

(Prep + Cooking Time: 2 hours 25 Minutes | **Servings:** 4)

Ingredients:

- 4 big chicken legs
- 2 tablespoon ginger; grated
- 4 tablespoon coconut cream
- 5 teaspoon turmeric powder
- Salt and black pepper to the taste

Directions:

1. In a bowl, mix cream with turmeric, ginger, salt and pepper, whisk, add chicken pieces, toss them well and leave aside for 2 hours
2. Transfer chicken to your preheated air fryer, cook at 370°F, for 25 minutes; divide among plates and serve with a side salad

Chicken and Peaches Recipe

(Prep + Cooking Time: 40 Minutes | **Servings:** 6)

Ingredients:
- 1 whole chicken; cut into medium pieces
- 1/4 cup olive oil
- 4 peaches; halved
- 3/4 cup water
- 1/3 cup honey
- Salt and black pepper to the taste

Directions:
1. Put the water in a pot, bring to a simmer over medium heat, add honey, whisk really well and leave aside.
2. Rub chicken pieces with the oil, season with salt and pepper, place in your air fryer's basket and cook at 350°F, for 10 minutes
3. Brush chicken with some of the honey mix, cook for 6 minutes more, flip again, brush one more time with the honey mix and cook for 7 minutes more.
4. Divide chicken pieces on plates and keep warm
5. Brush peaches with what's left of the honey marinade, place them in your air fryer and cook them for 3 minutes. Divide among plates next to chicken pieces and serve.

Chicken and Apricot Sauce Recipe

(Prep + Cooking Time: 30 Minutes | **Servings:** 4)

Ingredients:
- 1 whole chicken; cut into medium pieces
- 2 tablespoon honey
- 1 tablespoon olive oil
- 1/4 cup apricot preserves
- 1 ½ teaspoon ginger; grated
- 1/2 teaspoon marjoram; dried
- 1/2 teaspoon smoked paprika
- 1/4 cup white wine
- 2 tablespoon white vinegar
- 1/4 cup chicken stock
- Salt and black pepper to the taste

Directions:
1. Season chicken with salt, pepper, marjoram and paprika; toss to coat, add oil, rub well, place in your air fryer and cook at 360°F, for 10 minutes.
2. Transfer chicken to a pan that fits your air fryer, add stock, wine, vinegar, ginger, apricot preserves and honey; toss, put in your air fryer and cook at 360°F, for 10 minutes more. Divide chicken and apricot sauce on plates and serve

Chicken and Capers Recipe

(Prep + Cooking Time: 30 Minutes | **Servings:** 2)

Ingredients:
- 4 chicken thighs
- 3 tablespoon capers
- 4 green onions; chopped
- 3 tablespoon butter; melted
- 4 garlic cloves; minced
- 1/2 cup chicken stock
- 1 lemon; sliced
- Salt and black pepper to the taste

Directions:
1. Brush chicken with butter, sprinkle salt and pepper to the taste, place them in a baking dish that fits your air fryer
2. Also add capers, garlic, chicken stock and lemon slices, toss to coat, introduce in your air fryer and cook at 370°F, for 20 minutes; shaking halfway. Sprinkle green onions, divide among plates and serve

Marinated Duck Breasts Recipe

(Prep + Cooking Time: 1 day 15 Minutes | **Servings:** 2)

Ingredients:
- 2 duck breasts
- 1/4 cup sherry wine
- 1 cup white wine
- 1/4 cup soy sauce
- 2 garlic cloves; minced
- 6 tarragon springs
- 1 tablespoon butter
- Salt and black pepper to the taste

Directions:
1. In a bowl, mix duck breasts with white wine, soy sauce, garlic, tarragon, salt and pepper; toss well and keep in the fridge for 1 day
2. Transfer duck breasts to your preheated air fryer at 350°F and cook for 10 minutes; flipping halfway.
3. Meanwhile; pour the marinade in a pan, heat up over medium heat, add butter and sherry; stir, bring to a simmer, cook for 5 minutes and take off heat. Divide duck breasts on plates, drizzle sauce all over and serve

Chicken Breasts with Passion Fruit Sauce

(Prep + Cooking Time: 20 Minutes | **Servings:** 4)

Ingredients:
- 4 chicken breasts
- 2-star anise
- 2-ounce maple syrup
- 4 passion fruits; halved, deseeded and pulp reserved
- 1 tablespoon whiskey
- 1 bunch chives; chopped
- Salt and black pepper to the taste

Directions:
1. Heat up a pan with the passion fruit pulp over medium heat, add whiskey, star anise, maple syrup and chives; stir well, simmer for 5 - 6 minutes and take off heat
2. Season chicken with salt and pepper, put in preheated air fryer and cook at 360°F, for 10 minutes; flipping halfway. Divide chicken on plates, heat up the sauce a bit, drizzle it over chicken and serve

Duck Breasts with Endives

(Prep + Cooking Time: 35 Minutes | **Servings:** 4)

Ingredients:
- 2 duck breasts
- 1 tablespoon sugar
- 8-ounce white wine
- 1 tablespoon garlic; minced
- 1 tablespoon olive oil
- 6 endives; julienned
- 2 tablespoon cranberries
- 2 tablespoon heavy cream
- Salt and black pepper to the taste

Directions:
1. Score duck breasts and season them with salt and pepper, put in preheated air fryer and cook at 350°F, for 20 minutes; flipping them halfway
2. Meanwhile; heat up a pan with the oil over medium heat, add sugar and endives; stir and cook for 2 minutes.
3. Add salt, pepper, wine, garlic, cream and cranberries; stir and cook for 3 minutes. Divide duck breasts on plates, drizzle the endives sauce all over and serve

Chicken and Black Olives Sauce

(Prep + Cooking Time: 18 Minutes | Servings: 2)

Ingredients:
- 1 chicken breast cut into 4 pieces
- 3 garlic cloves; minced

For the sauce:
- 1 cup black olives; pitted
- 1/4 cup parsley; chopped
- 1 tablespoon lemon juice
- 2 tablespoon olive oil

- 2 tablespoon olive oil
- Salt and black pepper to the taste

Directions:
1. In your food processor, mix olives with salt, pepper, 2 tablespoon olive oil, lemon juice and parsley, blend very well and transfer to a bowl
2. Season chicken with salt and pepper, rub with the oil and garlic, place in your preheated air fryer and cook at 370°F, for 8 minutes. Divide chicken on plates, top with olives sauce and serve

Chicken Salad Recipe

(Prep + Cooking Time: 20 Minutes | Servings: 4)

Ingredients:
- 1-pound chicken breast; boneless, skinless and halved
- 1/2 cup feta cheese; cubed
- 1 ½ teaspoon red wine vinegar
- 1/2 teaspoon anchovies; minced
- 3/4 teaspoon garlic; minced
- 1 tablespoon water
- 2 tablespoon lemon juice
- 1½ teaspoon mustard
- 1 tablespoon olive oil
- 8 cups lettuce leaves; cut into strips
- 4 tablespoon parmesan; grated
- Cooking spray
- Salt and black pepper to the taste

Directions:
1. Spray chicken breasts with cooking oil, season with salt and pepper, introduce in your air fryer's basket and cook at 370°F, for 10 minutes; flipping halfway
2. Transfer chicken beasts to a cutting board, shred using 2 forks, put in a salad bowl and mix with lettuce leaves.
3. In your blender, mix feta cheese with lemon juice, olive oil, mustard, vinegar, garlic, anchovies, water and half of the parmesan and blend very well. Add this over chicken mix; toss, sprinkle the rest of the parmesan and serve

Duck Breasts and Raspberry Sauce

(Prep + Cooking Time: 25 Minutes | Servings: 4)

Ingredients:
- 2 duck breasts; skin on and scored
- 1 tablespoon sugar
- 1/2 cup water
- 1/2 teaspoon cinnamon powder
- Salt and black pepper to the taste
- 1 teaspoon red wine vinegar
- 1/2 cup raspberries
- Cooking spray

Directions:
1. Season duck breasts with salt and pepper, spray them with cooking spray, put in preheated air fryer skin side down and cook at 350°F, for 10 minutes
2. Heat up a pan with the water over medium heat, add raspberries, cinnamon, sugar and wine; stir, bring to a simmer, transfer to your blender, puree and return to pan. Add air fryer duck breasts to pan as well; toss to coat, divide among plates and serve right away

Chicken and Radish Mix Recipe

(Prep + Cooking Time: 40 Minutes | **Servings:** 4)

Ingredients:

- 6 radishes; halved
- 2 tablespoon chives; chopped
- 1 cup chicken stock
- 1 teaspoon sugar
- 4 chicken things; bone-in
- 1 tablespoon olive oil
- 3 carrots; cut into thin sticks
- Salt and black pepper to the taste

Directions:

1. Heat up a pan that fits your air fryer over medium heat, add stock, carrots, sugar and radishes; stir gently, reduce heat to medium, cover pot partly and simmer for 20 minutes
2. Rub chicken with olive oil, season with salt and pepper, put in your air fryer and cook at 350°F, for 4 minutes. Add chicken to radish mix; toss, introduce everything in your air fryer, cook for 4 minutes more, divide among plates and serve

Turkey, Mushrooms and Peas Casserole

(Prep + Cooking Time: 30 Minutes | **Servings:** 4)

Ingredients:

- 2-pound turkey breasts; skinless, boneless
- 1/2 cup peas
- 1 cup chicken stock
- 1 cup cream of mushrooms soup
- 1 cup bread cubes
- 1 yellow onion; chopped
- 1 celery stalk; chopped.
- Salt and black pepper to the taste

Directions:

1. In a pan that fits your air fryer, mix turkey with salt, pepper, onion, celery, peas and stock, introduce in your air fryer and cook at 360°F, for 15 minutes
2. Add bread cubes and cream of mushroom soup; stir toss and cook at 360°F, for 5 minutes more. Divide among plates and serve hot

Duck Breasts with Orange Sauce

(Prep + Cooking Time: 45 Minutes | **Servings:** 4)

Ingredients:

- 2 duck breasts; skin on and halved
- 2 cups chicken stock
- 2 tablespoon olive oil
- 2 tablespoon butter
- 1/2 cup honey
- 2 tablespoon sherry vinegar
- 2 cups orange juice
- 2 teaspoon pumpkin pie spice
- 4 cups red wine
- Salt and black pepper to the taste

Directions:

1. Heat up a pan with the orange juice over medium heat, add honey; stir well and cook for 10 minutes
2. Add wine, vinegar, stock, pie spice and butter; stir well, cook for 10 minutes more and take off heat.
3. Season duck breasts with salt and pepper, rub with olive oil, place in preheated air fryer at 370°F and cook for 7 minutes on each side
4. Divide duck breasts on plates, drizzle wine and orange juice all over and serve right away.

Chicken and Chestnuts Mix Recipe

(Prep + Cooking Time: 22 Minutes | Servings: 2)

Ingredients:

- 1/2-pound chicken pieces
- 1 small yellow onion; chopped
- 4 tablespoon water chestnuts
- 2 tablespoon chicken stock
- 2 tablespoon balsamic vinegar
- 2 tortillas for serving
- 2 teaspoon garlic; minced
- 2 tablespoon soy sauce
- A pinch of ginger; grated
- A pinch of allspice; ground

Directions:

1. In a pan that fits your air fryer, mix chicken meat with onion, garlic, ginger, allspice, chestnuts, soy sauce, stock and vinegar; stir, transfer to your air fryer and cook at 360°F, for 12 minutes. Divide everything on plates and serve

Duck and Cherries Recipe

(Prep + Cooking Time: 30 Minutes | Servings: 4)

Ingredients:

- 4 duck breasts; boneless, skin on and scored
- 1/3 cup balsamic vinegar
- 1/2 cup yellow onion; chopped
- 1/2 teaspoon cinnamon powder
- 4 sage leaves; chopped
- 1 teaspoon garlic; minced
- 1 jalapeno; chopped
- 1 tablespoon ginger; grated
- 1 teaspoon cumin; ground
- 1/2 teaspoon clove; ground
- 2 cups cherries; pitted
- 1/2 cup sugar
- 1/4 cup honey
- 2 cups rhubarb; sliced
- Salt and black pepper to the taste

Directions:

1. Season duck breast with salt and pepper, put in your air fryer and cook at 350°F, for 5 minutes on each side
2. Meanwhile; heat up a pan over medium heat, add sugar, honey, vinegar, garlic, ginger, cumin, clove, cinnamon, sage, jalapeno, rhubarb, onion and cherries; stir, bring to a simmer and cook for 10 minutes.
3. Add duck breasts; toss well, divide everything on plates and serve

Greek Chicken Recipe

(Prep + Cooking Time: 25 Minutes | Servings: 4)

Ingredients:

- 1-pound chicken thighs
- 3 garlic cloves; minced
- 1/2-pound asparagus; trimmed
- 1 zucchini; roughly chopped
- 1 lemon sliced
- 2 tablespoon olive oil
- Juice from 1 lemon
- 1 teaspoon oregano; dried
- Salt and black pepper to the taste

Directions:

1. In a heat proof dish that fits your air fryer, mix chicken pieces with oil, lemon juice, oregano, garlic, salt, pepper, asparagus, zucchini and lemon slices; toss, introduce in preheated air fryer and cook at 380°F, for 15 minutes. Divide everything on plates and serve

Chicken and Garlic Sauce Recipe

(Prep + Cooking Time: 30 Minutes | **Servings:** 4)

Ingredients:

- 4 chicken breasts; skin on and bone-in
- 40 garlic cloves; peeled and chopped.
- 2 thyme springs
- 1/4 cup chicken stock
- 2 tablespoon parsley; chopped
- 1 tablespoon butter; melted
- 1 tablespoon olive oil
- Salt and black pepper to the taste
- 1/4 cup dry white wine

Directions:

1. Season chicken breasts with salt and pepper, rub with the oil, place in your air fryer, cook at 360°F, for 4 minutes on each side and transfer to a heat proof dish that fits your air fryer
2. Add melted butter, garlic, thyme, stock, wine and parsley; toss, introduce in your air fryer and cook at 350°F, for 15 minutes more. Divide everything on plates and serve

Duck and Tea Sauce Recipe

(Prep + Cooking Time: 30 Minutes | **Servings:** 4)

Ingredients:

- 2 duck breast halves; boneless
- 3 teaspoon earl gray tea leaves
- 3 tablespoon butter; melted
- 1 tablespoon honey
- 3/4 cup shallot; chopped
- 2 ¼ cup chicken stock
- 1 ½ cup orange juice
- Salt and black pepper to the taste

Directions:

1. Season duck breast halves with salt and pepper, put in preheated air fryer and cook at 360°F, for 10 minutes.
2. Meanwhile; heat up a pan with the butter over medium heat, add shallot; stir and cook for 2 - 3 minutes
3. Add stock; stir and cook for another minute.
4. Add orange juice, tea leaves and honey; stir, cook for 2 - 3 minutes more and strain into a bowl
5. Divide duck on plates, drizzle tea sauce all over and serve

Chicken and Spinach Salad Recipe

(Prep + Cooking Time: 22 Minutes | **Servings:** 2)

Ingredients:

- 2 chicken breasts; skinless and boneless
- 2 teaspoon parsley; dried
- 1/2 teaspoon onion powder
- 5 cups baby spinach
- 8 strawberries; sliced
- 1 small red onion; sliced
- 2 tablespoon balsamic vinegar
- 1 avocado; pitted, peeled and chopped
- 1/4 cup olive oil
- 1 tablespoon tarragon; chopped
- 2 teaspoon sweet paprika
- 1/2 cup lemon juice
- Salt and black pepper to the taste

Directions:

1. Put chicken in a bowl, add lemon juice, parsley, onion powder and paprika and toss
2. Transfer chicken to your air fryer and cook at 360°F, for 12 minutes.
3. In a bowl, mix spinach, onion, strawberries and avocado and toss
4. In another bowl, mix oil with vinegar, salt, pepper and tarragon, whisk well, add to the salad and toss. Divide chicken on plates, add spinach salad on the side and serve

Vegetable Recipes

Beets and Arugula Salad Time Recipe

(Prep + Cooking Time: 20 Minutes | Servings: 4)

Ingredients:

- 1 ½-pound beets; peeled and quartered
- 2 tablespoon brown sugar
- 2 scallions; chopped
- 2 tablespoon cider vinegar
- 1/2 cup orange juice
- 2 cups arugula
- 2 teaspoon mustard
- A drizzle of olive oil
- 2 teaspoon orange zest; grated

Directions:

1. Rub beets with the oil and orange juice, place them in your air fryer and cook at 350°F, for 10 minutes.
2. Transfer beet quarters to a bowl, add scallions, arugula and orange zest and toss.
3. In a separate bowl, mix sugar with mustard and vinegar, whisk well, add to salad, toss and serve

Sweet Baby Carrots Dish Recipe

(Prep + Cooking Time: 20 Minutes | Servings: 4)

Ingredients:

- 2 cups baby carrots
- 1 tablespoon brown sugar
- 1/2 tablespoon butter; melted
- A pinch of salt and black pepper

Directions:

1. In a dish that fits your air fryer, mix baby carrots with butter, salt, pepper and sugar, toss, introduce in your air fryer and cook at 350°F, for 10 minutes. Divide among plates and serve.

Fried Leeks Recipe

(Prep + Cooking Time: 17 Minutes | Servings: 4)

Ingredients:

- 4 leeks; washed, ends cut off and halved
- 1 tablespoon butter; melted
- 1 tablespoon lemon juice
- Salt and black pepper to the taste

Directions:

1. Rub leeks with melted butter, season with salt and pepper, put in your air fryer and cook at 350°F, for 7 minutes
2. Arrange on a platter, drizzle lemon juice all over and serve.

Brussels Sprouts and Tomatoes Mix

(Prep + Cooking Time: 15 Minutes | Servings: 4)

Ingredients:

- 1-pound Brussels sprouts; trimmed
- 1/4 cup green onions; chopped.
- 6 cherry tomatoes; halved
- 1 tablespoon olive oil
- Salt and black pepper to the taste

Directions:

1. Season Brussels sprouts with salt and pepper, put them in your air fryer and cook at 350°F, for 10 minutes.
2. Transfer them to a bowl, add salt, pepper, cherry tomatoes, green onions and olive oil, toss well and serve

Swiss Chard and Sausage Recipe

(Prep + Cooking Time: 30 Minutes **| Servings:** 8)

Ingredients:

- 8 cups Swiss chard; chopped
- 1/2 cup onion; chopped
- 1/4 cup parmesan; grated
- 3 eggs
- 2 cups ricotta cheese
- 1 cup mozzarella; shredded.
- 1-pound sausage; chopped
- 1 tablespoon olive oil
- 1 garlic clove; minced
- Salt and black pepper to the taste
- A pinch of nutmeg

Directions:

1. Heat up a pan that fits your air fryer with the oil over medium heat, add onions, garlic, Swiss chard, salt, pepper and nutmeg; stir, cook for 2 minutes and take off heat.
2. In a bowl; whisk eggs with mozzarella, parmesan and ricotta; stir, pour over Swiss chard mix, toss, introduce in your air fryer and cook at 320°F, for 17 minutes. Divide among plates and serve

Crispy Potatoes and Parsley

(Prep + Cooking Time: 20 Minutes **| Servings:** 4)

Ingredients:

- 1-pound gold potatoes; cut into wedges
- 2 tablespoon olive
- 1/4 cup parsley leaves; chopped
- Juice from 1/2 lemon
- Salt and black pepper to the taste

Directions:

1. Rub potatoes with salt, pepper, lemon juice and olive oil, put them in your air fryer and cook at 350°F, for 10 minutes.
2. Divide among plates, sprinkle parsley on top and serve

Fried Asparagus Recipe

(Prep + Cooking Time: 25 Minutes **| Servings:** 4)

Ingredients:

- 2-pound fresh asparagus; trimmed
- 1/2 teaspoon oregano; dried
- 4-ounce feta cheese; crumbled
- 4 garlic cloves; minced
- 2 tablespoon parsley; finely chopped.
- 1/4 teaspoon red pepper flakes
- 1/4 cup olive oil
- Salt and black pepper to the taste
- 1 teaspoon lemon zest
- Juice from 1 lemon

Directions:

1. In a bowl; mix oil with lemon zest, garlic, pepper flakes and oregano and whisk
2. Add asparagus, cheese, salt and pepper, toss, transfer to your air fryer's basket and cook at 350°F, for 8 minutes.
3. Divide asparagus on plates, drizzle lemon juice and sprinkle parsley on top and serve.

Stuffed Baby Peppers Recipe

(Prep + Cooking Time: 16 Minutes **| Servings:** 4)

Ingredients:

- 12 baby bell peppers; cut into halves lengthwise
- 6 tablespoon jarred basil pesto
- 1 tablespoon lemon juice
- 1 tablespoon olive oil
- 1-pound shrimp; cooked, peeled and deveined
- 1/4 teaspoon red pepper flakes; crushed
- Salt and black pepper to the taste
- A handful parsley; chopped

Directions:

1. In a bowl; mix shrimp with pepper flakes, pesto, salt, black pepper, lemon juice, oil and parsley, whisk very well and stuff bell pepper halves with this mix.
2. Place them in your air fryer and cook at 320°F, for 6 minutes; Arrange peppers on plates and serve

Flavored Fennel Recipe

(Prep + Cooking Time: 18 Minutes **| Servings:** 4)

Ingredients:

- 2 fennel bulbs; cut into quarters
- 1 red chili pepper; chopped
- 3/4 cup veggie stock
- 1/4 cup white wine
- 3 tablespoon olive oil
- Juice from 1/2 lemon
- Salt and black pepper to the taste
- 1 garlic clove; minced
- 1/4 cup parmesan; grated

Directions:

1. Heat up a pan that fits your air fryer with the oil over medium high heat, add garlic and chili pepper; stir and cook for 2 minutes.
2. Add fennel, salt, pepper, stock, wine, lemon juice, and parmesan, toss to coat, introduce in your air fryer and cook at 350°F, for 6 minutes. Divide among plates and serve right away

Balsamic Artichokes Recipe

(Prep + Cooking Time: 17 Minutes **| Servings:** 4)

Ingredients:

- 4 big artichokes; trimmed
- 1/4 cup extra virgin olive oil
- 2 garlic cloves; minced
- 2 tablespoon lemon juice
- 2 teaspoon balsamic vinegar
- 1 teaspoon oregano; dried
- Salt and black pepper to the taste

Directions:

1. Season artichokes with salt and pepper, rub them with half of the oil and half of the lemon juice, put them in your air fryer and cook at 360°F, for 7 minutes.
2. Meanwhile; in a bowl, mix the rest of the lemon juice with vinegar, the remaining oil, salt, pepper, garlic and oregano and stir very well
3. Arrange artichokes on a platter, drizzle the balsamic vinaigrette over them and serve

Flavored Fried Tomatoes Recipe

(Prep + Cooking Time: 25 Minutes **| Servings:** 8)

Ingredients:

- 1 jalapeno pepper; chopped
- 4 garlic cloves; minced
- 1/2 teaspoon oregano; dried
- 1/4 cup olive oil
- 1/2 cup parmesan; grated
- 1/4 cup basil; chopped
- 2-pound cherry tomatoes; halved
- Salt and black pepper to the taste

Directions:
1. In a bowl; mix tomatoes with garlic, jalapeno, season with salt, pepper and oregano and drizzle the oil, toss to coat, introduce in your air fryer and cook at 380°F, for 15 minutes
2. Transfer tomatoes to a bowl, add basil and parmesan, toss and serve

Peppers Stuffed with Beef Recipe

(Prep + Cooking Time: 65 Minutes | **Servings:** 4)

Ingredients:
- 1-pound beef; ground
- 4 bell peppers; cut into halves and seeds removed
- 1/3 cup raisins
- 1/3 cup walnuts; chopped
- 1 teaspoon coriander; ground
- 1 onion; chopped
- 3 garlic cloves; minced
- 1/2 teaspoon turmeric powder
- 1 tablespoon hot curry powder
- 1 egg
- 2 tablespoon olive oil
- 1 tablespoon ginger; grated
- 1/2 teaspoon cumin; ground
- Salt and black pepper to the taste

Directions:
1. Heat up a pan with the oil over medium high heat, add onion; stir and cook for 4 minutes.
2. Add garlic and beef; stir and cook for 10 minutes.
3. Add coriander, ginger, cumin, curry powder, salt, pepper, turmeric, walnuts and raisins; stir take off heat and mix with the egg
4. Stuff pepper halves with this mix, introduce them in your air fryer and cook at 320°F, for 20 minutes. Divide among plates and serve.

Beet, Tomato and Goat Cheese Mix

(Prep + Cooking Time: 44 Minutes | **Servings:** 8)

Ingredients:
- 8 small beets; trimmed, peeled and halved
- 2 tablespoon olive oil
- 4-ounce goat cheese; crumbled
- 1 tablespoon balsamic vinegar
- 1 red onion; sliced
- 2 tablespoon sugar
- 1 pint mixed cherry tomatoes; halved
- 2-ounce pecans
- Salt and black pepper to the taste

Directions:
1. Put beets in your air fryer, season them with salt and pepper, cook at 350°F, for 14 minutes and transfer to a salad bowl.
2. Add onion, cherry tomatoes and pecans and toss.
3. In another bowl, mix vinegar with sugar and oil, whisk well until sugar dissolves and add to salad. Also add goat cheese, toss and serve

Cherry Tomatoes Skewers

(Prep + Cooking Time: 36 Minutes | **Servings:** 4)

Ingredients:
- 3 tablespoon balsamic vinegar
- 24 cherry tomatoes
- 2 tablespoon olive oil

For the dressing:
- 2 tablespoon balsamic vinegar
- 4 tablespoon olive oil

- 3 garlic cloves; minced
- 1 tablespoon thyme; chopped
- Salt and black pepper to the taste

- Salt and black pepper to the taste

Directions:

1. In a bowl; mix 2 tablespoon oil with 3 tablespoon vinegar, 3 garlic cloves, thyme, salt and black pepper and whisk well.
2. Add tomatoes, toss to coat and leave aside for 30 minutes.
3. Arrange 6 tomatoes on one skewer and repeat with the rest of the tomatoes
4. Introduce them in your air fryer and cook at 360°F, for 6 minutes.
5. In another bowl, mix 2 tablespoon vinegar with salt, pepper and 4 tablespoon oil and whisk well. Arrange tomato skewers on plates and serve with the dressing drizzled on top

Herbed Eggplant and Zucchini Mix

(Prep + Cooking Time: 18 Minutes | Servings: 4)

Ingredients:

- 1 eggplant; roughly cubed
- 3 zucchinis; roughly cubed
- 2 tablespoon lemon juice
- 1 teaspoon oregano; dried
- 3 tablespoon olive oil
- 1 teaspoon thyme; dried
- Salt and black pepper to the taste

Directions:

1. Put eggplant in a dish that fits your air fryer, add zucchinis, lemon juice, salt, pepper, thyme, oregano and olive oil, toss, introduce in your air fryer and cook at 360°F, for 8 minutes.
2. Divide among plates and serve right away

Beet Salad and Parsley Dressing

(Prep + Cooking Time: 24 Minutes | Servings: 4)

Ingredients:

- 4 beets
- 1 garlic clove; chopped
- 2 tablespoon capers
- 2 tablespoon balsamic vinegar
- A bunch of parsley; chopped
- 1 tablespoon extra virgin olive oil
- Salt and black pepper to the taste

Directions:

1. Put beets in your air fryer and cook them at 360°F, for 14 minutes
2. Meanwhile; in a bowl, mix parsley with garlic, salt, pepper, olive oil and capers and stir very well
3. Transfer beets to a cutting board, leave them to cool down, peel them, slice put them in a salad bowl
4. Add vinegar, drizzle the parsley dressing all over and serve

Spinach Pie Recipe

(Prep + Cooking Time: 25 Minutes | Servings: 4)

Ingredients:

- 7-ounce flour
- 2 tablespoon butter
- 2 eggs
- 2 tablespoon milk
- 3-ounce cottage cheese
- 7oz. spinach
- 1 tablespoon olive oil
- 1 yellow onion; chopped
- Salt and black pepper to the taste

Directions:

1. In your food processor, mix flour with butter, 1 egg, milk, salt and pepper, blend well, transfer to a bowl, knead, cover and leave for 10 minutes.
2. Heat up a pan with the oil over medium high heat, add onion and spinach; stir and cook for 2 minutes.
3. Add salt, pepper, the remaining egg and cottage cheese; stir well and take off heat.
4. Divide dough in 4 pieces, roll each piece, place on the bottom of a ramekin, add spinach filling over dough, place ramekins in your air fryer's basket and cook at 360°F, for 15 minutes

Broccoli Salad Recipe

(**Prep + Cooking Time:** 18 Minutes | **Servings:** 4)

Ingredients:
- 1 broccoli head; florets separated
- 6 garlic cloves; minced
- 1 tablespoon Chinese rice wine vinegar
- 1 tablespoon peanut oil
- Salt and black pepper to the taste

Directions:
1. In a bowl; mix broccoli with salt, pepper and half of the oil, toss, transfer to your air fryer and cook at 350°F, for 8 minutes; shaking the fryer halfway.
2. Transfer broccoli to a salad bowl, add the rest of the peanut oil, garlic and rice vinegar, toss really well and serve

Okra and Corn Salad Recipe

(**Prep + Cooking Time:** 22 Minutes | **Servings:** 6)

Ingredients:
- 1-pound okra; trimmed
- 28-ounce canned tomatoes; chopped.
- 6 scallions; chopped
- 2 tablespoon olive oil
- 1 teaspoon sugar
- 1 cup con
- 3 green bell peppers; chopped
- Salt and black pepper to the taste

Directions:
1. Heat up a pan that fits your air fryer with the oil over medium high heat, add scallions and bell peppers; stir and cook for 5 minutes.
2. Add okra, salt, pepper, sugar, tomatoes and corn; stir, introduce in your air fryer and cook at 360°F, for 7 minutes. Divide okra mix on plates and serve warm

Mexican Peppers Recipe

(**Prep + Cooking Time:** 35 Minutes | **Servings:** 4)

Ingredients:
- 4 bell peppers; tops cut off and seeds removed
- 1/2 cup tomato juice
- 1/4 cup yellow onion; chopped
- 1/4 cup green peppers; chopped
- 2 cups tomato sauce
- 2 tablespoon jarred jalapenos; chopped.
- 1/2 teaspoon red pepper; crushed
- 1 teaspoon chili powder
- 1/2 teaspoon garlic powder
- 4 chicken breasts
- 1 cup tomatoes; chopped
- Salt and black pepper to the taste
- 2 teaspoon onion powder
- 1 teaspoon cumin; ground

Directions:
1. In a pan that fits your air fryer, mix chicken breasts with tomato juice, jalapenos, tomatoes, onion, green peppers, salt, pepper, onion powder, red pepper, chili powder, garlic powder, oregano and cumin; stir well, introduce in your air fryer and cook at 350°F, for 15 minutes.
2. Shred meat using 2 forks; stir, stuff bell peppers with this mix, place them in your air fryer and cook at 320°F, for 10 minutes more. Divide stuffed peppers on plates and serve.

Artichokes and Special Sauce

(Prep + Cooking Time: 16 Minutes | **Servings:** 2)

Ingredients:

- 2 artichokes; trimmed
- 1 tablespoon lemon juice

For the sauce:

- 3 anchovy fillets
- 1/4 cup extra virgin olive oil

- 2 garlic cloves; minced
- A drizzle of olive oil

- 1/4 cup coconut oil
- 3 garlic cloves

Directions:

1. In a bowl; mix artichokes with oil, 2 garlic cloves and lemon juice, toss well, transfer to your air fryer, cook at 350°F, for 6 minutes and divide among plates.
2. In your food processor, mix coconut oil with anchovy, 3 garlic cloves and olive oil, blend very well, drizzle over artichokes and serve

Creamy Green Beans Recipe

(Prep + Cooking Time: 25 Minutes | **Servings:** 4)

Ingredients:

- 2-pound green beans
- 1/2 cup heavy cream
- 1 cup mozzarella; shredded.
- 2/3 cup parmesan; grated

- 2 teaspoon lemon zest; grated
- Salt and black pepper to the taste
- A pinch of red pepper flakes

Directions:

1. Put the beans in a dish that fits your air fryer, add heavy cream, salt, pepper, lemon zest, pepper flakes, mozzarella and parmesan, toss, introduce in your air fryer and cook at 350°F, for 15 minutes.
2. Divide among plates and serve right away

Green Beans and Potatoes Recipe

(Prep + Cooking Time: 25 Minutes | **Servings:** 5)

Ingredients:

- 2-pound green beans
- 6 bacon slices; cooked and chopped
- 6 new potatoes; halved

- Salt and black pepper to the taste
- A drizzle of olive oil

Directions:

1. In a bowl; mix green beans with potatoes, salt, pepper and oil, toss, transfer to your air fryer and cook at 390°F, for 15 minutes. Divide among plates and serve with bacon sprinkled on top.

Eggplant and Garlic Sauce Recipe

(Prep + Cooking Time: 20 Minutes | **Servings:** 4)

Ingredients:

- 3 eggplants; halved and sliced
- 1 red chili pepper; chopped.
- 2 garlic cloves; minced
- 2 tablespoon olive oil

- 1 tablespoon ginger; grated
- 1 tablespoon soy sauce
- 1 green onion stalk; chopped
- 1 tablespoon balsamic vinegar

Directions:

1. Heat up a pan that fits your air fryer with the oil over medium high heat, add eggplant slices and cook for 2 minutes.
2. Add chili pepper, garlic, green onions, ginger, soy sauce and vinegar, introduce in your air fryer and cook at 320°F, for 7 minutes. Divide among plates and serve

Radish Hash Recipe

(Prep + Cooking Time: 17 Minutes **| Servings:** 4)

Ingredients:

- 1-pound radishes; sliced
- 1/2 teaspoon onion powder
- 1/2 teaspoon garlic powder
- 1/3 cup parmesan; grated
- 4 eggs
- Salt and black pepper to the taste

Directions:

1. In a bowl; mix radishes with salt, pepper, onion and garlic powder, eggs and parmesan and stir well
2. Transfer radishes to a pan that fits your air fryer and cook at 350°F, for 7 minutes.
3. Divide hash on plates and serve

Beets and Blue Cheese Salad

(Prep + Cooking Time: 24 Minutes **| Servings:** 6)

Ingredients:

- 6 beets; peeled and quartered
- 1 tablespoon olive oil
- 1/4 cup blue cheese; crumbled
- Salt and black pepper to the taste

Directions:

1. Put beets in your air fryer, cook them at 350°F, for 14 minutes and transfer them to a bowl
2. Add blue cheese, salt, pepper and oil, toss and serve.

Sesame Mustard Greens Recipe

(Prep + Cooking Time: 21 Minutes **| Servings:** 4)

Ingredients:

- 2 garlic cloves; minced
- 1 tablespoon olive oil
- 1/2 cup yellow onion; sliced
- 3 tablespoon veggie stock
- 1/4 teaspoon dark sesame oil
- 1-pound mustard greens; torn
- Salt and black pepper to the taste

Directions:

1. Heat up a pan that fits your air fryer with the oil over medium heat, add onions; stir and brown them for 5 minutes
2. Add garlic, stock, greens, salt and pepper; stir, introduce in your air fryer and cook at 350°F, for 6 minutes. Add sesame oil, toss to coat, divide among plates and serve.

Collard Greens and Turkey Wings

(Prep + Cooking Time: 30 Minutes **| Servings:** 6)

Ingredients:

- 1 sweet onion; chopped
- 2 smoked turkey wings
- 1/2 teaspoon crushed red pepper
- 2 tablespoon apple cider vinegar
- 1 tablespoon brown sugar
- 2 tablespoon olive oil
- 3 garlic cloves; minced
- 2 ½-pound collard greens; chopped.
- Salt and black pepper to the taste

Directions:

1. Heat up a pan that fits your air fryer with the oil over medium high heat, add onions; stir and cook for 2 minutes.
2. Add garlic, greens, vinegar, salt, pepper, crushed red pepper, sugar and smoked turkey, introduce in preheated air fryer and cook at 350°F, for 15 minutes
3. Divide greens and turkey on plates and serve

Asian Turnips Salad Recipe

(Prep + Cooking Time: 22 Minutes **| Servings:** 4)

Ingredients:

- 20-ounce turnips; peeled and chopped
- 1 teaspoon garlic; minced
- 2 tomatoes; chopped
- 1 teaspoon cumin; ground
- 1 teaspoon coriander; ground
- 2 green chilies; chopped
- 1 teaspoon ginger; grated
- 1/2 teaspoon turmeric powder
- 2 tablespoon butter
- 2 yellow onions; chopped
- Salt and black pepper to the taste
- A handful coriander leaves; chopped

Directions:

1. Heat up a pan that fits your air fryer with the butter, melt it, add green chilies, garlic and ginger; stir and cook for 1 minute.
2. Add onions, salt, pepper, tomatoes, turmeric, cumin, ground coriander and turnips; stir, introduce in your air fryer and cook at 350°F, for 10 minutes
3. Divide among plates, sprinkle fresh coriander on top and serve

Brussels Sprouts and Butter Sauce

(Prep + Cooking Time: 14 Minutes **| Servings:** 4)

Ingredients:

- 1-pound Brussels sprouts; trimmed
- 2 tablespoon dill; finely chopped.
- 1 tablespoon mustard
- 1/2 cup bacon; cooked and chopped
- 1 tablespoon butter
- Salt and black pepper to the taste

Directions:

1. Put Brussels sprouts in your air fryer and cook them at 350°F, for 10 minutes.
2. Heat up a pan with the butter over medium high heat, add bacon, mustard and dill and whisk well. Divide Brussels sprouts on plates, drizzle butter sauce all over and serve

Cheesy Brussels Sprouts Recipe

(Prep + Cooking Time: 18 Minutes **| Servings:** 4)

Ingredients:

- 1-pound Brussels sprouts; washed
- 3 tablespoon parmesan; grated
- Juice of 1 lemon
- 2 tablespoon butter
- Salt and black pepper to the taste

Directions:

1. Put Brussels sprouts in your air fryer, cook them at 350°F, for 8 minutes and transfer them to a bowl.
2. Heat up a pan with the butter over medium heat, add lemon juice, salt and pepper, whisk well and add to Brussels sprouts. Add parmesan, toss until parmesan melts and serve

Stuffed Poblano Peppers Recipe

(Prep + Cooking Time: 25 Minutes **| Servings:** 4)

Ingredients:

- 10 poblano peppers; tops cut off and deseeded
- 2 teaspoon garlic; minced
- 8-ounce mushrooms; chopped.
- 1/2 cup cilantro; chopped
- 1 white onion; chopped
- 1 tablespoon olive oil
- Salt and black pepper to the taste

Directions:

1. Heat up a pan with the oil over medium high heat, add onion and mushrooms; stir and cook for 5 minutes.

2. Add garlic, cilantro, salt and black pepper; stir and cook for 2 minutes.
3. Divide this mix into poblanos, introduce them in your air fryer and cook at 350°F, for 15 minutes. Divide among plates and serve.

Stuffed Tomatoes Recipe

(Prep + Cooking Time: 25 Minutes | **Servings:** 4)

Ingredients:
- 4 tomatoes; tops cut off and pulp scooped and chopped
- 1 yellow onion; chopped.
- 1/2 cup mushrooms; chopped
- 1 tablespoon bread crumbs
- 1 tablespoon butter
- 1/4 teaspoon caraway seeds
- 1 tablespoon parsley; chopped
- 2 tablespoon celery; chopped
- 1 cup cottage cheese
- Salt and black pepper to the taste

Directions:
1. Heat up a pan with the butter over medium heat, melt it, add onion and celery; stir and cook for 3 minutes.
2. Add tomato pulp and mushrooms; stir and cook for 1 minute more.
3. Add salt, pepper, crumbled bread, cheese, caraway seeds and parsley; stir, cook for 4 minutes more and take off heat.
4. Stuff tomatoes with this mix, place them in your air fryer and cook at 350°F, for 8 minutes. Divide stuffed tomatoes on plates and serve.

Portobello Mushrooms Recipe

(Prep + Cooking Time: 22 Minutes | **Servings:** 4)

Ingredients:
- 4 Portobello mushrooms; stems removed and chopped.
- 10 basil leaves
- 1 tablespoon parsley
- 1/4 cup olive oil
- 8 cherry tomatoes; halved
- 1 cup baby spinach
- 3 garlic cloves; chopped
- 1 cup almonds; roughly chopped
- Salt and black pepper to the taste

Directions:
1. In your food processor, mix basil with spinach, garlic, almonds, parsley, oil, salt, black pepper to the taste and mushroom stems and blend well.
2. Stuff each mushroom with this mix, place them in your air fryer and cook at 350°F, for 12 minutes. Divide mushrooms on plates and serve

Broccoli and Tomatoes Fried Stew

(Prep + Cooking Time: 30 Minutes | **Servings:** 4)

Ingredients:
- 28-ounce canned tomatoes; pureed
- A pinch of red pepper; crushed
- 1 small ginger piece; chopped
- 1 garlic clove; minced
- 1 broccoli head; florets separated
- 2 teaspoon coriander seeds
- 1 tablespoon olive oil
- 1 yellow onion; chopped
- Salt and black pepper to the taste

Directions:
1. Heat up a pan that fits your air fryer with the oil over medium heat, add onions, salt, pepper and red pepper; stir and cook for 7 minutes.
2. Add ginger, garlic, coriander seeds, tomatoes and broccoli; stir, introduce in your air fryer and cook at 360°F, for 12 minutes. Divide into bowls and serve

Simple Tomatoes & Bell Pepper Sauce

(Prep + Cooking Time: 25 Minutes | **Servings:** 4)

Ingredients:

- 2 red bell peppers; chopped
- 1-pound cherry tomatoes; halved
- 1 teaspoon rosemary; dried
- 3 bay leaves
- 2 garlic cloves; minced
- 2 tablespoon olive oil
- 1 tablespoon balsamic vinegar
- Salt and black pepper to the taste

Directions:

1. In a bowl mix tomatoes with garlic, salt, black pepper, rosemary, bay leaves, half of the oil and half of the vinegar, toss to coat, introduce in your air fryer and roast them at 320°F, for 15 minutes.
2. Meanwhile; in your food processor, mix bell peppers with a pinch of sea salt, black pepper, the rest of the oil and the rest of the vinegar and blend very well
3. Divide roasted tomatoes on plates, drizzle the bell peppers sauce over them and serve.

Asian Potatoes Recipe

(Prep + Cooking Time: 22 Minutes | **Servings:** 4)

Ingredients:

- 1 tablespoon coriander seeds
- 1/2 teaspoon turmeric powder
- 1/2 teaspoon red chili powder
- 1 teaspoon pomegranate powder
- 1 tablespoon pickled mango; chopped
- 1 tablespoon cumin seeds
- 2 teaspoon fenugreek; dried
- 5 potatoes; boiled, peeled and cubed
- Salt and black pepper to the taste
- 2 tablespoon olive oil

Directions:

1. Heat up a pan that fits your air fryer with the oil over medium heat, add coriander and cumin seeds; stir and cook for 2 minutes.
2. Add salt, pepper, turmeric, chili powder, pomegranate powder, mango, fenugreek and potatoes, toss, introduce in your air fryer and cook at 360°F, for 10 minutes
3. Divide among plates and serve hot.

Cheesy Artichokes Recipe

(Prep + Cooking Time: 16 Minutes | **Servings:** 6)

Ingredients:

- 14-ounce canned artichoke hearts
- 8-ounce cream cheese
- 16-ounce parmesan cheese; grated
- 10-ounce spinach
- 1/2 cup chicken stock
- 1/2 cup mayonnaise
- 8-ounce mozzarella; shredded.
- 1/2 cup sour cream
- 3 garlic cloves; minced
- 1 teaspoon onion powder

Directions:

1. In a pan that fits your air fryer, mix artichokes with stock, garlic, spinach, cream cheese, sour cream, onion powder and mayo, toss, introduce in your air fryer and cook at 350°F, for 6 minutes.
2. Add mozzarella and parmesan; stir well and serve

Spanish Greens Recipe

(Prep + Cooking Time: 18 Minutes **| Servings:** 4)

Ingredients:

- 1 apple; cored and chopped.
- 1 yellow onion; sliced
- 1/4 cup raisins
- 6 garlic cloves; chopped
- 5 cups mixed spinach and chard
- 1/4 cup pine nuts; toasted
- 1/4 cup balsamic vinegar
- 3 tablespoon olive oil
- Salt and black pepper to the taste
- A pinch of nutmeg

Directions:

1. Heat up a pan that fits your air fryer with the oil over medium high heat, add onion; stir and cook for 3 minutes
2. Add apple, garlic, raisins, vinegar, mixed spinach and chard, nutmeg, salt and pepper; stir, introduce in preheated air fryer and cook at 350°F, for 5 minutes.
3. Divide among plates, sprinkle pine nuts on top and serve

Collard Greens Mix Recipe

(Prep + Cooking Time: 20 Minutes **| Servings:** 4)

Ingredients:

- 1 bunch collard greens; trimmed
- 2 tablespoon olive oil
- 1 teaspoon sugar
- 1 yellow onion; chopped
- 3 garlic cloves; minced
- 2 tablespoon tomato puree
- 1 tablespoon balsamic vinegar
- Salt and black pepper to the taste

Directions:

1. In a dish that fits your air fryer, mix oil, garlic, vinegar, onion and tomato puree and whisk.
2. Add collard greens, salt, pepper and sugar, toss, introduce in your air fryer and cook at 320°F, for 10 minutes. Divide collard greens mix on plates and serve.

Green Beans and Parmesan Recipe

(Prep + Cooking Time: 18 Minutes **| Servings:** 4)

Ingredients:

- 12-ounce green beans
- 2 teaspoon garlic; minced
- 2 tablespoon olive oil
- 1 egg; whisked
- 1/3 cup parmesan; grated
- Salt and black pepper to the taste

Directions:

1. In a bowl; mix oil with salt, pepper, garlic and egg and whisk well
2. Add green beans to this mix, toss well and sprinkle parmesan all over.
3. Transfer green beans to your air fryer and cook them at 390°F, for 8 minutes. Divide green beans on plates and serve them right away

Swiss Chard Salad Recipe

(Prep + Cooking Time: 23 Minutes | **Servings:** 4)

Ingredients:
- 1 bunch Swiss chard; torn
- 1/4 cup pine nuts; toasted
- 1/4 cup raisins
- 2 tablespoon olive oil
- 1 tablespoon balsamic vinegar
- 1 small yellow onion; chopped
- A pinch of red pepper flakes
- Salt and black pepper to the taste

Directions:
1. Heat up a pan that fits your air fryer with the oil over medium heat, add chard and onions; stir and cook for 5 minutes.
2. Add salt, pepper, pepper flakes, raisins, pine nuts and vinegar; stir, introduce in your air fryer and cook at 350°F, for 8 minutes. Divide among plates and serve

Stuffed Eggplants Recipe

(Prep + Cooking Time: 40 Minutes | **Servings:** 4)

Ingredients:
- 4 small eggplants; halved lengthwise
- 1/2 cup cauliflower; chopped
- 1 teaspoon oregano; chopped
- 1/2 cup parsley; chopped
- Salt and black pepper to the taste
- 10 tablespoon olive oil
- 2 ½-pound tomatoes; cut into halves and grated
- 1 green bell pepper; chopped
- 1 yellow onion; chopped
- 1 tablespoon garlic; minced
- 3-ounce feta cheese; crumbled

Directions:
1. Season eggplants with salt, pepper and 4 tablespoon oil, toss, put them in your air fryer and cook at 350°F, for 16 minutes
2. Meanwhile; heat up a pan with 3 tablespoon oil over medium high heat, add onion; stir and cook for 5 minutes.
3. Add bell pepper, garlic and cauliflower; stir, cook for 5 minutes; take off heat, add parsley, tomato, salt, pepper, oregano and cheese and whisk everything.
4. Stuff eggplants with the veggie mix, drizzle the rest of the oil over them, put them in your air fryer and cook at 350°F, for 6 minutes more. Divide among plates and serve right away.

Garlic Tomatoes Recipe

(Prep + Cooking Time: 25 Minutes | **Servings:** 4)

Ingredients:
- 1-pound mixed cherry tomatoes
- 4 garlic cloves; crushed
- 3 thyme springs; chopped.
- 1/4 cup olive oil
- Salt and black pepper to the taste

Directions:
1. In a bowl; mix tomatoes with salt, black pepper, garlic, olive oil and thyme, toss to coat, introduce in your air fryer and cook at 360°F, for 15 minutes. Divide tomatoes mix on plates and serve.

Spicy Cabbage Recipe

(Prep + Cooking Time: 18 Minutes **| Servings:** 4)

Ingredients:

- 1/4 cups apple juice
- 1 carrot; grated
- 1/4 cup apple cider vinegar
- 1/2 teaspoon cayenne pepper
- 1 cabbage; cut into 8 wedges
- 1 tablespoon sesame seed oil
- 1 teaspoon red pepper flakes; crushed

Directions:

1. In a pan that fits your air fryer, combine cabbage with oil, carrot, vinegar, apple juice, cayenne and pepper flakes, toss, introduce in preheated air fryer and cook at 350°F, for 8 minutes.
2. Divide cabbage mix on plates and serve

Eggplant Hash Recipe

(Prep + Cooking Time: 30 Minutes **| Servings:** 4)

Ingredients:

- 1 eggplant; roughly chopped
- 1/2-pound cherry tomatoes; halved
- 1/4 cup mint; chopped
- 1/4 cup basil; chopped
- 1/2 cup olive oil
- 1 teaspoon Tabasco sauce
- Salt and black pepper to the taste

Directions:

1. Heat up a pan that fits your air fryer with half of the oil over medium high heat, add eggplant pieces, cook for 3 minutes; flip, cook them for 3 minutes more and transfer to a bowl.
2. Heat up the same pan with the rest of the oil over medium high heat, add tomatoes; stir and cook for 1 - 2 minutes
3. Return eggplant pieces to the pan, add salt, black pepper, basil, mint and Tabasco sauce, introduce in your air fryer and cook at 320°F, for 6 minutes. Divide among plates and serve.

Collard Greens and Bacon Recipe

(Prep + Cooking Time: 22 Minutes **| Servings:** 4)

Ingredients:

- 1-pound collard greens
- 2 tablespoon chicken stock
- 3 bacon strips; chopped
- 1/4 cup cherry tomatoes; halved
- 1 tablespoon apple cider vinegar
- Salt and black pepper to the taste

Directions:

1. Heat up a pan that fits your air fryer over medium heat, add bacon; stir and cook 1 - 2 minutes
2. Add tomatoes, collard greens, vinegar, stock, salt and pepper; stir, introduce in your air fryer and cook at 320°F, for 10 minutes. Divide among plates and serve.

Sweet Potatoes Mix Recipe

(Prep + Cooking Time: 25 Minutes **| Servings:** 4)

Ingredients:

- 3 sweet potatoes; cubed
- 4 tablespoon olive oil
- 4 garlic cloves; minced
- 1/2-pound bacon; chopped
- 2 tablespoon balsamic vinegar
- 2 green onions; chopped.
- Juice from 1 lime
- A handful dill; chopped
- Salt and black pepper to the taste
- A pinch of cinnamon powder
- A pinch of red pepper flakes

Directions:
1. Arrange bacon and sweet potatoes in your air fryer's basket, add garlic and half of the oil, toss well and cook at 350°F and bake for 15 minutes.
2. Meanwhile; in a bowl, mix vinegar with lime juice, olive oil, green onions, pepper flakes, dill, salt, pepper and cinnamon and whisk. Transfer bacon and sweet potatoes to a salad bowl, add salad dressing, toss well and serve right away.

Greek Potato Mix Recipe

(**Prep + Cooking Time:** 30 Minutes | **Servings:** 2)

Ingredients:
- 2 medium potatoes; cut into wedges
- 1 yellow onion; chopped.
- 1 bay leaf
- 1 small carrot; roughly chopped
- 1 ½ tablespoon flour
- 1/2 cup chicken stock
- 2 tablespoon Greek yogurt
- 2 tablespoon butter
- Salt and black pepper to the taste

Directions:
1. Heat up a pan that fits your air fryer with the butter over medium high heat, add onion and carrot; stir and cook for 3 - 4 minutes.
2. Add potatoes, flour, chicken stock, salt, pepper and bay leaf; stir, introduce in your air fryer and cook at 320°F, for 16 minutes. Add Greek yogurt, toss, divide among plates and serve.

Zucchini Noodles Recipe

(**Prep + Cooking Time:** 30 Minutes | **Servings:** 6)

Ingredients:
- 2 tablespoon olive oil
- 3 zucchinis; cut with a spiralizer
- 1/4 cup sun dried tomatoes; chopped
- 1 teaspoon garlic; minced
- 1/2 cup cherry tomatoes; halved
- 16-ounce mushrooms; sliced
- 2 cups tomatoes sauce
- 2 cups spinach; torn
- Salt and black pepper to the taste
- A handful basil; chopped.

Directions:
1. Put zucchini noodles in a bowl, season salt and black pepper and leave them aside for 10 minutes
2. Heat up a pan that fits your air fryer with the oil over medium high heat, add garlic; stir and cook for 1 minute
3. Add mushrooms, sun dried tomatoes, cherry tomatoes, spinach, cayenne, sauce and zucchini noodles; stir, introduce in your air fryer and cook at 320°F, for 10 minutes.
4. Divide among plates and serve with basil sprinkled on top

Tomato and Basil Tart Recipe

(**Prep + Cooking Time:** 24 Minutes | **Servings:** 2)

Ingredients:
- 1 bunch basil; chopped
- 1/4 cup cheddar cheese; grated
- 1/2 cup cherry tomatoes; halved
- 4 eggs
- 1 garlic clove; minced
- Salt and black pepper to the taste

Directions:
1. In a bowl; mix eggs with salt, black pepper, cheese and basil and whisk well
2. Pour this into a baking dish that fits your air fryer, arrange tomatoes on top, introduce in the fryer and cook at 320°F, for 14 minutes.
3. Slice and serve right away

Broccoli Hash Recipe

(Prep + Cooking Time: 38 Minutes | **Servings:** 2)

Ingredients:

- 10-ounce mushrooms; halved
- 1 broccoli head; florets separated
- 1 yellow onion; chopped
- 1 tablespoon olive oil
- 1 garlic clove; minced
- 1 teaspoon basil; dried
- 1 tablespoon balsamic vinegar
- 1 avocado; peeled and pitted
- A pinch of red pepper flakes
- Salt and black pepper

Directions:

1. In a bowl; mix mushrooms with broccoli, onion, garlic and avocado
2. In another bowl, mix vinegar, oil, salt, pepper and basil and whisk well.
3. Pour this over veggies, toss to coat, leave aside for 30 minutes; transfer to your air fryer's basket and cook at 350°F, for 8 minutes; Divide among plates and serve with pepper flakes on top.

Delicious Green Beans Recipe

(Prep + Cooking Time: 25 Minutes | **Servings:** 4)

Ingredients:

- 1-pound red potatoes; cut into wedges
- 2 garlic cloves; minced
- 2 tablespoon olive oil
- 1/2 teaspoon oregano; dried
- 1-pound green beans
- Salt and black pepper to the taste

Directions:

1. In a pan that fits your air fryer, combine potatoes with green beans, garlic, oil, salt, pepper and oregano, toss, introduce in your air fryer and cook at 380°F, for 15 minutes. Divide among plates and serve.

Potatoes and Special Tomato Sauce

(Prep + Cooking Time: 26 Minutes | **Servings:** 4)

Ingredients:

- 2-pound potatoes; cubed
- 1/2 teaspoon oregano; dried
- 1/2 teaspoon parsley; dried
- 2 tablespoon basil; chopped
- 4 garlic cloves; minced
- 1 yellow onion; chopped.
- 1 cup tomato sauce
- 2 tablespoon olive oil

Directions:

1. Heat up a pan that fits your air fryer with the oil over medium heat, add onion; stir and cook for 1 - 2 minutes
2. Add garlic, potatoes, parsley, tomato sauce and oregano; stir, introduce in your air fryer and cook at 370°F and cook for 16 minutes. Add basil, toss everything, divide among plates and serve.

Zucchini Mix Recipe

(Prep + Cooking Time: 24 Minutes | **Servings:** 6)

Ingredients:

- 6 zucchinis; halved and then sliced
- 3 garlic cloves; minced
- 1 tablespoon butter
- 1 teaspoon oregano; dried
- 1/2 cup yellow onion; chopped
- 2-ounce parmesan; grated
- 3/4 cup heavy cream
- Salt and black pepper to the taste

Directions:

1. Heat up a pan that fits your air fryer with the butter over medium high heat, add onion; stir and cook for 4 minutes.
2. Add garlic, zucchinis, oregano, salt, pepper and heavy cream, toss, introduce in your air fryer and cook at 350°F, for 10 minutes. Add parmesan; stir, divide among plates and serve

Italian Eggplant Stew Recipe

(Prep + Cooking Time: 25 Minutes **| Servings:** 4)

Ingredients:
- 1 red onion; chopped
- 2 garlic cloves; chopped
- 1 bunch parsley; chopped
- 1 teaspoon oregano; dried
- 2 eggplants; cut into medium chunks
- 2 tablespoon olive oil
- 2 tablespoon capers; chopped
- 1 handful green olives; pitted and sliced
- Salt and black pepper to the taste
- 5 tomatoes; chopped
- 3 tablespoon herb vinegar

Directions:
1. Heat up a pan that fits your air fryer with the oil over medium heat, add eggplant, oregano, salt and pepper; stir and cook for 5 minutes.
2. Add garlic, onion, parsley, capers, olives, vinegar and tomatoes; stir, introduce in your air fryer and cook at 360°F, for 15 minutes. Divide into bowls and serve

Green Beans and Tomatoes

(Prep + Cooking Time: 25 Minutes **| Servings:** 4)

Ingredients:
- 1-pound green beans
- 1-pint cherry tomatoes
- 2 tablespoon olive oil
- Salt and black pepper to the taste

Directions:
1. In a bowl; mix cherry tomatoes with green beans, olive oil, salt and pepper, toss, transfer to your air fryer and cook at 400°F, for 15 minutes. Divide among plates and serve right away.

Rutabaga & Cherry Tomatoes Mix

(Prep + Cooking Time: 25 Minutes **| Servings:** 4)

Ingredients:
- 1 tablespoon shallot; chopped
- 1/2 cup veggie stock
- 2 teaspoon lemon juice
- 1 garlic clove; minced

For the pasta:
- 1 cup cherry tomatoes; halved
- 1/4 teaspoon garlic powder
- 3/4 cup cashews; soaked for a couple of hours and drained
- 2 tablespoon nutritional yeast
- Salt and black pepper to the taste
- 2 rutabagas; peeled and cut into thick noodles
- 5 teaspoon olive oil

Directions:
1. Place tomatoes and rutabaga noodles into a pan that fits your air fryer, drizzle the oil over them, season with salt, black pepper and garlic powder, toss to coat and cook in your air fryer at 350°F, for 15 minutes.
2. Meanwhile; in a food processor, mix garlic with shallots, cashews, veggie stock, nutritional yeast, lemon juice, a pinch of sea salt and black pepper to the taste and blend well.
3. Divide rutabaga pasta on plates, top with tomatoes, drizzle the sauce over them and serve.

Potatoes and Tomatoes Mix

(Prep + Cooking Time: 26 Minutes **| Servings:** 4)

Ingredients:

- 1 ½-pound red potatoes; quartered
- 1 tablespoon rosemary; chopped
- 1-pint cherry tomatoes
- 3 garlic cloves; minced
- 2 tablespoon olive oil
- 1 teaspoon sweet paprika
- Salt and black pepper to the taste

Directions:

1. In a bowl; mix potatoes with tomatoes, oil, paprika, rosemary, garlic, salt and pepper, toss, transfer to your air fryer and cook at 380°F, for 16 minutes. Divide among plates and serve.

Balsamic Potatoes Recipe

(Prep + Cooking Time: 30 Minutes **| Servings:** 4)

Ingredients:

- 1 ½-pound baby potatoes; halved
- 2 thyme springs; chopped
- 9-ounce cherry tomatoes
- 3 tablespoon olive oil
- 2 garlic cloves; chopped.
- 2 red onions; chopped
- 1 ½ tablespoon balsamic vinegar
- Salt and black pepper to the taste

Directions:

1. In your food processor, mix garlic with onions, oil, vinegar, thyme, salt and pepper and pulse really well
2. In a bowl; mix potatoes with tomatoes and balsamic marinade, toss well, transfer to your air fryer and cook at 380°F, for 20 minutes. Divide among plates and serve.

Snack & Appetizer Recipes

Tasty Cheese Sticks

(Prep + Cooking Time: 1 hour and 18 minutes | **Servings:** 4)

Ingredients:

- 2 eggs; whisked
- 1 garlic clove; minced
- 1 cup parmesan; grated
- 1 tablespoon Italian seasoning
- Salt and black pepper to the taste
- 8 mozzarella cheese strings; cut into halves
- Cooking spray

Directions:

1. In a bowl; mix parmesan with salt, pepper, Italian seasoning and garlic and stir well
2. Put whisked eggs in another bowl.
3. Dip mozzarella sticks in egg mixture; then in cheese mix
4. Dip them again in egg and in parmesan mix and keep them in the freezer for 1 hour.
5. Spray cheese sticks with cooking oil; place them in your air fryer's basket and cook at 390°F, for 8 minutes flipping them halfway. Arrange them on a platter and serve as an appetizer

Delicious Wrapped Shrimp

(Prep + Cooking Time: 18 Minutes | **Servings:** 16)

Ingredients:

- 10-ounce already cooked shrimp; peeled and deveined
- 2 tablespoon olive oil
- 11 prosciutto sliced
- 1/3 cup red wine
- 1/3 cup blackberries; ground
- 1 tablespoon mint; chopped

Directions:

1. Wrap each shrimp in a prosciutto slices, drizzle the oil over them, rub well, place in your preheated air fryer at 390°F and fry them for 8 minutes
2. Meanwhile; heat up a pan with ground blackberries over medium heat, add mint and wine; stir, cook for 3 minutes and take off heat. Arrange shrimp on a platter, drizzle blackberries sauce over them and serve as an appetizer

Salmon Patties

(Prep + Cooking Time: 30 Minutes | **Servings:** 4)

Ingredients:

- 3 big potatoes; boiled, drained and mashed
- 2 tablespoon bread crumbs
- 2 tablespoon parsley; chopped
- 2 tablespoon dill; chopped
- 1 egg
- 1 big salmon fillet; skinless, boneless
- Salt and black pepper to the taste
- Cooking spray

Directions:

1. Place salmon in your air fryer's basket and cook for 10 minutes at 360 degrees F
2. Transfer salmon to a cutting board, cool it down; flake it and put it in a bowl
3. Add mashed potatoes, salt, pepper, dill, parsley, egg and bread crumbs; stir well and shape 8 patties out of this mix. Place salmon patties in your air fryer's basket, spry them with cooking oil, cook at 360°F, for 12 minutes; flipping them halfway, transfer them to a platter and serve as an appetizer

Sweet Potato Spread

(Prep + Cooking Time: 20 Minutes | **Servings:** 10)

Ingredients:

- 19-ounce canned garbanzo beans; drained
- 5 garlic cloves; minced
- 1/2 teaspoon cumin; ground
- 1/4 cup tahini
- 2 tablespoon lemon juice
- 1 tablespoon olive oil
- 2 tablespoon water
- 1 cup sweet potatoes; peeled and chopped.
- A pinch of salt and white pepper

Directions:

1. Put potatoes in your air fryer's basket, cook them at 360°F, for 15 minutes; cool them down, peel, put them in your food processor and pulse well. basket
2. Add sesame paste, garlic, beans, lemon juice, cumin, water and oil and pulse really well. Add salt and pepper, pulse again; divide into bowls and serve.

Crispy Shrimp Snack

(Prep + Cooking Time: 15 Minutes | **Servings:** 4)

Ingredients:

- 12 big shrimp; deveined and peeled
- 1 cup panko bread crumbs
- 2 egg whites
- 1 cup coconut; shredded.
- 1 cup white flour
- Salt and black pepper to the taste

Directions:

1. In a bowl; mix panko with coconut and stir
2. Put flour, salt and pepper in a second bowl and whisk egg whites in a third one.
3. Dip shrimp in flour, egg whites mix and coconut, place them all in your air fryer's basket; cook at 350°F, for 10 minutes flipping halfway. Arrange on a platter and serve as an appetizer

Sweet Popcorn Snack

(Prep + Cooking Time: 15 Minutes | **Servings:** 4)

Ingredients:

- 2 ½ tablespoon butter
- 2-ounce brown sugar
- 2 tablespoon corn kernels

Directions:

1. Put corn kernels in your air fryer's pan, cook at 400°F, for 6 minutes; transfer them to a tray, spread and leave aside for now
2. Heat up a pan over low heat, add butter, melt it, add sugar and stir until it dissolves
3. Add popcorn, toss to coat, take off heat and spread on the tray again. Cool down, divide into bowls and serve as a snack.

Cheering Chicken Breast Rolls

(Prep + Cooking Time: 32 Minutes | **Servings:** 4)

Ingredients:

- 4 chicken breasts; boneless and skinless
- 1 cup sun dried tomatoes; chopped
- 1 ½ tablespoon Italian seasoning
- 4 mozzarella slices
- 2 cups baby spinach
- A drizzle of olive oil
- Salt and black pepper to the taste

Directions:

1. Flatten chicken breasts using a meat tenderizer, divide tomatoes, mozzarella and spinach, season with salt, pepper and Italian seasoning, roll and seal them.
2. Place them in your air fryer's basket; drizzle some oil over them and cook at 375°F, for 17 minutes; flipping once. Arrange chicken rolls on a platter and serve them as an appetizer

Succulent Chicken Dip

(Prep + Cooking Time: 35 Minutes **| Servings:** 10)

Ingredients:
- 2 cups chicken meat; cooked and shredded.
- 2 teaspoon curry powder
- 4 scallions; chopped.
- 1/3 cup raisins
- 1/4 cup cilantro; chopped
- 1/2 cup almonds; sliced
- 3 tablespoon butter; melted
- 1 cup yogurt
- 12-ounce cream cheese
- 6-ounce Monterey jack cheese; grated
- 1/2 cup chutney
- Salt and black pepper to the taste

Directions:
1. In a bowl mix cream cheese with yogurt and whisk using your mixer
2. Add curry powder, scallions, chicken meat, raisins, cheese, cilantro, salt and pepper and stir everything. Spread this into a baking dish that fist your air fryer; sprinkle almonds on top, place in your air fryer, bake at 300 degrees for 25 minutes; divide into bowls, top with chutney and serve as an appetizer.

Tasty Apple Chips

(Prep + Cooking Time: 20 Minutes **| Servings:** 2)

Ingredients:
- 1 apple; cored and sliced
- 1 tablespoon white sugar
- 1/2 teaspoon cinnamon powder
- A pinch of salt

Directions:
1. In a bowl; mix apple slices with salt, sugar and cinnamon; toss, transfer to your air fryer's basket, cook for 10 minutes at 390°F, flipping once. Divide apple chips in bowls and serve as a snack

Cheesy Tasty Zucchini Snack

(Prep + Cooking Time: 18 Minutes **| Servings:** 4)

Ingredients:
- 1 cup mozzarella; shredded.
- 1 zucchini; sliced
- 1/4 cup tomato sauce
- Salt and black pepper to the taste
- A pinch of cumin
- Cooking spray

Directions:
1. Arrange zucchini slices in your air fryer's basket; spray them with cooking oil, spread tomato sauce all over, them, season with salt, pepper, cumin, sprinkle mozzarella at the end and cook them at 320°F, for 8 minutes. Arrange them on a platter and serve as a snack

Bread Sticks Snack

(Prep + Cooking Time: 20 Minutes **| Servings:** 2)

Ingredients:
- 4 bread slices; each cut into 4 sticks
- 1/4 cup milk
- 1 teaspoon cinnamon powder
- 1 tablespoon honey
- 1/4 cup brown sugar
- 2 eggs
- A pinch of nutmeg

Directions:
1. In a bowl; mix eggs with milk, brown sugar, cinnamon, nutmeg and honey and whisk well.
2. Dip bread sticks in this mix; place them in your air fryer's basket and cook at 360°F, for 10 minutes. Divide bread sticks into bowls and serve as a snack

Herbed Tomatoes

(Prep + Cooking Time: 30 Minutes | **Servings:** 2)

Ingredients:

- 2 tomatoes; halved
- 1 teaspoon oregano; dried
- 1 teaspoon rosemary; dried
- 1 teaspoon parsley; dried
- 1 teaspoon basil; dried
- Cooking spray
- Salt and black pepper to the taste

Directions:

1. Spray tomato halves with cooking oil, season with salt, pepper, parsley, basil, oregano and rosemary over them
2. Place them in your air fryer's basket and cook at 320°F, for 20 minutes. Arrange them on a platter and serve as an appetizer.

Chestnut and Shrimp Rolls

(Prep + Cooking Time: 25 Minutes | **Servings:** 4)

Ingredients:

- 1/2-pound already cooked shrimp; chopped.
- 8-ounce water chestnuts; chopped
- 3 scallions; chopped
- 1 tablespoon water
- 1 egg yolk
- 1/2-pound shiitake mushrooms; chopped.
- 2 cups cabbage; chopped
- 2 tablespoon olive oil
- 1 garlic clove; minced
- 1 teaspoon ginger; grated
- 6 spring roll wrappers
- Salt and black pepper to the taste

Directions:

1. Heat up a pan with the oil over medium high heat, add cabbage, shrimp, chestnuts, mushrooms, garlic, ginger, scallions, salt and pepper; stir and cook for 2 minutes
2. In a bowl; mix egg with water and stir well. Arrange roll wrappers on a working surface, divide shrimp and veggie mix on them, seal edges with egg wash, place them all in your air fryer's basket, cook at 360°F, for 15 minutes; transfer to a platter and serve as an appetizer

Greek Style Lamb Meatballs

(Prep + Cooking Time: 18 Minutes | **Servings:** 10)

Ingredients:

- 4-ounce lamb meat; minced
- 1/2 tablespoon lemon peel; grated
- 1 tablespoon oregano; chopped
- 1 slice of bread; toasted and crumbled
- 2 tablespoon feta cheese; crumbled
- Salt and black pepper to the taste

Directions:

1. In a bowl; combine meat with bread crumbs, salt, pepper, feta, oregano and lemon peel; stir well, shape 10 meatballs and place them in you air fryer. Cook at 400°F, for 8 minutes; arrange them on a platter and serve as an appetizer

Spicy Fish Nuggets

(Prep + Cooking Time: 22 Minutes | **Servings:** 4)

Ingredients:

- 28-ounce fish fillets; skinless and cut into medium pieces
- 5 tablespoon flour
- 1 egg; whisked
- 5 tablespoon water
- 4 tablespoon homemade mayonnaise
- 3-ounce panko bread crumbs
- 1 tablespoon garlic powder
- 1 tablespoon smoked paprika
- 1 teaspoon dill; dried
- Lemon juice from 1/2 lemon
- Salt and black pepper to the taste
- Cooking spray

Directions:

1. In a bowl; mix flour with water and stir well
2. Add egg, salt and pepper and whisk well
3. In a second bowl; mix panko with garlic powder and paprika and stir well
4. Dip fish pieces in flour and egg mix and then in panko mix, place them in your air fryer's basket, spray them with cooking oil and cook at 400°F, for 12 minutes.
5. Meanwhile; in a bowl mix mayo with dill and lemon juice and whisk well. Arrange fish nuggets on a platter and serve with dill mayo on the side

Tasty Crab Sticks

(Prep + Cooking Time: 30 Minutes | **Servings:** 4)

Ingredients:

- 10 crabsticks; halved
- 2 teaspoon sesame oil
- 2 teaspoon Cajun seasoning

Directions:

1. Put crab sticks in a bowl; add sesame oil and Cajun seasoning; toss, transfer them to your air fryer's basket and cook at 350°F, for 12 minutes. Arrange on a platter and serve as an appetizer

Tasty Banana Snack

(Prep + Cooking Time: 15 Minutes | **Servings:** 8)

Ingredients:

- 16 baking cups crust
- 1/4 cup peanut butter
- 3/4 cup chocolate chips
- 1 banana; peeled and sliced into 16 pieces
- 1 tablespoon vegetable oil

Directions:

1. Put chocolate chips in a small pot, heat up over low heat; stir until it melts and take off heat.
2. In a bowl; mix peanut butter with coconut oil and whisk well
3. Spoon 1 teaspoon chocolate mix in a cup, add 1 banana slice and top with 1 teaspoon butter mix. Repeat with the rest of the cups, place them all into a dish that fits your air fryer, cook at 320°F, for 5 minutes; transfer to a freezer and keep there until you serve them as a snack

Chicken Breast Sticks

(Prep + Cooking Time: 26 Minutes | **Servings:** 4)

Ingredients:

- 1-pound chicken breast; skinless, boneless and cut into medium sticks
- 1 teaspoon sweet paprika
- 3/4 cup white flour
- 1/2 tablespoon olive oil
- 1 cup panko bread crumbs
- 1 egg; whisked
- Salt and black pepper to the taste
- Zest from 1 lemon; grated

Directions:

1. In a bowl; mix paprika with flour, salt, pepper and lemon zest and stir
2. Put whisked egg in another bowl and the panko breadcrumbs in a third one.
3. Dredge chicken pieces in flour, egg and panko and place them in your lined air fryer's basket; drizzle the oil over them, cook at 400°F, for 8 minutes; flip and cook for 8 more minutes. Arrange them on a platter and serve as a snack

Special Empanadas

(Prep + Cooking Time: 35 Minutes | **Servings:** 4)

Ingredients:

- 1 package empanada shells
- 1 tablespoon olive oil
- 1-pound beef meat; ground
- 1 yellow onion; chopped
- 1/2 teaspoon cumin; ground
- 1/4 cup tomato salsa
- 2 garlic cloves; minced
- 1 green bell pepper; chopped
- 1 egg yolk whisked with 1 tablespoon water
- Salt and black pepper to the taste

Directions:

1. Heat up a pan with the oil over medium high heat; add beef and brown on all sides
2. Add onion, garlic, salt, pepper, bell pepper and tomato salsa; stir and cook for 15 minutes
3. Divide cooked meat in empanada shells, brush them with egg wash and seal.
4. Place them in your air fryer's steamer basket and cook at 350°F, for 10 minutes. Arrange on a platter and serve as an appetizer.

Quick Zucchini Cakes

(Prep + Cooking Time: 22 Minutes | **Servings:** 12)

Ingredients:

- 1/2 cup whole wheat flour
- 1 egg
- 1 yellow onion; chopped.
- 2 garlic cloves; minced
- 1/2 cup dill; chopped
- 3 zucchinis; grated
- Cooking spray
- Salt and black pepper to the taste

Directions:

1. In a bowl; mix zucchinis with garlic, onion, flour, salt, pepper, egg and dill; stir well, shape small patties out of this mix, spray them with cooking spray; place them in your air fryer's basket and cook at 370°F, for 6 minutes on each side. Serve them as a snack right away

Yummy Spring Rolls

(Prep + Cooking Time: 35 Minutes | **Servings:** 8)

Ingredients:
- 2 cups green cabbage; shredded.
- 2 yellow onions; chopped
- 1/2 chili pepper; minced
- 1 tablespoon ginger; grated
- 3 garlic cloves; minced
- 1 carrot; grated
- 10 spring roll sheets
- 2 tablespoon corn flour
- 2 tablespoon water
- 1 teaspoon sugar
- 1 teaspoon soy sauce
- 2 tablespoon olive oil
- Salt and black pepper to the taste

Directions:
1. Heat up a pan with the oil over medium heat, add cabbage, onions, carrots, chili pepper, ginger, garlic, sugar, salt, pepper and soy sauce; stir well, cook for 2 - 3 minutes; take off heat and cool down
2. Cut spring roll sheets in squares, divide cabbage mix on each and roll them.
3. In a bowl; mix corn flour with water; stir well and seal spring rolls with this mix.
4. Place spring rolls in your air fryer's basket and cook them at 360°F, for 10 minutes
5. Flip roll and cook them for 10 minutes more. Arrange on a platter and serve them as an appetizer.

Tasty Stuffed Peppers

(Prep + Cooking Time: 18 Minutes | **Servings:** 8)

Ingredients:
- 8 small bell peppers; tops cut off and seeds removed
- 1 tablespoon olive oil
- 3.5-ounce goat cheese; cut into 8 pieces
- Salt and black pepper to the taste

Directions:
1. In a bowl; mix cheese with oil with salt and pepper and toss to coat. Stuff each pepper with goat cheese, place them in your air fryer's basket, cook at 400°F, for 8 minutes; arrange on a platter and serve as an appetizer

Radish Chips

(Prep + Cooking Time: 20 Minutes | **Servings:** 4)

Ingredients:
- 15 radishes; sliced
- Cooking spray
- 1 tablespoon chives; chopped.
- Salt and black pepper to the taste

Directions:
1. Arrange radish slices in your air fryer's basket, spray them with cooking oil, season with salt and black pepper to the taste, cook them at 350°F, for 10 minutes.
2. Flipping them halfway, transfer to bowls and serve with chives sprinkled on top

Coco Chicken Bites

(Prep + Cooking Time: 23 Minutes | **Servings:** 4)

Ingredients:
- 8 chicken tenders
- 2 teaspoon garlic powder
- 3/4 cup panko bread crumbs
- 3/4 cup coconut; shredded.
- 2 eggs
- Salt and black pepper to the taste
- Cooking spray

Directions:
1. In a bowl; mix eggs with salt, pepper and garlic powder and whisk well
2. In another bowl; mix coconut with panko and stir well.
3. Dip chicken tenders in eggs mix and then coat in coconut one well
4. Spray chicken bites with cooking spray, place them in your air fryer's basket and cook them at 350°F, for 10 minutes. Arrange them on a platter and serve as an appetizer

Tasty Banana Chips

(Prep + Cooking Time: 25 Minutes | **Servings:** 4)

Ingredients:
- 1/2 teaspoon turmeric powder
- 4 bananas; peeled and sliced
- 1/2 teaspoon chaat masala
- 1 teaspoon olive oil
- A pinch of salt

Directions:
1. In a bowl; mix banana slices with salt, turmeric, chaat masala and oil; toss and leave aside for 10 minutes.
2. Transfer banana slices to your preheated air fryer at 360°F and cook them for 15 minutes flipping them once. Serve as a snack

Appetizing Cajun Shrimp

(Prep + Cooking Time: 15 Minutes | **Servings:** 2)

Ingredients:
- 20 tiger shrimp; peeled and deveined
- 1/2 teaspoon old bay seasoning
- 1/4 teaspoon smoked paprika
- 1 tablespoon olive oil
- Salt and black pepper to the taste

Directions:
1. In a bowl; mix shrimp with oil, salt, pepper, old bay seasoning and paprika and toss to coat
2. Place shrimp in your air fryer's basket and cook at 390°F, for 5 minutes. Arrange them on a platter and serve as an appetizer

Tasty Fish Sticks

(Prep + Cooking Time: 22 Minutes | **Servings:** 2)

Ingredients:
- 4 white fish filets; boneless, skinless and cut into medium sticks
- 1 egg; whisked
- 4-ounce bread crumbs
- 4 tablespoon olive oil
- Salt and black pepper to the taste

Directions:
1. In a bowl; mix bread crumbs with oil and stir well
2. Put egg in a second bowl; add salt and pepper and whisk well.
3. Dip fish stick in egg and them in bread crumb mix, place them in your air fryer's basket and cook at 360°F, for 12 minutes. Arrange fish sticks on a platter and serve as an appetizer

Fried Dill Pickles

(Prep + Cooking Time: 15 Minutes | **Servings:** 4)

Ingredients:

- 16-ounce jarred dill pickles; cut into wedges and pat dried
- 1/2 cup white flour
- 1/4 cup milk
- 1/2 teaspoon garlic powder
- 1/2 teaspoon sweet paprika
- 1 egg
- 1/4 cup ranch sauce
- Cooking spray

Directions:

1. In a bowl; combine milk with egg and whisk well
2. In a second bowl; mix flour with salt, garlic powder and paprika and stir as well.
3. Dip pickles in flour, then in egg mix and again in flour and place them in your air fryer. Grease them with cooking spray, cook pickle wedges at 400°F, for 5 minutes; transfer to a bowl and serve with ranch sauce on the side.

Honey Chicken Wings

(Prep + Cooking Time: 1 hour and 22 minutes | **Servings:** 8)

Ingredients:

- 16 chicken wings; halved
- 2 tablespoon honey
- 2 tablespoon lime juice
- 2 tablespoon soy sauce
- Salt and black pepper to the taste

Directions:

1. In a bowl; mix chicken wings with soy sauce, honey, salt, pepper and lime juice; toss well and keep in the fridge for 1 hour
2. Transfer chicken wings to your air fryer and cook them at 360°F, for 12 minutes; flipping them halfway. Arrange them on a platter and serve as an appetizer

Chicken Wings

(Prep + Cooking Time: 1 hours 10 Minutes | **Servings:** 2)

Ingredients:

- 16 pieces' chicken wings
- 3/4 cup potato starch
- 4 tablespoon garlic; minced
- 1/4 cup honey
- 1/4 cup butter
- Salt and black pepper to the taste

Directions:

1. In a bowl; mix chicken wings with salt, pepper and potato starch; toss well, transfer to your air fryer's basket, cook them at 380°F, for 25 minutes and at 400°F, for 5 minutes more
2. Meanwhile; heat up a pan with the butter over medium high heat, melt it, add garlic; stir, cook for 5 minutes and then mix with salt, pepper and honey.
3. Whisk well, cook over medium heat for 20 minutes and take off heat. Arrange chicken wings on a platter; drizzle honey sauce all over and serve as an appetizer

Delicious Tuna Cakes

(Prep + Cooking Time: 20 Minutes **| Servings:** 12**)**

Ingredients:

- 15-ounce canned tuna; drain and flaked
- 1 teaspoon parsley; dried
- 1/2 cup red onion; chopped
- 1/2 teaspoon dill; dried
- 1 teaspoon garlic powder
- 3 eggs
- Salt and black pepper to the taste
- Cooking spray

Directions:

1. In a bowl; mix tuna with salt, pepper, dill, parsley, onion, garlic powder and eggs; stir well and shape medium cakes out of this mix
2. Place tuna cakes in your air fryer's basket, spray them with cooking oil and cook at 350°F, for 10 minutes; flipping them halfway. Arrange them on a platter and serve as an appetizer

Cauliflower Snack

(Prep + Cooking Time: 25 Minutes **| Servings:** 4**)**

Ingredients:

- 4 cups cauliflower florets
- 1/4 cup buffalo sauce
- 1/4 cup butter; melted
- 1 cup panko bread crumbs
- Mayonnaise for serving

Directions:

1. In a bowl; mix buffalo sauce with butter and whisk well
2. Dip cauliflower florets in this mix and coat them in panko bread crumbs.
3. Place them in your air fryer's basket and cook at 350°F, for 15 minutes. Arrange them on a platter and serve with mayo on the side

Amazing Pesto Crackers

(Prep + Cooking Time: 27 Minutes **| Servings:** 6**)**

Ingredients:

- 1/2 teaspoon baking powder
- 1 garlic clove; minced
- 2 tablespoon basil pesto
- 3 tablespoon butter
- 1/4 teaspoon basil; dried
- 1¼ cups flour
- Salt and black pepper to the taste

Directions:

1. In a bowl; mix salt, pepper, baking powder, flour, garlic, cayenne, basil, pesto and butter and stir until you obtain a dough
2. Spread this dough on a lined baking sheet that fits your air fryer; introduce in the fryer at 325°F and bake for 17 minutes. Leave aside to cool down, cut crackers and serve them as a snack

Mexican Style Apple Snack

(Prep + Cooking Time: 15 Minutes **| Servings:** 4**)**

Ingredients:

- 3 big apples; cored, peeled and cubed
- 1/2 cup clean caramel sauce
- 1/4 cup pecans; chopped.
- 2 teaspoon lemon juice
- 1/2 cup dark chocolate chips

Directions:

1. In a bowl; mix apples with lemon juice; stir and transfer to a pan that fits your air fryer
2. Add chocolate chips, pecans, drizzle the caramel sauce, toss; introduce in your air fryer and cook at 320°F, for 5 minutes. Toss gently, divide into small bowls and serve right away as a snack

Healthy Spinach Balls

(Prep + Cooking Time: 17 Minutes | **Servings:** 30)

Ingredients:

- 4 tablespoon butter; melted
- 2 eggs
- 1 cup flour
- 1/3 cup feta cheese; crumbled
- 1 tablespoon onion powder
- 3 tablespoon whipping cream
- 1/4 teaspoon nutmeg; ground
- 1/3 cup parmesan; grated
- 16-ounce spinach
- 1 teaspoon garlic powder
- Salt and black pepper to the taste

Directions:

1. In your blender, mix spinach with butter, eggs, flour, feta cheese, parmesan, nutmeg, whipping cream, salt, pepper, onion and garlic pepper, blend very well and keep in the freezer for 10 minutes
2. Shape 30 spinach balls; place them in your air fryer's basket and cook at 300°F, for 7 minutes. Serve as a party appetizer

Pure Pumpkin Muffins

(Prep + Cooking Time: 25 Minutes | **Servings:** 18)

Ingredients:

- 3/4 cup pumpkin puree
- 2 tablespoon flaxseed meal
- 1/4 cup flour
- 1/2 cup sugar
- 1/4 cup butter
- 1/2 teaspoon nutmeg; ground
- 1 teaspoon cinnamon powder
- 1/2 teaspoon baking soda
- 1 egg
- 1/2 teaspoon baking powder

Directions:

1. In a bowl; mix butter with pumpkin puree and egg and blend well
2. Add flaxseed meal, flour, sugar, baking soda, baking powder, nutmeg and cinnamon and stir well.
3. Spoon this into a muffin pan that fits your fryer introduce in the fryer at 350°F and bake for 15 minutes. Serve muffins cold as a snack

Roasted Pepper Rolls

(Prep + Cooking Time: 20 Minutes | **Servings:** 8)

Ingredients:

- 1 yellow bell pepper; halved
- 2 tablespoon oregano; chopped
- 1 orange bell pepper; halved
- 4-ounce feta cheese; crumbled
- 1 green onion; chopped
- Salt and black pepper to the taste

Directions:

1. In a bowl; mix cheese with onion, oregano, salt and pepper and whisk well
2. Place bell pepper halves in your air fryer's basket, cook at 400°F, for 10 minutes; transfer to a cutting board, cool down and peel. Divide cheese mix on each bell pepper half, roll, secure with toothpicks, arrange on a platter and serve as an appetizer

Jerky Beef Snack

(Prep + Cooking Time: 3 hour and 30 minutes | **Servings:** 6)

Ingredients:
- 2 tablespoon black peppercorns
- 2-pound beef round; sliced
- 2 cups soy sauce
- 2 tablespoon black pepper
- 1/2 cup Worcestershire sauce

Directions:
1. In a bowl; mix soy sauce with black peppercorns, black pepper and Worcestershire sauce and whisk well.
2. Add beef slices; toss to coat and leave aside in the fridge for 6 hours
3. Introduce beef rounds in your air fryer and cook them at 370°F, for 1 hour and 30 minutes. Transfer to a bowl and serve cold

Mouthwatering Beef Rolls

(Prep + Cooking Time: 24 Minutes | **Servings:** 4)

Ingredients:
- 2-pound beef steak; opened and flattened with a meat tenderizer
- 3-ounce red bell pepper; roasted and chopped.
- 6 slices provolone cheese
- 1 cup baby spinach
- 3 tablespoon pesto
- Salt and black pepper to the taste

Directions:
1. Arrange flattened beef steak on a cutting board, spread pesto all over, add cheese in a single layer, add bell peppers, spinach, salt and pepper to the taste
2. Roll your steak, secure with toothpicks, season again with salt and pepper; place roll in your air fryer's basket and cook at 400°F, for 14 minutes; rotating roll halfway. Leave aside to cool down, cut into 2 inch smaller rolls, arrange on a platter and serve them as an appetizer

Spicy Stuffed Peppers

(Prep + Cooking Time: 30 Minutes | **Servings:** 6)

Ingredients:
- 1-pound mini bell peppers; halved
- 1-pound beef meat; ground
- 1/2 teaspoon oregano; dried
- 1/4 teaspoon red pepper flakes
- 1 tablespoon chili powder
- 1½ cups cheddar cheese; shredded.
- Salt and black pepper to the taste
- 1 teaspoon garlic powder
- 1 teaspoon sweet paprika
- 1 teaspoon cumin; ground
- Sour cream for serving

Directions:
1. In a bowl; mix chili powder with paprika, salt, pepper, cumin, oregano, pepper flakes and garlic powder and stir
2. Heat up a pan over medium heat, add beef; stir and brown for 10 minutes
3. Add chili powder mix; stir, take off heat and stuff pepper halves with this mix
4. Sprinkle cheese all over, place peppers in your air fryer's basket and cook them at 350°F, for 6 minutes. Arrange peppers on a platter and serve them with sour cream on the side.

Easy Zucchini Chips

(Prep + Cooking Time: 1 hour 10 Minutes | **Servings:** 6)

Ingredients:
- 3 zucchinis; thinly sliced
- 2 tablespoon balsamic vinegar
- 2 tablespoon olive oil
- Salt and black pepper to the taste

Directions:
1. In a bowl; mix oil with vinegar, salt and pepper and whisk well
2. Add zucchini slices, toss to coat well; introduce in your air fryer and cook at 200°F, for 1 hour. Serve zucchini chips cold as a snack

Shrimp and Calamari Snack

(Prep + Cooking Time: 30 Minutes | **Servings:** 1)

Ingredients:
- 8-ounce calamari; cut into medium rings
- 1/2 teaspoon turmeric powder
- 1 tablespoon olive oil
- 1 teaspoon tomato paste
- 1 tablespoon mayonnaise
- 1 teaspoon lemon juice
- 2 tablespoon avocado; chopped
- 7-ounce shrimp; peeled and deveined
- 1 eggs
- 3 tablespoon white flour
- A splash of Worcestershire sauce
- Salt and black pepper to the taste

Directions:
1. In a bowl; whisk egg with oil, add calamari rings and shrimp and toss to coat
2. In another bowl; mix flour with salt, pepper and turmeric and stir
3. Dredge calamari and shrimp in this mix, place them in your air fryer's basket and cook at 350°F, for 9 minutes; flipping them once
4. Meanwhile; in a bowl, mix avocado with mayo and tomato paste and mash using a fork.
5. Add Worcestershire sauce, lemon juice, salt and pepper and stir well. Arrange calamari and shrimp on a platter and serve with the sauce on the side

Delicious Shrimp Muffins

(Prep + Cooking Time: 36 Minutes | **Servings:** 6)

Ingredients:
- 1 spaghetti squash; peeled and halved
- 2 tablespoon mayonnaise
- 8-ounce shrimp; peeled, cooked and chopped
- 1 garlic clove; minced
- Salt and black pepper to the taste
- 1 ½ cups panko
- 1 teaspoon parsley flakes
- 1 cup mozzarella; shredded.
- Cooking spray

Directions:
1. Put squash halves in your air fryer; cook at 350°F, for 16 minutes; leave aside to cool down and scrape flesh into a bowl
2. Add salt, pepper, parsley flakes, panko, shrimp, mayo and mozzarella and stir well
3. Spray a muffin tray that fits your air fryer with cooking spray and divide squash and shrimp mix in each cup.
4. Introduce in the fryer and cook at 360°F, for 10 minutes. Arrange muffins on a platter and serve as a snack.

Holyday Beef Patties

(Prep + Cooking Time: 18 Minutes | Servings: 4)

Ingredients:
- 14-ounce beef; minced
- 1 leek; chopped
- 3 tablespoon bread crumbs
- Salt and black pepper to the taste
- 1/2 teaspoon nutmeg; ground
- 2 tablespoon ham; cut into strips

Directions:
1. In a bowl; mix beef with leek, salt, pepper, ham, breadcrumbs and nutmeg; stir well and shape small patties out of this mix. Place them in your air fryer's basket, cook at 400°F, for 8 minutes; arrange on a platter and serve as an appetizer

Amazing Seafood Appetizer

(Prep + Cooking Time: 35 Minutes | Servings: 4)

Ingredients:
- 1/2 cup yellow onion; chopped
- 1 cup green bell pepper; chopped.
- 1 cup celery; chopped
- 1 cup baby shrimp; peeled and deveined
- 2 tablespoon bread crumbs
- 1 cup crabmeat; flaked
- 1 cup homemade mayonnaise
- 1 teaspoon Worcestershire sauce
- 1 tablespoon butter
- 1 teaspoon sweet paprika
- Salt and black pepper to the taste

Directions:
1. In a bowl; mix shrimp with crab meat, bell pepper, onion, mayo, celery, salt and pepper and stir
2. Add Worcestershire sauce; stir again and pour everything into a baking dish that fits your air fryer.
3. Sprinkle bread crumbs and add butter, introduce in your air fryer and cook at 320°F, for 25 minutes; shaking halfway. Divide into bowl and serve with paprika sprinkled on top as an appetizer

Salmon Meatballs Snack

(Prep + Cooking Time: 22 Minutes | Servings: 4)

Ingredients:
- 1-pound salmon; skinless and chopped.
- 1/2 teaspoon oregano; ground
- 1 small yellow onion; chopped
- 1 egg white
- 3 tablespoon cilantro; minced
- 2 garlic cloves; minced
- 1/2 teaspoon paprika
- 1/4 cup panko
- Salt and black pepper to the taste
- Cooking spray

Directions:
1. In your food processor, mix salmon with onion, cilantro, egg white, garlic cloves, salt, pepper, paprika and oregano and stir well
2. Add panko, blend again and shape meatballs from this mix using your palms.
3. Place them in your air fryer's basket; spray them with cooking spray and cook at 320°F, for 12 minutes shaking the fryer halfway. Arrange meatballs on a platter and serve them as an appetizer

Easy Broccoli Patties

(**Prep + Cooking Time:** 20 Minutes | **Servings:** 12)

Ingredients:
- 4 cups broccoli florets
- 1 ½ cup almond flour
- 2 cups cheddar cheese; grated
- 1 teaspoon garlic powder
- 1/2 teaspoon apple cider vinegar
- 1/2 teaspoon baking soda
- 1 teaspoon paprika
- 2 eggs
- 1/4 cup olive oil
- Salt and black pepper to the taste

Directions:
1. Put broccoli florets in your food processor; add salt and pepper, blend well and transfer to a bowl
2. Add almond flour, salt, pepper, paprika, garlic powder, baking soda, cheese, oil, eggs and vinegar; stir well and shape 12 patties out of this mix.
3. Place them in your preheated air fryer's basket and cook at 350°F, for 10 minutes. Arrange patties on a platter and serve as an appetizer

Party Pork Rolls

(**Prep + Cooking Time:** 50 Minutes | **Servings:** 4)

Ingredients:
- 1 (15-ounce) pork fillet
- 3 tablespoon parsley; chopped
- 1 garlic clove; minced
- 2 tablespoon olive oil
- 1/2 teaspoon chili powder
- 1 teaspoon cinnamon powder
- 1 red onion; chopped
- 1 ½ teaspoon cumin; ground
- Salt and black pepper to the taste

Directions:
1. In a bowl; mix cinnamon with garlic, salt, pepper, chili powder, oil, onion, parsley and cumin and stir well
2. Put pork fillet on a cutting board, flatten it using a meat tenderizer. And use a meat tenderizer to flatten it
3. Spread onion mix on pork, roll tight, cut into medium rolls, place them in your preheated air fryer at 360°F and cook them for 35 minutes. Arrange them on a platter and serve as an appetizer.

Kale and Celery Crackers

(**Prep + Cooking Time:** 30 Minutes | **Servings:** 6)

Ingredients:
- 2 cups flax seed; ground
- 2 cups flax seed; soaked overnight and drained
- 4 bunches kale; chopped
- 4 garlic cloves; minced
- 1 bunch basil; chopped
- 1/2 bunch celery; chopped
- 1/3 cup olive oil

Directions:
1. In your food processor mix ground flaxseed with celery, kale, basil and garlic and blend well
2. Add oil and soaked flaxseed and blend again, spread in your air fryer's pan; cut into medium crackers and cook them at 380°F, for 20 minutes. Divide into bowls and serve as an appetizer

Yummy Olives Balls

(Prep + Cooking Time: 14 Minutes | **Servings:** 6)

Ingredients:
- 8 black olives; pitted and minced
- 4-ounce cream cheese
- 1 tablespoon basil; chopped.
- 2 tablespoon sun dried tomato pesto
- 14 pepperoni slices; chopped
- Salt and black pepper to the taste

Directions:
1. In a bowl; mix cream cheese with salt, pepper, basil, pepperoni, pesto and black olives; stir well and shape small balls out of this mix. Place them in your air fryer's basket, cook at 350°F, for 4 minutes; arrange on a platter and serve as a snack

Sausage Balls Snack

(Prep + Cooking Time: 25 Minutes | **Servings:** 9)

Ingredients:
- 4-ounce sausage meat; ground
- 1 small onion; chopped.
- 3 tablespoon breadcrumbs
- 1 teaspoon sage
- 1/2 teaspoon garlic; minced
- Salt and black pepper to the taste

Directions:
1. In a bowl; mix sausage with salt, pepper, sage, garlic, onion and breadcrumbs; stir well and shape small balls out of this mix. Put them in your air fryer's basket, cook at 360°F, for 15 minutes; divide into bowls and serve as a snack

Party Beef Rolls

(Prep + Cooking Time: 25 Minutes | **Servings:** 4)

Ingredients:
- 14-ounce beef stock
- 8 sage leaves
- 7-ounce white wine
- 4 beef cutlets
- 4 ham slices
- 1 tablespoon butter; melted
- Salt and black pepper to the taste

Directions:
1. Heat up a pan with the stock over medium high heat, add wine, cook until it reduces, take off heat and divide into small bowls.
2. Season cutlets with salt and pepper; cover with sage and roll each in ham slices
3. Brush rolls with butter, place them in your air fryer's basket and cook at 400°F, for 15 minutes. Arrange rolls on a platter and serve them with the gravy on the side

White Mushrooms Appetizer

(Prep + Cooking Time: 20 Minutes | **Servings:** 4)

Ingredients:
- 1/2 cup Mexican cheese; shredded.
- 4-ounce cream cheese; soft
- 1 teaspoon garlic powder
- 1 small yellow onion; chopped
- 24-ounce white mushroom caps
- 1/4 cup sour cream
- 1 cup shrimp; cooked, peeled, deveined and chopped.
- 1/4 cup mayonnaise
- Salt and black pepper to the taste
- 1 teaspoon curry powder

Directions:
1. In a bowl; mix mayo with garlic powder, onion, curry powder, cream cheese, sour cream, Mexican cheese, shrimp, salt and pepper to the taste and whisk well
2. Stuff mushrooms with this mix; place them in your air fryer's basket and cook at 300°F, for 10 minutes. Arrange on a platter and serve as an appetizer

Delightful Chickpeas Snack

(Prep + Cooking Time: 20 Minutes **| Servings:** 4)

Ingredients:
- 15-ounce canned chickpeas; drained
- 1/2 teaspoon cumin; ground
- 1 tablespoon olive oil
- 1 teaspoon smoked paprika
- Salt and black pepper to the taste

Directions:
1. In a bowl; mix chickpeas with oil, cumin, paprika, salt and pepper; toss to coat, place them in your fryer's basket and cook at 390°F, for 10 minutes. Divide into bowls and serve as a snack

Egg White Chips Snack

(Prep + Cooking Time: 13 Minutes **| Servings:** 2)

Ingredients:
- 1/2 tablespoon water
- 2 tablespoon parmesan; shredded.
- 4 eggs whites
- Salt and black pepper to the taste

Directions:
1. In a bowl; mix egg whites with salt, pepper and water and whisk well
2. Spoon this into a muffin pan that fits your air fryer, sprinkle cheese on top; introduce in your air fryer and cook at 350°F, for 8 minutes. Arrange egg white chips on a platter and serve as a snack

Cheesy Chicken Wings

(Prep + Cooking Time: 22 Minutes **| Servings:** 6)

Ingredients:
- 6-pound chicken wings; halved
- 1 egg
- 2 tablespoon butter
- 1/2 cup parmesan cheese; grated
- 1/2 teaspoon Italian seasoning
- 1 teaspoon garlic powder
- A pinch of red pepper flakes; crushed
- Salt and black pepper to the taste

Directions:
1. Arrange chicken wings in your air fryer's basket and cook at 390°F and cook for 9 minutes.
2. Meanwhile; in your blender, mix butter with cheese, egg, salt, pepper, pepper flakes, garlic powder and Italian seasoning and blend very well
3. Take chicken wings out; pour cheese sauce over them, toss to coat well and cook in your air fryer's basket at 390°F, for 3 minutes. Serve them as an appetizer

Bacon Jalapeno Balls

(Prep + Cooking Time: 14 Minutes **| Servings:** 3)

Ingredients:
- 3 bacon slices; cooked and crumbled
- 1/2 teaspoon parsley; dried
- 1/4 teaspoon garlic powder
- 3-ounce cream cheese
- 1/4 teaspoon onion powder
- 1 jalapeno pepper; chopped
- Salt and black pepper to the taste

Directions:
1. In a bowl; mix cream cheese with jalapeno pepper, onion and garlic powder, parsley, bacon salt and pepper and stir well. Shape small balls out of this mix, place them in your air fryer's basket, cook at 350°F, for 4 minutes; arrange on a platter and serve as an appetizer

Cheesy Chicken Rolls

(Prep + Cooking Time: 30 Minutes | **Servings:** 12)

Ingredients:

- 4-ounce blue cheese; crumbled
- 2 cups chicken; cooked and chopped.
- 2 green onions; chopped
- 2 celery stalks; finely chopped
- 1/2 cup tomato sauce
- 12 egg roll wrappers
- Salt and black pepper to the taste
- Cooking spray

Directions:

1. In a bowl; mix chicken meat with blue cheese, salt, pepper, green onions, celery and tomato sauce; stir well and keep in the fridge for 2 hours
2. Place egg wrappers on a working surface, divide chicken mix on them, roll and seal edges. Place rolls in your air fryer's basket, spray them with cooking oil and cook at 350°F, for 10 minutes; flipping them halfway

Traditional Sweet Bacon Snack

(Prep + Cooking Time: 40 Minutes | **Servings:** 16)

Ingredients:

- 1/2 teaspoon cinnamon powder
- 1 tablespoon avocado oil
- 3-ounce dark chocolate
- 16 bacon slices
- 1 teaspoon maple extract

Directions:

1. Arrange bacon slices in your air fryer's basket; sprinkle cinnamon mix over them and cook them at 300°F, for 30 minutes.
2. Heat up a pot with the oil over medium heat, add chocolate and stir until it melts
3. Add maple extract; stir, take off heat and leave aside to cool down a bit.
4. Take bacon strips out of the oven; leave them to cool down, dip each in chocolate mix; place them on a parchment paper and leave them to cool down completely. Serve cold as a snack

Side Dish Recipes

Easy Creamy Endives

(Prep + Cooking Time: 20 Minutes | Servings: 6)

Ingredients:
- 6 endives; trimmed and halved
- 3 tablespoon lemon juice
- 1/2 teaspoon curry powder
- 1/2 cup Greek yogurt
- 1 teaspoon garlic powder
- Salt and black pepper to the taste

Directions:
1. In a bowl mix endives with garlic powder, yogurt, curry powder, salt, pepper and lemon juice; toss, leave aside for 10 minutes and transfer to your preheated air fryer at 350 degrees F. Cook endives for 10 minutes; divide them on plates and serve as a side dish

Amazing Potato Wedges

(Prep + Cooking Time: 35 Minutes | Servings: 4)

Ingredients:
- 2 potatoes; cut into wedges
- 2 tablespoon sweet chili sauce
- 1 tablespoon olive oil
- 3 tablespoon sour cream
- Salt and black pepper to the taste

Directions:
1. In a bowl; mix potato wedges with oil, salt and pepper, toss well, add to air fryer's basket and cook at 360°F, for 25 minutes; flipping them once. Divide potato wedges on plates; drizzle sour cream and chili sauce all over and serve them as a side dish

Zucchini Fries Dish

(Prep + Cooking Time: 22 Minutes | Servings: 4)

Ingredients:
- 1 zucchini; cut into medium sticks
- 1 cup bread crumbs
- 1/2 cup flour
- A drizzle of olive oil
- 2 eggs; whisked
- Salt and black pepper to the taste

Directions:
1. Put flour in a bowl and mix with salt and pepper and stir
2. Put breadcrumbs in another bowl.
3. In a third bowl mix eggs with a pinch of salt and pepper
4. Dredge zucchini fries in flour; then in eggs and in bread crumbs at the end.
5. Grease your air fryer with some olive oil, heat up at 400 degrees F; add zucchini fries and cook them for 12 minutes. Serve them as a side dish

Roasted Parsnips Dish

(Prep + Cooking Time: 50 Minutes | Servings: 6)

Ingredients:
- 2-pound parsnips; peeled and cut into medium chunks
- 1 tablespoon olive oil
- 1 tablespoon parsley flakes; dried
- 2 tablespoon maple syrup

Directions:
1. Preheat your air fryer at 360 degrees F; add oil and heat it up as well
2. Add parsnips, parsley flakes and maple syrup; toss and cook them for 40 minutes. Divide among plates and serve as a side dish

Eggplant Fries Dish

(Prep + Cooking Time: 15 Minutes | Servings: 4)

Ingredients:

- 1 eggplant; peeled and cut into medium fries
- 2 cups panko bread crumbs
- 1/2 cup Italian cheese; shredded.
- 2 tablespoon milk
- 1 egg; whisked
- A pinch of salt and black pepper to the taste
- Cooking spray

Directions:

1. In a bowl; mix egg with milk, salt and pepper and whisk well
2. In another bowl; mix panko with cheese and stir
3. Dip eggplant fries in egg mix, then coat in panko mix, place them in your air fryer greased with cooking spray and cook at 400°F, for 5 minutes. Divide among plates and serve as a side dish.

Creamy Potatoes Dish

(Prep + Cooking Time: 30 Minutes | Servings: 4)

Ingredients:

- 1 ½-pound potatoes; peeled and cubed
- 2 tablespoon olive oil
- 1 cup Greek yogurt
- 1 tablespoon hot paprika
- Salt and black pepper to the taste

Directions:

1. Put potatoes in a bowl; add water to cover, leave aside for 10 minutes; drain, pat dry them, transfer to another bowl; add salt, pepper, paprika and half of the oil and toss them well
2. Put potatoes in your air fryer's basket and cook at 360°F, for 20 minutes.
3. In a bowl; mix yogurt with salt, pepper and the rest of the oil and whisk. Divide potatoes on plates, drizzle yogurt dressing all over; toss them and serve as a side dish

Yellow Squash and Zucchinis Dish

(Prep + Cooking Time: 45 Minutes | Servings: 4)

Ingredients:

- 1 yellow squash; halved, deseeded and cut into chunks
- 1/2-pound carrots; cubed
- 1 tablespoon tarragon; chopped
- 6 teaspoon olive oil
- 1-pound zucchinis; sliced
- Salt and white pepper to the taste

Directions:

1. In your air fryer's basket; mix zucchinis with carrots, squash, salt, pepper and oil; toss well and cook at 400°F, for 25 minutes. Divide them on plates and serve as a side dish with tarragon sprinkled on top

Air Fried Red Cabbage

(Prep + Cooking Time: 25 Minutes | Servings: 4)

Ingredients:

- 1/2 cup yellow onion; chopped
- 4 garlic cloves; minced
- 6 cups red cabbage; chopped
- 1 cup veggie stock
- 1 tablespoon apple cider vinegar
- 1 cup applesauce
- 1 tablespoon olive oil
- Salt and black pepper to the taste

Directions:

1. In a heat proof dish that fits your air fryer; mix cabbage with onion, garlic, oil, stock, vinegar, applesauce, salt and pepper; toss really well, place dish in your air fryer's basket and cook at 380°F, for 15 minutes. Divide among plates and serve as a side dish

Parmesan Button Mushrooms

(Prep + Cooking Time: 25 Minutes | **Servings:** 3)

Ingredients:

- 9 button mushroom caps
- 3 cream cracker slices; crumbled
- 2 tablespoon parmesan; grated
- 1 teaspoon Italian seasoning
- 1 tablespoon butter; melted
- 1 egg white
- A pinch of salt and black pepper

Directions:

1. In a bowl; mix crackers with egg white, parmesan, Italian seasoning, butter, salt and pepper; stir well and stuff mushrooms with this mix
2. Arrange mushrooms in your air fryer's basket and cook them at 360°F, for 15 minutes. Divide among plates and serve as a side dish

Herbed Tomatoes Dish

(Prep + Cooking Time: 25 Minutes | **Servings:** 4)

Ingredients:

- 4 big tomatoes; halved and insides scooped out
- 2 garlic cloves; minced
- 1/2 teaspoon thyme; chopped.
- 1 tablespoon olive oil
- Salt and black pepper to the taste

Directions:

1. In your air fryer, mix tomatoes with salt, pepper, oil, garlic and thyme; toss and cook at 390°F, for 15 minutes. Divide among plates and serve them as a side dish

Potato Chips

(Prep + Cooking Time: 60 Minutes | **Servings:** 4)

Ingredients:

- 4 potatoes; scrubbed, peeled into thin chips, soaked in water for 30 minutes, drained and pat dried
- 2 teaspoon rosemary; chopped
- 1 tablespoon olive oil
- Salt to taste

Directions:

1. In a bowl; mix potato chips with salt and oil toss to coat, place them in your air fryer's basket and cook at 330°F, for 30 minutes. Divide among plates; sprinkle rosemary all over and serve as a side dish

Roasted Carrots

(Prep + Cooking Time: 30 Minutes | **Servings:** 4)

Ingredients:

- 1-pound baby carrots
- 2 teaspoon olive oil
- 4 tablespoon orange juice
- 1 teaspoon herbs de Provence

Directions:

1. In your air fryer's basket, mix carrots with herbs de Provence, oil and orange juice; toss and cook at 320°F, for 20 minutes. Divide among plates and serve as a side dish

Tasty Barley Risotto

(Prep + Cooking Time: 40 Minutes | **Servings:** 8)

Ingredients:

- 2-pound sweet potato; peeled and chopped.
- 5 cups veggie stock
- 1 teaspoon thyme; dried
- 1 teaspoon tarragon; dried
- 3/4-pound barley
- 3-ounce mushrooms; sliced
- 2-ounce skim milk
- 3 tablespoon olive oil
- 2 yellow onions; chopped
- 2 garlic cloves; minced
- Salt and black pepper to the taste

Directions:

1. Put stock in a pot, add barley; stir, bring to a boil over medium heat and cook for 15 minutes.
2. Heat up your air fryer at 350 degrees F; add oil and heat it up
3. Add barley, onions, garlic, mushrooms, milk, salt, pepper, tarragon and sweet potato; stir and cook for 15 minutes more. Divide among plates and serve as a side dish

Delightful Cauliflower and Broccoli

(Prep + Cooking Time: 17 Minutes | **Servings:** 4)

Ingredients:

- 2 cauliflower heads; florets separated and steamed
- 1 broccoli head; florets separated and steamed
- 1 tablespoon capers; chopped.
- 4 anchovies
- Zest from 1 orange; grated
- Juice from 1 orange
- A pinch of hot pepper flakes
- Salt and black pepper to the taste
- 4 tablespoon olive oil

Directions:

1. In a bowl; mix orange zest with orange juice, pepper flakes, anchovies, capers salt, pepper and olive oil and whisk well
2. Add broccoli and cauliflower; toss well, transfer them to your air fryer's basket and cook at 400°F, for 7 minutes. Divide among plates and serve as a side dish with some of the orange vinaigrette drizzled on to

Brussels Sprouts Dish

(Prep + Cooking Time: 25 Minutes | **Servings:** 4)

Ingredients:

- 1-pound Brussels sprouts; trimmed and halved
- 6 teaspoon olive oil
- 2 tablespoon roasted garlic; crushed
- 1/2 teaspoon thyme; chopped
- 1/2 cup mayonnaise
- Salt and black pepper to the taste

Directions:

1. In your air fryer; mix Brussels sprouts with salt, pepper and oil; toss well and cook them at 390°F, for 15 minutes
2. Meanwhile; in a bowl, mix thyme with mayo and garlic and whisk well. Divide Brussels sprouts on plates; drizzle garlic sauce all over and serve as a side dish

Special Risotto

(Prep + Cooking Time: 40 Minutes | **Servings:** 4)

Ingredients:
- 2 tablespoon olive oil
- 2 yellow onions; chopped.
- 2 cups beer
- 1 teaspoon basil; dried
- 1 teaspoon oregano; dried
- 1 ½ cups rice
- 2 cups chicken stock
- 1 tablespoon butter
- 1 cup mushrooms; sliced
- 1/2 cup parmesan; grated

Directions:
1. In a dish that fits your air fryer, mix oil with onions, mushrooms, basil and oregano and stir
2. Add rice, beer, butter, stock and butter; stir again, place in your air fryer's basket and cook at 350°F, for 30 minutes. Divide among plates and serve with grated parmesan on top as a side dish

Yummy Biscuits

(Prep + Cooking Time: 30 Minutes | **Servings:** 8)

Ingredients:
- 2 ⅓ cup self-rising flour
- 1/2 cup cheddar cheese; grated
- 1 ⅓ cup buttermilk
- 1/2 cup butter+ 1 tablespoon; melted
- 1 cup flour
- 2 tablespoon sugar

Directions:
1. In a bowl; mix self-rising flour with 1/2 cup butter, sugar, cheddar cheese and buttermilk and stir until you obtain a dough
2. Spread 1 cup flour on a working surface, roll dough, flatten it, cut 8 circles with a cookie cutter and coat them with flour.
3. Line your air fryer's basket with tin foil, add biscuits, brush them with melted butter and cook them at 380°F, for 20 minutes. Divide among plates and serve as a side

Eggplant Dish

(Prep + Cooking Time: 20 Minutes | **Servings:** 4)

Ingredients:
- 8 baby eggplants; scooped in the center and pulp reserved
- 1/2 teaspoon garlic powder
- 1 tablespoon olive oil
- 1 yellow onion; chopped
- 1 tablespoon tomato paste
- 1 bunch coriander; chopped
- 1 tomato chopped
- A pinch of oregano; dried
- 1 green bell pepper; chopped.
- Salt and black pepper to the taste

Directions:
1. Heat up a pan with the oil over medium heat, add onion; stir and cook for 1 minute
2. Add salt, pepper, eggplant pulp, oregano, green bell pepper, tomato paste, garlic power, coriander and tomato; stir, cook for 1 - 2 minutes more, take off heat and cool down
3. Stuff eggplants with this mix, place them in your air fryer's basket and cook at 360°F, for 8 minutes. Divide eggplants on plates and serve them as a side dish

Mushrooms and Cream

(Prep + Cooking Time: 20 Minutes | **Servings:** 6)

Ingredients:

- 2 bacon strips; chopped
- 1 yellow onion; chopped.
- 1 green bell pepper; chopped
- 24 mushrooms; stems removed
- 1 carrot; grated
- 1/2 cup sour cream
- 1 cup cheddar cheese; grated
- Salt and black pepper to the taste

Directions:

1. Heat up a pan over medium high heat; add bacon, onion, bell pepper and carrot; stir and cook for 1 minute.
2. Add salt, pepper and sour cream, stir cook for 1 minute more; take off heat and cool down
3. Stuff mushrooms with this mix, sprinkle cheese on top and cook at 360°F, for 8 minutes. Divide among plates and serve as a side dish

Creamy Fried Potato Dish

(Prep + Cooking Time: 1 hour and 30 minutes | **Servings:** 2)

Ingredients:

- 2 bacon strips; cooked and chopped.
- 1 teaspoon olive oil
- 1/3 cup cheddar cheese; shredded.
- 1 tablespoon butter
- 2 tablespoon heavy cream
- 1 big potato
- 1 tablespoon green onions; chopped
- Salt and black pepper to the taste

Directions:

1. Rub potato with oil, season with salt and pepper, place in preheated air fryer and cook at 400°F, for 30 minutes
2. Flip potato, cook for 30 minutes more; transfer to a cutting board, cool it down, slice in half lengthwise and scoop pulp in a bowl
3. Add bacon, cheese, butter, heavy cream, green onions, salt and pepper; stir well and stuff potato skins with this mix.
4. Return potatoes to your air fryer and cook them at 400°F, for 20 minutes. Divide among plates and serve as a side dish

Veggie Fries Dish

(Prep + Cooking Time: 40 Minutes | **Servings:** 4)

Ingredients:

- 4 parsnips; cut into medium sticks
- 2 sweet potatoes cut into medium sticks
- 4 mixed carrots cut into medium sticks
- 1 tablespoon flour
- 1/2 teaspoon garlic powder
- 2 tablespoon rosemary; chopped
- 2 tablespoon olive oil
- Salt and black pepper to the taste

Directions:

1. Put veggie fries in a bowl; add oil, garlic powder, salt, pepper, flour and rosemary and toss to coat
2. Put sweet potatoes in your preheated air fryer; cook them for 10 minutes at 350°F and transfer them to a platter.
3. Put parsnip fries in your air fryer; cook for 5 minutes and transfer over potato fries
4. Put carrot fries in your air fryer; cook for 15 minutes at 350°F and transfer to the platter with the other fries. Divide veggie fries on plates and serve them as a side dish.

Green Beans Dish

(Prep + Cooking Time: 35 Minutes | **Servings:** 4)

Ingredients:

- 1 ½-pound green beans; trimmed and steamed for 2 minutes
- 2 tablespoon olive oil
- 1/2-pound shallots; chopped.
- 1/4 cup almonds; toasted
- Salt and black pepper to the taste

Directions:

1. In your air fryer's basket, mix green beans with salt, pepper, shallots, almonds and oil; toss well and cook at 400°F, for 25 minutes. Divide among plates and serve as a side dish

Roasted Pumpkin Side Dish

(Prep + Cooking Time: 22 Minutes | **Servings:** 4)

Ingredients:

- 1 ½-pound pumpkin; deseeded, sliced and roughly chopped
- 3 garlic cloves; minced
- 1 tablespoon olive oil
- A pinch of nutmeg; ground
- A pinch of brown sugar
- A pinch of sea salt
- A pinch of cinnamon powder

Directions:

1. In your air fryer's basket, mix pumpkin with garlic, oil, salt, brown sugar, cinnamon and nutmeg; toss well, cover and cook at 370°F, for 12 minutes. Divide among plates and serve as a side dish

Special Sweet Potato Fries

(Prep + Cooking Time: 30 Minutes | **Servings:** 2)

Ingredients:

- 2 sweet potatoes; peeled and cut into medium fries
- 2 tablespoon mayonnaise
- 1/2 teaspoon cumin; ground
- 1/4 cup ketchup
- 2 tablespoon olive oil
- 1/2 teaspoon curry powder
- 1/4 teaspoon coriander; ground
- Salt and black pepper to the taste
- A pinch of ginger powder
- A pinch of cinnamon powder

Directions:

1. In your air fryer's basket; mix sweet potato fries with salt, pepper, coriander, curry powder and oil; toss well and cook at 370°F, for 20 minutes; flipping them once
2. Meanwhile; in a bowl, mix ketchup with mayo, cumin, ginger and cinnamon and whisk well. Divide fries on plates; drizzle ketchup mix over them and serve as a side dish

Delicious Cauliflower Cakes

(Prep + Cooking Time: 20 Minutes | **Servings:** 6)

Ingredients:

- 2 eggs
- 1/4 cup white flour
- 3 ½ cups cauliflower rice
- 1/2 cup parmesan; grated
- Salt and black pepper to the taste
- Cooking spray

Directions:

1. In a bowl; mix cauliflower rice with salt and pepper, stir and squeeze excess water
2. Transfer cauliflower to another bowl; add eggs, salt, pepper, flour and parmesan; stir really well and shape your cakes.
3. Grease your air fryer with cooking spray, heat it up at 400 degrees; add cauliflower cakes and cook them for 10 minutes flipping them halfway. Divide cakes on plates and serve as a side dish

Button Mushroom Dish

(Prep + Cooking Time: 18 Minutes | **Servings:** 4)

Ingredients:

- 10 button mushrooms; stems removed
- 1 tablespoon Italian seasoning
- 2 tablespoon mozzarella; grated
- 1 tablespoon dill; chopped
- 2 tablespoon cheddar cheese; grated
- 1 tablespoon olive oil
- Salt and black pepper to the taste

Directions:

1. In a bowl; mix mushrooms with Italian seasoning, salt, pepper, oil and dill and rub well
2. Arrange mushrooms in your air fryer's basket; sprinkle mozzarella and cheddar in each and cook them at 360°F, for 8 minutes. Divide them on plates and serve them as a side dish

Air Fried Tomatoes

(Prep + Cooking Time: 15 Minutes | **Servings:** 4)

Ingredients:

- 1/2 tablespoon Creole seasoning
- 1/2 cup flour
- 1 cup buttermilk
- 1 cup panko bread crumbs
- 2 green tomatoes; sliced
- Salt and black pepper to the taste
- Cooking spray

Directions:

1. Season tomato slices with salt and pepper
2. Put flour in a bowl; buttermilk in another and panko crumbs and Creole seasoning in a third one.
3. Dredge tomato slices in flour; then in buttermilk and panko bread crumbs, place them in your air fryer's basket greased with cooking spray and cook them at 400°F, for 5 minutes. Divide among plates and serve as a side dish

Yummy Garlic Potatoes

(Prep + Cooking Time: 30 Minutes | **Servings:** 6)

Ingredients:

- 2 tablespoon parsley; chopped.
- 5 garlic cloves; minced
- 1/2 teaspoon basil; dried
- 1/2 teaspoon oregano; dried
- 3-pound red potatoes; halved
- 1 teaspoon thyme; dried
- 2 tablespoon butter
- 1/3 cup parmesan; grated
- 2 tablespoon olive oil
- Salt and black pepper to the taste

Directions:

1. In a bowl; mix potato halves with parsley, garlic, basil, oregano, thyme, salt, pepper, oil and butter; toss really well and transfer to your air fryer's basket
2. Cover and cook at 400°F, for 20 minutes; flipping them once. Sprinkle parmesan on top, divide potatoes on plates and serve as a side dish

Roasted Eggplant Dish

(Prep + Cooking Time: 30 Minutes | **Servings:** 6)

Ingredients:

- 1 ½-pound eggplant; cubed
- 1 teaspoon onion powder
- 1 teaspoon garlic powder
- 2 teaspoon za'atar
- 1 teaspoon sumac
- 1 tablespoon olive oil
- Juice from 1/2 lemon
- 2 bay leaves

Directions:

1. In your air fryer; mix eggplant cubes with oil, garlic powder, onion powder, sumac, za'atar, lemon juice and bay leaves; toss and cook at 370°F, for 20 minutes. Divide among plates and serve as a side dish

Flavored Cauliflower Dish

(Prep + Cooking Time: 20 Minutes | **Servings:** 4)

Ingredients:

- 12 cauliflower florets; steamed
- 1/4 teaspoon turmeric powder
- 2 teaspoon lemon juice
- 3 tablespoon white flour
- 1/2 teaspoon corn flour
- 1½ teaspoon red chili powder
- 1 tablespoon ginger; grated
- 2 tablespoon water
- Salt and black pepper to the taste
- Cooking spray

Directions:

1. In a bowl; mix chili powder with turmeric powder, ginger paste, salt, pepper, lemon juice, white flour, corn flour and water, stir, add cauliflower, toss well and transfer them to your air fryer's basket. Coat them with cooking spray, cook them at 400°F, for 10 minutes, divide among plates and serve as a side dish

Cauliflower Rice Dish

(Prep + Cooking Time: 50 Minutes | **Servings:** 8)

Ingredients:

- 1 tablespoon peanut oil
- 1 tablespoon sesame oil
- 15-ounce mushrooms; chopped
- 1 tablespoon ginger; grated
- Juice from 1/2 lemon
- 4 tablespoon soy sauce
- 3 garlic cloves; minced
- 9-ounce water chestnuts; drained
- 3/4 cup peas
- 1 cauliflower head; riced
- 1 egg; whisked

Directions:

1. In your air fryer; mix cauliflower rice with peanut oil, sesame oil, soy sauce, garlic, ginger and lemon juice; stir, cover and cook at 350°F, for 20 minutes
2. Add chestnuts, peas, mushrooms and egg; toss and cook at 360°F, for 20 minutes more. Divide among plates and serve for breakfast

Hassel-Back Potatoes

(Prep + Cooking Time: 30 Minutes | Servings: 2)

Ingredients:
- 2 potatoes; peeled and thinly sliced almost all the way horizontally
- 1/2 teaspoon oregano; dried
- 1/2 teaspoon basil; dried
- 1/2 teaspoon sweet paprika
- 2 tablespoon olive oil
- 1 teaspoon garlic; minced
- Salt and black pepper to the taste

Directions:
1. In a bowl; mix oil with garlic, salt, pepper, oregano, basil and paprika and whisk really well
2. Rub potatoes with this mix; place them in your air fryer's basket and fry them at 360°F, for 20 minutes. Divide them on plates and serve as a side dish

Easy Mushroom Cakes

(Prep + Cooking Time: 18 Minutes | Servings: 8)

Ingredients:
- 4-ounce mushrooms; chopped
- 1 yellow onion; chopped.
- 1/2 teaspoon nutmeg; ground
- 1 ½ tablespoon flour
- 1 tablespoon bread crumbs
- 14-ounce milk
- 2 tablespoon olive oil
- 1 tablespoon butter
- Salt and black pepper to the taste

Directions:
1. Heat up a pan with the butter over medium high heat; add onion and mushrooms; stir, cook for 3 minutes, add flour, stir well again and take off heat
2. Add milk gradually, salt, pepper and nutmeg; stir and leave aside to cool down completely.
3. In a bowl; mix oil with bread crumbs and whisk
4. Take spoonfuls of the mushroom filling, add to breadcrumbs mix, coat well, shape patties out of this mix; place them in your air fryer's basket and cook at 400°F, for 8 minutes. Divide among plates and serve as a side for a steak.

Beet Wedges Dish

(Prep + Cooking Time: 25 Minutes | Servings: 4)

Ingredients:
- 4 beets; washed, peeled and cut into large wedges
- 1 teaspoon lemon juice
- 1 tablespoon olive oil
- 2 garlic cloves; minced
- Salt and black to the taste

Directions:
1. In a bowl; mix beets with oil, salt, pepper, garlic and lemon juice; toss well, transfer to your air fryer's basket and cook them at 400°F, for 15 minutes. Divide beets wedges on plates and serve as a side dish

Roasted Peppers Dish

(Prep + Cooking Time: 20 Minutes | **Servings:** 4)

Ingredients:
- 1 tablespoon lemon juice
- 1 red bell pepper
- 1 green bell pepper
- 1-ounce rocket leaves
- 3 tablespoon Greek yogurt
- 2 tablespoon olive oil
- 1 yellow bell pepper
- 1 lettuce head; cut into strips
- Salt and black pepper to the taste

Directions:
1. Place bell peppers in your air fryer's basket, cook at 400°F, for 10 minutes; transfer to a bowl, leave aside for 10 minutes; peel them, discard seeds, cut them in strips, transfer to a larger bowl; add rocket leaves and lettuce strips and toss
2. In a bowl; mix oil with lemon juice, yogurt, salt and pepper and whisk well. Add this over bell peppers mix, toss to coat, divide among plates and serve as a side salad

Vermouth White Mushrooms

(Prep + Cooking Time: 35 Minutes | **Servings:** 4)

Ingredients:
- 1 tablespoon olive oil
- 2-pound white mushrooms
- 2 tablespoon white vermouth
- 2 teaspoon herbs de Provence
- 2 garlic cloves; minced

Directions:
1. In your air fryer; mix oil with mushrooms, herbs de Provence and garlic; toss and cook at 350°F, for 20 minutes
2. Add vermouth, toss and cook for 5 minutes more. Divide among plates and serve as a side dish

Pumpkin Rice Dish

(Prep + Cooking Time: 35 Minutes | **Servings:** 4)

Ingredients:
- 12-ounce white rice
- 1 teaspoon thyme; chopped
- 1/2 teaspoon ginger; grated
- 1/2 teaspoon cinnamon powder
- 4 cups chicken stock
- 6-ounce pumpkin puree
- 2 tablespoon olive oil
- 1 small yellow onion; chopped
- 2 garlic cloves; minced
- 1/2 teaspoon nutmeg
- 1/2 teaspoon allspice
- 4-ounce heavy cream

Directions:
1. In a dish that fits your air fryer; mix oil with onion, garlic, rice, stock, pumpkin puree, nutmeg, thyme, ginger, cinnamon, allspice and cream; stir well.
2. place in your air fryer's basket and cook at 360°F, for 30 minutes. Divide among plates and serve as a side dish.

Fried Creamy Cabbage

(Prep + Cooking Time: 30 Minutes | **Servings:** 4)

Ingredients:
- 1 green cabbage head; chopped.
- 1 cup whipped cream
- 2 tablespoon cornstarch
- 1 yellow onion; chopped
- 4 bacon slices; chopped.
- Salt and black pepper to the taste

Directions:
1. Put cabbage, bacon and onion in your air fryer
2. In a bowl; mix cornstarch with cream, salt and pepper, stir and add over cabbage. Toss, cook at 400°F, for 20 minutes; divide among plates and serve as a side dish

Onion Rings Dish

(Prep + Cooking Time: 20 Minutes | **Servings:** 3)

Ingredients:
- 1 onion cut into medium slices and rings separated
- 1 egg
- 1 cup milk
- 1¼ cups white flour
- 1 teaspoon baking powder
- A pinch of salt
- 3/4 cup bread crumbs

Directions:
1. In a bowl; mix flour with salt and baking powder; stir, dredge onion rings in this mix and place them on a separate plate.
2. Add milk and egg to flour mix and whisk well
3. Dip onion rings in this mix, dredge them in breadcrumbs; put them in your air fryer's basket and cook them at 360°F, for 10 minutes. Divide among plates and serve as a side dish for a steak

Cajun Onion Wedges Dish

(Prep + Cooking Time: 25 Minutes | **Servings:** 4)

Ingredients:
- 2 big white onions; cut into wedges
- 2 eggs
- 1/2 teaspoon Cajun seasoning
- 1/4 cup milk
- 1 ½ teaspoon paprika
- 1 teaspoon garlic powder
- 1/3 cup panko
- A drizzle of olive oil
- Salt and black pepper to the taste

Directions:
1. In a bowl; mix panko with Cajun seasoning and oil and stir
2. In another bowl; mix egg with milk, salt and pepper and stir
3. Sprinkle onion wedges with paprika and garlic powder, dip them in egg mix, then in bread crumbs mix; place in your air fryer's basket, cook at 360°F, for 10 minutes; flip and cook for 5 minutes more. Divide among plates and serve as a side dish

Delicious Tortilla Chips

(Prep + Cooking Time: 16 Minutes | **Servings:** 4)

Ingredients:
- 8 corn tortillas; cut into triangles
- 1 tablespoon olive oil
- A pinch of sweet paprika
- A pinch of garlic powder
- Salt and black pepper to the taste

Directions:
1. In a bowl; mix tortilla chips with oil, add salt, pepper, garlic powder and paprika; toss well, place them in your air fryer's basket and cook them at 400°F, for 6 minutes. Serve them as a side for a fish dish

Rice and Sausage Dish

(Prep + Cooking Time: 30 Minutes | **Servings:** 4)

Ingredients:
- 2 cups white rice; already boiled
- 1 tablespoon butter
- 3 tablespoon cheddar cheese; grated
- 1 pork sausage; chopped
- Salt and black pepper to the taste
- 4 garlic cloves; minced
- 2 tablespoon carrot; chopped
- 2 tablespoon mozzarella cheese; shredded.

Directions:
1. Heat up your air fryer at 350 degrees F; add butter, melt it, add garlic, stir and brown for 2 minutes
2. Add sausage, salt, pepper, carrots and rice; stir and cook at 350°F, for 10 minutes. Add cheddar and mozzarella; toss, divide among plates and serve as a side dish

Coconut Potatoes

(Prep + Cooking Time: 30 Minutes | **Servings:** 4)

Ingredients:
- 2 eggs; whisked
- 1 tablespoon cheddar cheese; grated
- 1 tablespoon flour
- 2 potatoes; sliced
- 4-ounce coconut cream
- Salt and black pepper to the taste

Directions:
1. Place potato slices in your air fryer's basket and cook at 360°F, for 10 minutes
2. Meanwhile; in a bowl, mix eggs with coconut cream, salt, pepper and flour
3. Arrange potatoes in your air fryer's pan, add coconut cream mix over them, sprinkle cheese, return to air fryer's basket and cook at 400°F, for 10 minutes more. Divide among plates and serve as a side dish

Maple Glazed Beets

(Prep + Cooking Time: 50 Minutes | **Servings:** 8)

Ingredients:
- 3-pound small beets; trimmed
- 1 tablespoon duck fat
- 4 tablespoon maple syrup

Directions:
1. Heat up your air fryer at 360 degrees F; add duck fat and heat it up
2. Add beets and maple syrup; toss and cook for 40 minutes. Divide among plates and serve as a side dish.

Colored Veggie Rice Recipe

(Prep + Cooking Time: 35 Minutes | **Servings:** 4)

Ingredients:

- 1 cup mixed carrots; peas, corn and green beans
- 2 cups basmati rice
- 2 cups water
- 1/2 teaspoon green chili; minced
- 1/2 teaspoon ginger; grated
- 5 black peppercorns
- 2 whole cardamoms
- 1 tablespoon cumin seeds
- 2 bay leaves
- 3 whole cloves
- 3 garlic cloves; minced
- 2 tablespoon butter
- 1 teaspoon cinnamon powder
- 1 tablespoon sugar
- Salt to the taste

Directions:

1. Pour the water in a heat proof dish that fits your air fryer.
2. Add rice, mixed veggies, green chili, grated ginger, garlic cloves, cinnamon, cloves, butter, cumin seeds, bay leaves, cardamoms, black peppercorns, salt and sugar; stir, put in your air fryer's basket and cook at 370°F, for 25 minutes.
3. Divide among plates and serve as a side dish

Lemony Artichokes Side Dish

(Prep + Cooking Time: 25 Minutes | **Servings:** 4)

Ingredients:

- 2 medium artichokes; trimmed and halved
- 2 tablespoon lemon juice
- Cooking spray
- Salt and black pepper to the taste

Directions:

1. Grease your air fryer with cooking spray, add artichokes; drizzle lemon juice and sprinkle salt and black pepper and cook them at 380°F, for 15 minutes. Divide them on plates and serve as a side dish

Carrots and Rhubarb Dish

(Prep + Cooking Time: 50 Minutes | **Servings:** 4)

Ingredients:

- 1 orange; peeled, cut into medium segments and zest grated
- 1-pound rhubarb; roughly chopped.
- 1/2 cup walnuts; halved
- 1-pound baby carrots
- 2 teaspoon walnut oil
- 1/2 teaspoon stevia

Directions:

1. Put the oil in your air fryer, add carrots; toss and fry them at 380°F, for 20 minutes
2. Add rhubarb, orange zest, stevia and walnuts; toss and cook for 20 minutes more. Add orange segments; toss and serve as a side dish

Potato Casserole Dish

(Prep + Cooking Time: 55 Minutes | **Servings:** 4)

Ingredients:
- 3-pound sweet potatoes; scrubbed
- 1/4 cup milk
- 2 tablespoon white flour

For the topping:
- 1/2 cup almond flour
- 1/2 cup walnuts; soaked, drained and ground
- 1/4 cup pecans; soaked, drained and ground

- 1/2 teaspoon nutmeg; ground
- 1/4 teaspoon allspice; ground
- Salt to the taste

- 1/4 cup coconut; shredded.
- 1 teaspoon cinnamon powder
- 5 tablespoon butter
- 1/4 cup sugar
- 1 tablespoon chia seeds

Directions:
1. Place potatoes in your air fryer's basket, prick them with a fork and cook at 360°F, for 30 minutes.
2. Meanwhile; in a bowl, mix almond flour with pecans, walnuts, 1/4 cup coconut, 1/4 cup sugar, chia seeds, 1 teaspoon cinnamon and the butter and stir everything
3. Transfer potatoes to a cutting board, cool them, peel and place them in a baking dish that fits your air fryer.
4. Add milk, flour, salt, nutmeg and allspice and stir.
5. Add crumble mix you've made earlier on top; place dish in your air fryer's basket and cook at 400°F, for 8 minutes. Divide among plates and serve as a side dish

Tasty Potatoes Patties

(Prep + Cooking Time: 18 Minutes | **Servings:** 4)

Ingredients:
- 4 potatoes; cubed, boiled and mashed
- 1 cup parmesan; grated
- 3 tablespoon chives; chopped
- 2 tablespoon white flour

For the breading:
- 3 tablespoon vegetable oil
- 1/4 cup bread crumbs

- 2 egg yolks
- A pinch of nutmeg
- Salt and black pepper to the taste

- 1/4 cup white flour
- 2 eggs; whisked

Directions:
1. In a bowl; mix mashed potatoes with egg yolks, salt, pepper, nutmeg, parmesan, chives and 2 tablespoon flour; stir well, shape medium cakes and place them on a plate
2. In another bowl; mix vegetable oil with bread crumbs and stir
3. Put whisked eggs in a third bowl and 1/4 cup flour in a forth one. Dip cakes in flour, then in eggs and in breadcrumbs at the end; place them in your air fryer's basket, cook them at 390°F, for 8 minutes; divide among plates and serve as a side dish.

Fried Broccoli

(**Prep + Cooking Time:** 30 Minutes | **Servings:** 4)

Ingredients:
- 1 broccoli head; florets separated
- 3 garlic cloves; minced
- 1 tablespoon duck fat
- 1 tablespoon sesame seeds
- Juice from 1/2 lemon

Directions:
1. Heat up your air fryer at 350 degrees F; add duck fat and heat as well
2. Add broccoli, garlic, lemon juice and sesame seeds; toss and cook for 20 minutes. Divide among plates and serve as a side dish.

Corn with Cheese and Lime

(**Prep + Cooking Time:** 25 Minutes | **Servings:** 2)

Ingredients:
- 2 corns on the cob; husks removed
- 2 teaspoon sweet paprika
- 1/2 cup feta cheese; grated
- A drizzle of olive oil
- Juice from 2 limes

Directions:
1. Rub corn with oil and paprika, place in your air fryer and cook at 400°F, for 15 minutes; flipping once. Divide corn on plates; sprinkle cheese on top, drizzle lime juice and serve as a side dish

Greek Veggie Dish

(**Prep + Cooking Time:** 55 Minutes | **Servings:** 4)

Ingredients:
- 1 eggplant; sliced
- 1 zucchini; sliced
- 4 tomatoes; cut into quarters
- 2 red bell peppers; chopped.
- 2 garlic cloves; minced
- 3 tablespoon olive oil
- 1 thyme spring; chopped
- 2 onions; chopped
- 1 bay leaf
- Salt and black pepper to the taste

Directions:
1. In your air fryer's pan; mix eggplant slices with zucchini ones, bell peppers, garlic, oil, bay leaf, thyme, onions, tomatoes, salt and pepper; toss and cook them at 300°F, for 35 minutes. Divide among plates and serve as a side dish

Roasted Peppers Dish

(**Prep + Cooking Time:** 30 Minutes | **Servings:** 4)

Ingredients:
- 4 red bell peppers; cut into medium strips
- 4 green bell peppers; cut into medium strips
- 1 yellow onion; chopped
- 1 tablespoon sweet paprika
- 1 tablespoon olive oil
- 4 yellow bell peppers; cut into medium strips
- Salt and black pepper to the taste

Directions:
1. In your air fryer; mix red bell peppers with green and yellow ones
2. Add paprika, oil, onion, salt and pepper; toss and cook at 350°F, for 20 minutes. Divide among plates and serve as a side dish

Brussels Sprouts & Pomegranate Seeds

(Prep + Cooking Time: 15 Minutes | **Servings:** 4)

Ingredients:

- 1-pound Brussels sprouts; trimmed and halved
- 1 tablespoon olive oil
- 2 tablespoon veggie stock
- 1 cup pomegranate seeds
- 1/4 cup pine nuts; toasted
- Salt and black pepper to the taste

Directions:

1. In a heat proof dish that fits your air fryer; mix Brussels sprouts with salt, pepper, pomegranate seeds, pine nuts, oil and stock; stir, place in your air fryer's basket and cook at 390°F, for 10 minutes
2. Divide among plates and serve as a side dish

Yummy Zucchini Croquettes

(Prep + Cooking Time: 20 Minutes | **Servings:** 4)

Ingredients:

- 1 carrot; grated
- 1 zucchini; grated
- 2 slices of bread; crumbled
- 2 tablespoon parmesan cheese; grated
- 1 tablespoon corn flour
- 1 egg
- 1/2 teaspoon sweet paprika
- 1 teaspoon garlic; minced
- Salt and black pepper to the taste

Directions:

1. Put zucchini in a bowl; add salt, leave aside for 10 minutes; squeeze excess water and transfer them to another bowl
2. Add carrots, salt, pepper, paprika, garlic, flour, parmesan, egg and bread crumbs; stir well, shape 8 croquettes, place them in your air fryer and cook at 360°F, for 10 minutes. Divide among plates and serve as a side dish.

Brussels Sprouts and Potatoes

(Prep + Cooking Time: 18 Minutes | **Servings:** 4)

Ingredients:

- 1 ½-pound Brussels sprouts; washed and trimmed
- 1 ½ tablespoon butter
- 1 ½ tablespoon bread crumbs
- 1 cup new potatoes; chopped
- Salt and black pepper to the taste

Directions:

1. Put Brussels sprouts and potatoes in your air fryer's pan, add bread crumbs, salt, pepper and butter
2. Toss well and cook at 400°F, for 8 minutes.
3. Divide among plates and serve as a side dish

Avocado Fries Dish

(**Prep + Cooking Time:** 20 Minutes | **Servings:** 4)

Ingredients:

- 1 avocado; pitted, peeled, sliced and cut into medium fries
- 1 tablespoon lemon juice
- 1 egg; whisked
- 1 tablespoon olive oil
- 1/2 cup panko bread crumbs
- Salt and black pepper to the taste

Directions:

1. In a bowl; mix panko with salt and pepper and stir.
2. In another bowl; mix egg with a pinch of salt and whisk
3. In a third bowl; mix avocado fries with lemon juice and oil and toss.
4. Dip fries in egg, then in panko, place them in your air fryer's basket and cook at 390°F, for 10 minutes; shaking halfway. Divide among plates and serve as a side dish

Artichokes and Tarragon Sauce Dish

(**Prep + Cooking Time:** 28 Minutes | **Servings:** 4)

Ingredients:

- 4 artichokes; trimmed
- 1 celery stalk; chopped.
- 1/2 cup olive oil
- 2 tablespoon chicken stock
- 2 tablespoon tarragon; chopped
- 2 tablespoon lemon juice
- Lemon zest from 2 lemons; grated
- Salt to the taste

Directions:

1. In your food processor; mix tarragon, chicken stock, lemon zest, lemon juice, celery, salt and olive oil and pulse very well
2. In a bowl; mix artichokes with tarragon and lemon sauce; toss well, transfer them to your air fryer's basket and cook at 380°F, for 18 minutes.
3. Divide artichokes on plates; drizzle the rest of the sauce all over and serve as a side dish

Simple Cauliflower Bars

(**Prep + Cooking Time:** 35 Minutes | **Servings:** 12)

Ingredients:

- 1 big cauliflower head; florets separated
- 1/4 cup egg whites
- 1 teaspoon Italian seasoning
- 1/2 cup mozzarella; shredded.
- Salt and black pepper to the taste

Directions:

1. Put cauliflower florets in your food processor; pulse well, spread on a lined baking sheet that fits your air fryer, introduce in the fryer and cook at 360°F, for 10 minutes
2. Transfer cauliflower to a bowl; add salt, pepper, cheese, egg whites and Italian seasoning; stir really well, spread this into a rectangle pan that fits your air fryer; press well, introduce in the fryer and cook at 360°F, for 15 minutes more. Cut into 12 bars, arrange them on a platter and serve as a snack.

Quick Wild Rice Pilaf

(Prep + Cooking Time: 35 Minutes | **Servings:** 12)

Ingredients:

- 1 shallot; chopped
- 1 teaspoon garlic; minced
- 3/4 cup cherries; dried
- 3/4 cup wild rice
- 4 cups chicken stock
- 1 tablespoon parsley; chopped.
- 1 cup farro
- 1/2 cup hazelnuts; toasted and chopped
- A drizzle of olive oil
- Salt and black pepper to the taste
- Chopped chives for serving

Directions:

1. In a dish that fits your air fryer; mix shallot with garlic, oil, faro, wild rice, stock, salt, pepper, parsley, hazelnuts and cherries; stir, place in your air fryer's basket and cook at 350°F, for 25 minutes.
2. Divide among plates and serve as a side dish

Creamy Brussels Sprouts Side Dish

(Prep + Cooking Time: 35 Minutes | **Servings:** 8)

Ingredients:

- 3-pound Brussels sprouts; halved
- 2 cups heavy cream
- 4 tablespoon butter
- 3 shallots; chopped
- 1 cup milk
- 1/4 teaspoon nutmeg; ground
- 3 tablespoon prepared horseradish
- 1-pound bacon; chopped
- A drizzle of olive oil
- Salt and black pepper to the taste

Directions:

1. Preheated you air fryer at 370 degrees F; add oil, bacon, salt and pepper and Brussels sprouts and toss
2. Add butter, shallots, heavy cream, milk, nutmeg and horseradish; toss again and cook for 25 minutes. Divide among plates and serve as a side dish

Dessert Recipes

Chocolate Cake Recipe

(Prep + Cooking Time: 40 Minutes | **Servings:** 12)

Ingredients:

- 3/4 cup white flour
- 3/4 cup whole wheat flour
- 1 teaspoon baking soda
- 1/2 teaspoon baking powder
- 3/4 cup sugar
- 1/2 teaspoon vanilla extract
- 2/3 cup chocolate chips
- 2 tablespoon canola oil
- 1/2 cup Greek yogurt
- 8-ounce canned pumpkin puree
- 1 egg
- 3/4 teaspoon pumpkin pie spice
- 1 banana; mashed
- Cooking spray

Directions:

1. In a bowl; mix white flour with whole wheat flour, salt, baking soda and powder and pumpkin spice and stir.
2. In another bowl, mix sugar with oil, banana, yogurt, pumpkin puree, vanilla and egg and stir using a mixer
3. Combine the 2 mixtures, add chocolate chips; stir, pour this into a greased Bundt pan that fits your air fryer.
4. Introduce in your air fryer and cook at 330°F, for 30 minutes.
5. Leave the cake to cool down, before cutting and serving it.

Pumpkin Cookies Recipe

(Prep + Cooking Time: 25 Minutes | **Servings:** 24)

Ingredients:

- 2 ½ cups flour
- 1/2 teaspoon baking soda
- 1/2 cup pumpkin flesh; mashed
- 1/4 cup honey
- 2 tablespoon butter
- 1 teaspoon vanilla extract
- 1 tablespoon flax seed; ground
- 3 tablespoon water
- 1/2 cup dark chocolate chips

Directions:

1. In a bowl; mix flax seed with water; stir and leave aside for a few minutes
2. In another bowl, mix flour with salt and baking soda.
3. In a third bowl, mix honey with pumpkin puree, butter, vanilla extract and flaxseed
4. Combine flour with honey mix and chocolate chips and stir
5. Scoop 1 tablespoon of cookie dough on a lined baking sheet that fits your air fryer, repeat with the rest of the dough, introduce them in your air fryer and cook at 350°F, for 15 minutes
6. Leave cookies to cool down and serve.

Bread Dough & Amaretto Dessert

(Prep + Cooking Time: 22 Minutes | **Servings:** 12)

Ingredients:
- 1-pound bread dough
- 1 cup heavy cream
- 1 cup sugar
- 1/2 cup butter; melted
- 12-ounce chocolate chips
- 2 tablespoon amaretto liqueur

Directions:
1. Roll dough, cut into 20 slices and then cut each slice in halves
2. Brush dough pieces with butter, sprinkle sugar, place them in your air fryer's basket after you've brushed it some butter, cook them at 350°F, for 5 minutes; flip them, cook for 3 minutes more and transfer to a platter.
3. Heat up a pan with the heavy cream over medium heat, add chocolate chips and stir until they melt. Add liqueur; stir again, transfer to a bowl and serve bread dippers with this sauce.

Cinnamon Rolls & Cream Cheese Dip

(Prep + Cooking Time: 2 hours 15 Minutes | **Servings:** 8)

Ingredients:
- 1-pound bread dough
- 1/4 cup butter; melted

For the cream cheese dip:
- 2 tablespoon butter
- 1/2 teaspoon vanilla
- 3/4 cup brown sugar
- 1 ½ tablespoon cinnamon; ground

- 1 ¼ cups sugar
- 4-ounce cream cheese

Directions:
1. Roll dough on a floured working surface; shape a rectangle and brush with 1/4 cup butter
2. In a bowl; mix cinnamon with sugar; stir, sprinkle this over dough, roll dough into a log, seal well and cut into 8 pieces.
3. Leave rolls to rise for 2 hours, place them in your air fryer's basket, cook at 350°F, for 5 minutes; flip them, cook for 4 minutes more and transfer to a platter.
4. In a bowl; mix cream cheese with butter, sugar and vanilla and whisk really well. Serve your cinnamon rolls with this cream cheese dip

Pumpkin Pie Recipe

(Prep + Cooking Time: 25 Minutes | **Servings:** 9)

Ingredients:
- 1 tablespoon sugar
- 2 tablespoon water

For the pumpkin pie filling:
- 3.5-ounce pumpkin flesh; chopped
- 3-ounce water
- 1 teaspoon mixed spice
- 2 tablespoon flour
- 1 tablespoon butter

- 1 teaspoon nutmeg
- 1 egg; whisked
- 1 tablespoon sugar

Directions:
1. Put 3-ounce water in a pot, bring to a boil over medium high heat, add pumpkin, egg, 1 tablespoon sugar, spice and nutmeg; stir, boil for 20 minutes; take off heat and blend using an immersion blender.
2. In a bowl; mix flour with butter, 1 tablespoon sugar and 2 tablespoon water and knead your dough well
3. Grease a pie pan that fits your air fryer with butter, press dough into the pan, fill with pumpkin pie filling, place in your air fryer's basket and cook at 360°F, for 15 minutes. Slice and serve warm.

Banana Bread Recipe

(**Prep + Cooking Time:** 50 Minutes | **Servings:** 6)

Ingredients:
- 3/4 cup sugar
- 1/3 cup butter
- 1 teaspoon baking powder
- 1 ½ cups flour
- 1/2 teaspoon baking soda
- 1 ½ teaspoon cream of tartar
- 1/3 cup milk
- 1 teaspoon vanilla extract
- 1 egg
- 2 bananas; mashed
- Cooking spray

Directions:
1. In a bowl; mix milk with cream of tartar, sugar, butter, egg, vanilla and bananas and stir everything.
2. In another bowl, mix flour with baking powder and baking soda.
3. Combine the 2 mixtures; stir well, pour this into a cake pan greased with some cooking spray, introduce in your air fryer and cook at 320°F, for 40 minutes. Take bread out, leave aside to cool down, slice and serve it

Blueberry Pudding Recipe

(**Prep + Cooking Time:** 35 Minutes | **Servings:** 6)

Ingredients:
- 2 cups flour
- 3 tablespoon maple syrup
- 2 cups rolled oats
- 8 cups blueberries
- 1 stick butter; melted
- 1 cup walnuts; chopped
- 2 tablespoon rosemary; chopped

Directions:
1. Spread blueberries in a greased baking pan and leave aside.
2. In your food processor, mix rolled oats with flour, walnuts, butter, maple syrup and rosemary, blend well, layer this over blueberries, introduce everything in your air fryer and cook at 350 degrees for 25 minutes. Leave dessert to cool down, cut and serve.

Apple Bread Recipe

(**Prep + Cooking Time:** 50 Minutes | **Servings:** 6)

Ingredients:
- 3 cups apples; cored and cubed
- 1 tablespoon vanilla
- 2 eggs
- 1 tablespoon apple pie spice
- 1 cup sugar
- 1 tablespoon baking powder
- 1 stick butter
- 2 cups white flour
- 1 cup water

Directions:
1. In a bowl mix egg with 1 butter stick, apple pie spice and sugar and stir using your mixer
2. Add apples and stir again well.
3. In another bowl, mix baking powder with flour and stir
4. Combine the 2 mixtures; stir and pour into a spring form pan
5. Put spring form pan in your air fryer and cook at 320°F, for 40 minutes Slice and serve

Cocoa and Almond Bars Recipe

(Prep + Cooking Time: 34 Minutes | **Servings:** 6)

Ingredients:
- 8 dates; pitted and soaked
- 2 tablespoon cocoa powder
- 1/4 cup hemp seeds
- 1/4 cup cocoa nibs
- 1 cup almonds; soaked and drained
- 1/4 cup coconut; shredded.
- 1/4 cup goji berries

Directions:
1. Put almonds in your food processor, blend, add hemp seeds, cocoa nibs, cocoa powder, goji, coconut and blend very well.
2. Add dates, blend well again, spread on a lined baking sheet that fits your air fryer and cook at 320°F, for 4 minutes. Cut into equal parts and keep in the fridge for 30 minutes before serving

Cashew Bars Recipe

(Prep + Cooking Time: 25 Minutes | **Servings:** 6)

Ingredients:
- 1/4 cup almond meal
- 4 dates; chopped
- 3/4 cup coconut; shredded.
- 1/3 cup honey
- 1 tablespoon almond butter
- 1 ½ cups cashews; chopped
- 1 tablespoon chia seeds

Directions:
1. In a bowl; mix honey with almond meal and almond butter and stir well
2. Add cashews, coconut, dates and chia seeds and stir well again
3. Spread this on a lined baking sheet that fits your air fryer and press well
4. Introduce in the fryer and cook at 300°F, for 15 minutes. Leave mix to cool down, cut into medium bars and serve

Easy Granola Recipe

(Prep + Cooking Time: 45 Minutes | **Servings:** 4)

Ingredients:
- 1 cup coconut; shredded.
- 1/2 cup almonds
- 1/2 cup pecans; chopped.
- 1/2 cup sunflower seeds
- 2 tablespoon sunflower oil
- 1 teaspoon nutmeg; ground
- 2 tablespoon sugar
- 1/2 cup pumpkin seeds
- 1 teaspoon apple pie spice mix

Directions:
1. In a bowl; mix almonds and pecans with pumpkin seeds, sunflower seeds, coconut, nutmeg and apple pie spice mix and stir well.
2. Heat up a pan with the oil over medium heat, add sugar and stir well
3. Pour this over nuts and coconut mix and stir well
4. Spread this on a lined baking sheet that fits your air fryer, introduce in your air fryer and cook at 300°F and bake for 25 minutes. Leave your granola to cool down, cut and serve

Pears and Espresso Cream Recipe

(Prep + Cooking Time: 40 Minutes | **Servings:** 4)

Ingredients:
- 4 pears; halved and cored
- 1 tablespoon sugar
- 2 tablespoon butter
- 2 tablespoon water
- 2 tablespoon lemon juice

For the cream:
- 2 tablespoon espresso; cold
- 1 cup mascarpone
- 1 cup whipping cream
- 1/3 cup sugar

Directions:
1. In a bowl; mix pears halves with lemon juice, 1 tablespoon sugar, butter and water, toss well, transfer them to your air fryer and cook at 360°F, for 30 minutes.
2. Meanwhile; in a bowl, mix whipping cream with mascarpone, ⅓ cup sugar and espresso, whisk really well and keep in the fridge until pears are done
3. Divide pears on plates, top with espresso cream and serve them.

Easy Cheesecake Recipe

(Prep + Cooking Time: 25 Minutes | **Servings:** 15)

Ingredients:
- 1-pound cream cheese
- 2 tablespoon butter
- 2 eggs
- 1/2 teaspoon vanilla extract
- 1 cup graham crackers; crumbled
- 4 tablespoon sugar

Directions:
1. In a bowl; mix crackers with butter
2. Press crackers mix on the bottom of a lined cake pan, introduce in your air fryer and cook at 350°F, for 4 minutes.
3. Meanwhile; in a bowl, mix sugar with cream cheese, eggs and vanilla and whisk well.
4. Spread filling over crackers crust and cook your cheesecake in your air fryer at 310°F, for 15 minutes. Leave cake in the fridge for 3 hours, slice and serve.

Coffee Cheesecakes Recipe

(Prep + Cooking Time: 30 Minutes | **Servings:** 6)

Ingredients:
For the cheesecakes:
- 2 tablespoon butter
- 8-ounce cream cheese
- 3 tablespoon coffee
- 3 eggs
- 1/3 cup sugar
- 1 tablespoon caramel syrup

For the frosting:
- 3 tablespoon caramel syrup
- 3 tablespoon butter
- 2 tablespoon sugar
- 8-ounce mascarpone cheese; soft

Directions:
1. In your blender, mix cream cheese with eggs, 2 tablespoon butter, coffee, 1 tablespoon caramel syrup and ⅓ cup sugar and pulse very well, spoon into a cupcakes pan that fits your air fryer, introduce in the fryer and cook at 320°F and bake for 20 minutes.
2. Leave aside to cool down and then keep in the freezer for 3 hours. Meanwhile; in a bowl, mix 3 tablespoon butter with 3 tablespoon caramel syrup, 2 tablespoon sugar and mascarpone, blend well, spoon this over cheesecakes and serve them

Tomato Cake Recipe

(Prep + Cooking Time: 40 Minutes | **Servings:** 4)

Ingredients:
- 1 ½ cups flour
- 1 teaspoon baking powder
- 1 teaspoon baking soda
- 3/4 cup maple syrup
- 1 teaspoon cinnamon powder
- 1 cup tomatoes chopped
- 1/2 cup olive oil
- 2 tablespoon apple cider vinegar

Directions:
1. In a bowl; mix flour with baking powder, baking soda, cinnamon and maple syrup and stir well.
2. In another bowl, mix tomatoes with olive oil and vinegar and stir well.
3. Combine the 2 mixtures; stir well, pour into a greased round pan that fits your air fryer, introduce in the fryer and cook at 360°F, for 30 minutes. Leave cake to cool down, slice and serve

Plum Bars Recipe

(Prep + Cooking Time: 26 Minutes | **Servings:** 8)

Ingredients:
- 2 cups dried plums
- 2 cup rolled oats
- 1 cup brown sugar
- 1/2 teaspoon baking soda
- 6 tablespoon water
- 2 tablespoon butter; melted
- 1 egg; whisked
- 1 teaspoon cinnamon powder
- Cooking spray

Directions:
1. In your food processor, mix plums with water and blend until you obtain a sticky spread
2. In a bowl; mix oats with cinnamon, baking soda, sugar, egg and butter and whisk really well
3. Press half of the oats mix in a baking pan that fits your air fryer sprayed with cooking oil, spread plums mix and top with the other half of the oats mix.
4. Introduce in your air fryer and cook at 350°F, for 16 minutes. Leave mix aside to cool down, cut into medium bars and serve.

Crispy Apples Recipe

(Prep + Cooking Time: 20 Minutes | **Servings:** 4)

Ingredients:
- 2 teaspoon cinnamon powder
- 5 apples; cored and cut into chunks
- 3/4 cup old fashioned rolled oats
- 1/2 teaspoon nutmeg powder
- 1 tablespoon maple syrup
- 1/2 cup water
- 4 tablespoon butter
- 1/4 cup flour
- 1/4 cup brown sugar

Directions:
1. Put the apples in a pan that fits your air fryer, add cinnamon, nutmeg, maple syrup and water.
2. In a bowl; mix butter with oats, sugar, salt and flour; stir, drop spoonfuls of this mix on top of apples, introduce in your air fryer and cook at 350°F, for 10 minutes. Serve warm

Passion Fruit Pudding Recipe

(Prep + Cooking Time: 50 Minutes | **Servings:** 6)

Ingredients:
- 1 cup Paleo passion fruit curd
- 3 ½-ounce almond milk
- 3 ½-ounce maple syrup
- 3 eggs
- 2-ounce ghee; melted
- 1/2 cup almond flour
- 4 passion fruits; pulp and seeds
- 1/2 teaspoon baking powder

Directions:
1. In a bowl; mix the half of the fruit curd with passion fruit seeds and pulp; stir and divide into 6 heat proof ramekins
2. In a bowl; whisked eggs with maple syrup, ghee, the rest of the curd, baking powder, milk and flour and stir well
3. Divide this into the ramekins as well, introduce in the fryer and cook at 200°F, for 40 minutes. Leave puddings to cool down and serve!

Lentils Cookies Recipe

(Prep + Cooking Time: 35 Minutes | **Servings:** 36)

Ingredients:
- 1/2 cup brown sugar
- 1/2 cup white sugar
- 1 cup white flour
- 1 egg
- 1 cup water
- 1 teaspoon cinnamon powder
- 1/2 teaspoon nutmeg; ground
- 1 cup canned lentils; drained and mashed
- 1 teaspoon baking powder
- 2 teaspoon almond extract
- 1 cup raisins
- 1 cup rolled oats
- 1 cup butter; soft
- 1 cup whole wheat flour
- 1 cup coconut; unsweetened and shredded.

Directions:
1. In a bowl; mix white and whole wheat flour with salt, cinnamon, baking powder and nutmeg and stir
2. In a bowl; mix butter with white and brown sugar and stir using your kitchen mixer for 2 minutes.
3. Add egg, almond extract, lentils mix, flour mix, oats, raisins and coconut and stir everything well
4. Scoop tablespoon of dough on a lined baking sheet that fits your air fryer, introduce them in the fryer and cook at 350°F, for 15 minutes. Arrange cookies on a serving platter and serve.

Chocolate & Pomegranate Bars

(Prep + Cooking Time: 2 hours 10 Minutes | **Servings:** 6)

Ingredients:
- 1/2 cup milk
- 1/2 cup almonds; chopped
- 1 ½ cups dark chocolate; chopped
- 1 teaspoon vanilla extract
- 1/2 cup pomegranate seeds

Directions:
1. Heat up a pan with the milk over medium low heat, add chocolate; stir for 5 minutes; take off heat add vanilla extract, half of the pomegranate seeds and half of the nuts and stir.
2. Pour this into a lined baking pan, spread, sprinkle a pinch of salt, the rest of the pomegranate arils and nuts, introduce in your air fryer and cook at 300°F, for 4 minutes. Keep in the fridge for 2 hours before serving

Lime Cheesecake Recipe

(Prep + Cooking Time: 4 hours and 14 minutes | **Servings:** 10)

Ingredients:
- 2 tablespoon butter; melted
- 1/4 cup coconut; shredded.

For the filling:
- 1-pound cream cheese
- 2 sachets lime jelly
- Juice form 1 lime

- 4-ounce flour
- 2 teaspoon sugar

- 2 cups hot water
- Zest from 1 lime; grated

Directions:
1. In a bowl; mix coconut with flour, butter and sugar; stir well and press this on the bottom of a pan that fits your air fryer.
2. Meanwhile; put the hot water in a bowl, add jelly sachets and stir until it dissolves
3. Put cream cheese in a bowl, add jelly, lime juice and zest and whisk really well.
4. Add this over the crust, spread, introduce in the air fryer and cook at 300°F, for 4 minutes. Keep in the fridge for 4 hours before serving.

Macaroons Recipe

(Prep + Cooking Time: 18 Minutes | **Servings:** 20)

Ingredients:
- 2 tablespoon sugar
- 1 teaspoon vanilla extract

- 2 cup coconut; shredded.
- 4 egg whites

Directions:
1. In a bowl; mix egg whites with stevia and beat using your mixer.
2. Add coconut and vanilla extract, whisk again, shape small balls out of this mix, introduce them in your air fryer and cook at 340°F, for 8 minutes. Serve macaroons cold.

Cocoa Cake Recipe

(Prep + Cooking Time: 27 Minutes | **Servings:** 6)

Ingredients:
- 3.5-ounce butter; melted
- 3-ounce sugar
- 1 teaspoon cocoa powder

- 3-ounce flour
- 3 eggs
- 1/2 teaspoon lemon juice

Directions:
1. In a bowl; mix 1 tablespoon butter with cocoa powder and whisk
2. In another bowl, mix the rest of the butter with sugar, eggs, flour and lemon juice, whisk well and pour half into a cake pan that fits your air fryer.
3. Add half of the cocoa mix, spread, add the rest of the butter layer and top with the rest of cocoa
4. Introduce in your air fryer and cook at 360°F, for 17 minutes. Cool cake down before slicing and serving

Mini Lava Cakes Recipe

(Prep + Cooking Time: 30 Minutes | **Servings:** 3)

Ingredients:

- 1 egg
- 1/2 teaspoon baking powder
- 4 tablespoon milk
- 4 tablespoon flour
- 4 tablespoon sugar
- 2 tablespoon olive oil
- 1 tablespoon cocoa powder
- 1/2 teaspoon orange zest

Directions:

1. In a bowl; mix egg with sugar, oil, milk, flour, salt, cocoa powder, baking powder and orange zest; stir very well and pour this into greased ramekins.
2. Add ramekins to your air fryer and cook at 320°F, for 20 minutes. Serve lava cakes warm

Ginger Cheesecake Recipe

(Prep + Cooking Time: 2 hours and 30 Minutes | **Servings:** 6)

Ingredients:

- 2 teaspoon butter; melted
- 1/2 teaspoon nutmeg; ground
- 2 eggs
- 1/2 cup sugar
- 1/2 cup ginger cookies; crumbled
- 16-ounce cream cheese; soft
- 1/2 teaspoon vanilla extract
- 1 teaspoon rum

Directions:

1. Grease a pan with the butter and spread cookie crumbs on the bottom.
2. In a bowl; beat cream cheese with nutmeg, vanilla, rum and eggs, whisk well and spread over the cookie crumbs
3. Introduce in your air fryer and cook at 340°F, for 20 minutes. Leave cheesecake to cool down and keep in the fridge for 2 hours before slicing and serving it.

Fried Bananas Recipe

(Prep + Cooking Time: 25 Minutes | **Servings:** 4)

Ingredients:

- 3 tablespoon butter
- 2 eggs
- 8 bananas; peeled and halved
- 3 tablespoon cinnamon sugar
- 1 cup panko
- 1/2 cup corn flour

Directions:

1. Heat up a pan with the butter over medium high heat, add panko; stir and cook for 4 minutes and then transfer to a bowl.
2. Roll each in flour, eggs and panko mix, arrange them in your air fryer's basket, dust with cinnamon sugar and cook at 280°F, for 10 minutes. Serve right away

Wrapped Pears Recipe

(Prep + Cooking Time: 25 Minutes | **Servings:** 4)

Ingredients:

- 4 puff pastry sheets
- 14-ounce vanilla custard
- 2 pears; halved
- 1 egg; whisked
- 1/2 teaspoon cinnamon powder
- 2 tablespoon sugar

Directions:

1. Place puff pastry slices on a working surface, add spoonfuls of vanilla custard in the center of each, top with pear halves and wrap.
2. Brush pears with egg, sprinkle sugar and cinnamon, place them in your air fryer's basket and cook at 320°F, for 15 minutes. Divide parcels on plates and serve

Carrot Cake Recipe

(Prep + Cooking Time: 55 Minutes | **Servings:** 6)

Ingredients:

- 5-ounce flour
- 3/4 teaspoon baking powder
- 1/3 cup carrots; grated
- 1/3 cup pecans; toasted and chopped
- 1/4 teaspoon nutmeg; ground
- 1/2 teaspoon baking soda
- 1/2 teaspoon allspice
- 1 egg
- 3 tablespoon yogurt
- 4 tablespoon sunflower oil
- 1/2 teaspoon cinnamon powder
- 1/2 cup sugar
- 1/4 cup pineapple juice
- 1/3 cup coconut flakes; shredded.
- Cooking spray

Directions:

1. In a bowl; mix flour with baking soda and powder, salt, allspice, cinnamon and nutmeg and stir
2. In another bowl, mix egg with yogurt, sugar, pineapple juice, oil, carrots, pecans and coconut flakes and stir well.
3. Combine the two mixtures and stir well, pour this into a spring form pan that fits your air fryer which you've greased with some cooking spray, transfer to your air fryer and cook on 320°F, for 45 minutes.
4. Leave cake to cool down, then cut and serve it

Orange Cookies Recipe

(Prep + Cooking Time: 22 Minutes | **Servings:** 8)

Ingredients:

- 1/2 cup butter; soft
- 3/4 cup sugar
- 2 cups flour
- 1 egg; whisked
- 1 teaspoon vanilla extract
- 1 teaspoon baking powder
- 1 tablespoon orange zest; grated

For the filling:

- 1/2 cup butter
- 2 cups powdered sugar
- 4-ounce cream cheese; soft

Directions:

1. In a bowl; mix cream cheese with 1/2 cup butter and 2 cups powdered sugar; stir well using your mixer and leave aside for now.
2. In another bowl, mix flour with baking powder
3. In a third bowl, mix 1/2 cup butter with 3/4 cup sugar, egg, vanilla extract and orange zest and whisk well.
4. Combine flour with orange mix; stir well and scoop 1 tablespoon of the mix on a lined baking sheet that fits your air fryer.

5. Repeat with the rest of the orange batter, introduce in the fryer and cook at 340°F, for 12 minutes. Leave cookies to cool down, spread cream filling on half of them top with the other cookies and serve.

Ricotta and Lemon Cake

(Prep + Cooking Time: 1 hour and 10 Minutes | Servings: 4)

Ingredients:
- 8 eggs; whisked
- Zest from 1 orange; grated
- 1/2-pound sugar
- 3-pound ricotta cheese
- Zest from 1 lemon; grated
- Butter for the pan

Directions:
1. In a bowl; mix eggs with sugar, cheese, lemon and orange zest and stir very well
2. Grease a baking pan that fits your air fryer with some batter, spread ricotta mixture, introduce in the fryer at 390°F and bake for 30 minutes.
3. Reduce heat at 380°F and bake for 40 more minutes. Take out of the oven, leave cake to cool down and serve!

Cocoa Cookies Recipe

(Prep + Cooking Time: 24 Minutes | Servings: 12)

Ingredients:
- 6-ounce coconut oil; melted
- 6 eggs
- 4-ounce cream cheese
- 3-ounce cocoa powder
- 2 teaspoon vanilla
- 1/2 teaspoon baking powder
- 5 tablespoon sugar

Directions:
1. In a blender, mix eggs with coconut oil, cocoa powder, baking powder, vanilla, cream cheese and swerve and stir using a mixer.
2. Pour this into a lined baking dish that fits your air fryer, introduce in the fryer at 320°F and bake for 14 minutes. Slice cookie sheet into rectangles and serve

Figs and Coconut Butter Mix

(Prep + Cooking Time: 10 Minutes | Servings: 3)

Ingredients:
- 1/4 cup sugar
- 2 tablespoon coconut butter
- 12 figs; halved
- 1 cup almonds; toasted and chopped

Directions:
1. Put butter in a pan that fits your air fryer and melt over medium high heat.
2. Add figs, sugar and almonds, toss, introduce in your air fryer and cook at 300°F, for 4 minutes.
3. Divide into bowls and serve cold

Sponge Cake Recipe

(Prep + Cooking Time: 30 Minutes | **Servings:** 12)

Ingredients:

- 3 cups flour
- 1/2 cup cornstarch
- 1 teaspoon baking soda
- 1 cup olive oil
- 3 teaspoon baking powder
- 1 ½ cup milk
- 1 ⅔ cup sugar
- 2 cups water
- 1/4 cup lemon juice
- 2 teaspoon vanilla extract

Directions:

1. In a bowl; mix flour with cornstarch, baking powder, baking soda and sugar and whisk well
2. In another bowl, mix oil with milk, water, vanilla and lemon juice and whisk.
3. Combine the two mixtures; stir, pour in a greased baking dish that fits your air fryer, introduce in the fryer and cook at 350°F, for 20 minutes. Leave cake to cool down, cut and serve

Lentils and Dates Brownies

(Prep + Cooking Time: 25 Minutes | **Servings:** 8)

Ingredients:

- 28-ounce canned lentils; rinsed and drained
- 12 dates
- 1 tablespoon honey
- 1/2 teaspoon baking soda
- 4 tablespoon almond butter
- 1 banana; peeled and chopped.
- 2 tablespoon cocoa powder

Directions:

1. In your food processor, mix lentils with butter, banana, cocoa, baking soda and honey and blend really well
2. Add dates, pulse a few more times, pour this into a greased pan that fits your air fryer, spread evenly, introduce in the fryer at 360°F and bake for 15 minutes
3. Take brownies mix out of the oven, cut, arrange on a platter and serve.

Orange Cake Recipe

(Prep + Cooking Time: 42 Minutes | **Servings:** 12)

Ingredients:

- 1 orange, peeled and cut into quarters
- 1 teaspoon vanilla extract
- 4-ounce cream cheese
- 1 teaspoon baking powder
- 9-ounce flour
- 6 eggs
- 2 tablespoon orange zest
- 2-ounce sugar+ 2 tablespoon
- 4-ounce yogurt

Directions:

1. In your food processor, pulse orange very well.
2. Add flour, 2 tablespoon sugar, eggs, baking powder, vanilla extract and pulse well again.
3. Transfer this into 2 spring form pans, introduce each in your fryer and cook at 330°F, for 16 minutes
4. Meanwhile; in a bowl, mix cream cheese with orange zest, yogurt and the rest of the sugar and stir well.
5. Place one cake layer on a plate, add half of the cream cheese mix, add the other cake layer and top with the rest of the cream cheese mix. Spread it well, slice and serve

Peach Pie Recipe

(Prep + Cooking Time: 45 Minutes | **Servings:** 4)

Ingredients:

- 1 pie dough
- 2 ¼-pound peaches; pitted and chopped
- 1 tablespoon lemon juice
- 1/2 cup sugar
- 2 tablespoon flour
- 2 tablespoon cornstarch
- 1 tablespoon dark rum
- A pinch of nutmeg; ground
- 2 tablespoon butter; melted

Directions:

1. Roll pie dough into a pie pan that fits your air fryer and press well
2. In a bowl; mix peaches with cornstarch, sugar, flour, nutmeg, rum, lemon juice and butter and stir well.
3. Pour and spread this into pie pan, introduce in your air fryer and cook at 350°F, for 35 minutes. Serve warm or cold.

Bread Pudding Recipe

(Prep + Cooking Time: 1 hour 10 Minutes | **Servings:** 4)

Ingredients:

- 6 glazed doughnuts; crumbled
- 1 cup cherries
- 1/2 cup chocolate chips.
- 1 ½ cups whipping cream
- 4 egg yolks
- 1/4 cup sugar
- 1/2 cup raisins

Directions:

1. In a bowl; mix cherries with egg yolks and whipping cream and stir well
2. In another bowl, mix raisins with sugar, chocolate chips and doughnuts and stir
3. Combine the 2 mixtures, transfer everything to a greased pan that fits your air fryer and cook at 310°F, for 1 hour. Chill pudding before cutting and serving it.

Strawberry Donuts Recipe

(Prep + Cooking Time: 25 Minutes | **Servings:** 4)

Ingredients:

- 8-ounce flour
- 1 teaspoon baking powder
- 1 tablespoon white sugar
- 1 tablespoon brown sugar
- 4-ounce whole milk
- 1 egg
- 2 ½ tablespoon butter

For the strawberry icing:

- 1/2 teaspoon pink coloring
- 2 tablespoon butter
- 3.5-ounce icing sugar
- 1/4 cup strawberries; chopped.
- 1 tablespoon whipped cream

Directions:

1. In a bowl; mix butter, 1 tablespoon brown sugar, 1 tablespoon white sugar and flour and stir.
2. In a second bowl, mix egg with 1 ½ tablespoon butter and milk and stir well
3. Combine the 2 mixtures; stir, shape donuts from this mix, place them in your air fryer's basket and cook at 360°F, for 15 minutes
4. Put 1 tablespoon butter, icing sugar, food coloring, whipped cream and strawberry puree and whisk well. Arrange donuts on a platter and serve with strawberry icing on top.

Strawberry Shortcakes Recipe

(Prep + Cooking Time: 65 Minutes | **Servings:** 6)

Ingredients:

- 1/4 cup sugar+ 4 tablespoon
- 1 ½ cup flour
- 1 teaspoon baking powder
- 1/3 cup butter
- 1 cup buttermilk
- 1 egg; whisked
- 2 cups strawberries; sliced
- 1 tablespoon mint; chopped
- 1 teaspoon lime zest; grated
- 1/4 teaspoon baking soda
- Cooking spray
- 1 tablespoon rum
- 1/2 cup whipping cream

Directions:

1. In a bowl; mix flour with 1/4 cup sugar, baking powder and baking soda and stir.
2. In another bowl, mix buttermilk with egg; stir, add to flour mix and whisk.
3. Spoon this dough into 6 jars greased with cooking spray, cover with tin foil, arrange them in your air fryer cook at 360°F, for 45 minutes.
4. Meanwhile; in a bowl, mix strawberries with 3 tablespoon sugar, rum, mint and lime zest; stir and leave aside in a cold place
5. In another bowl, mix whipping cream with 1 tablespoon sugar and stir. Take jars out, divide strawberry mix and whipped cream on top and serve

Strawberry Pie Recipe

(Prep + Cooking Time: 30 Minutes | **Servings:** 12)

Ingredients:

For the crust:

- 1 cup coconut; shredded.
- 1 cup sunflower seeds
- 1/4 cup butter

For the filling:

- 1/4 teaspoon stevia
- 4-ounce strawberries
- 2 tablespoon water
- 1 teaspoon gelatin
- 8-ounce cream cheese
- 1/2 tablespoon lemon juice
- 1/2 cup heavy cream
- 8-ounce strawberries; chopped for serving

Directions:

1. In your food processor, mix sunflower seeds with coconut, a pinch of salt and butter, pulse and press this on the bottom of a cake pan that fits your air fryer.
2. Heat up a pan with the water over medium heat, add gelatin; stir until it dissolves, leave aside to cool down, add this to your food processor, mix with 4-ounce strawberries, cream cheese, lemon juice and stevia and blend well.
3. Add heavy cream; stir well and spread this over crust.
4. Top with 8-ounce strawberries, introduce in your air fryer and cook at 330°F, for 15 minutes. Keep in the fridge until you serve it

Maple Cupcakes Recipe

(Prep + Cooking Time: 30 Minutes | **Servings:** 4)

Ingredients:

- 1/2 cup pure applesauce
- 2 teaspoon cinnamon powder
- 4 eggs
- 4 teaspoon maple syrup
- 3/4 cup white flour
- 1 teaspoon vanilla extract
- 4 tablespoon butter
- 1/2 apple; cored and chopped
- 1/2 teaspoon baking powder

Directions:

1. Heat up a pan with the butter over medium heat, add applesauce, vanilla, eggs and maple syrup; stir, take off heat and leave aside to cool down.
2. Add flour, cinnamon, baking powder and apples, whisk, pour in a cupcake pan, introduce in your air fryer at 350°F and bake for 20 minutes
3. Leave cupcakes them to cool down, transfer to a platter and serve them

Banana Cake Recipe

(Prep + Cooking Time: 40 Minutes | **Servings:** 4)

Ingredients:

- 1 tablespoon butter; soft
- 1/2 teaspoon cinnamon powder
- 2 tablespoon honey
- 1 banana; peeled and mashed
- 1 egg
- 1/3 cup brown sugar
- 1 teaspoon baking powder
- 1 cup white flour
- Cooking spray

Directions:

1. Spray a cake pan with some cooking spray and leave aside
2. In a bowl; mix butter with sugar, banana, honey, egg, cinnamon, baking powder and flour and whisk
3. Pour this into a cake pan greased with cooking spray, introduce in your air fryer and cook at 350°F, for 30 minutes. Leave cake to cool down, slice and serve.

Chocolate Cookies Recipe

(Prep + Cooking Time: 35 Minutes | **Servings:** 12)

Ingredients:

- 1 teaspoon vanilla extract
- 1 egg
- 4 tablespoon sugar
- 2 cups flour
- 1/2 cup butter
- 1/2 cup unsweetened chocolate chips

Directions:

1. Heat up a pan with the butter over medium heat; stir and cook for 1 minute.
2. In a bowl; mix egg with vanilla extract and sugar and stir well
3. Add melted butter, flour and half of the chocolate chips and stir everything.
4. Transfer this to a pan that fits your air fryer, spread the rest of the chocolate chips on top, introduce in the fryer at 330°F and bake for 25 minutes. Slice when it's cold and serve.

Strawberry Cobbler Recipe

(**Prep + Cooking Time:** 35 Minutes | **Servings:** 6)

Ingredients:

- 3/4 cup sugar
- 6 cups strawberries; halved
- 1/2 cup flour
- 1/2 cup water
- 3 ½ tablespoon olive oil
- 1/8 teaspoon baking powder
- 1 tablespoon lemon juice
- A pinch of baking soda
- Cooking spray

Directions:

1. In a bowl; mix strawberries with half of sugar, sprinkle some flour, add lemon juice, whisk and pour into the baking dish that fits your air fryer and greased with cooking spray.
2. In another bowl, mix flour with the rest of the sugar, baking powder and soda and stir well
3. Add the olive oil and mix until the whole thing with your hands
4. Add 1/2 cup water and spread over strawberries
5. Introduce in the fryer at 355°F and bake for 25 minutes. Leave cobbler aside to cool down, slice and serve.

Plum and Currant Tart Recipe

(**Prep + Cooking Time:** 65 Minutes | **Servings:** 6)

Ingredients:

For the crumble:

- 1/4 cup almond flour
- 1 cup brown rice flour
- 1/2 cup cane sugar
- 1/4 cup millet flour
- 10 tablespoon butter; soft
- 3 tablespoon milk

For the filling:

- 1-pound small plums; pitted and halved
- 3 tablespoon sugar
- 1/2 teaspoon vanilla extract
- 1/2 teaspoon cinnamon powder
- 1 cup white currants
- 2 tablespoon cornstarch
- 1/4 teaspoon ginger powder
- 1 teaspoon lime juice

Directions:

1. In a bowl; mix brown rice flour with 1/2 cup sugar, millet flour, almond flour, butter and milk and stir until you obtain a sand like dough
2. Reserve 1/4 of the dough, press the rest of the dough into a tart pan that fits your air fryer and keep in the fridge for 30 minutes
3. Meanwhile; in a bowl, mix plums with currants, 3 tablespoon sugar, cornstarch, vanilla extract, cinnamon, ginger and lime juice and stir well
4. Pour this over tart crust, crumble reserved dough on top, introduce in your air fryer and cook at 350°F, for 35 minutes. Leave tart to cool down, slice and serve

Black Tea Cake Recipe

(Prep + Cooking Time: 45 Minutes | Servings: 12)

Ingredients:

- 6 tablespoon black tea powder
- 1/2 cup olive oil
- 1/2 cup butter
- 2 cups sugar
- 4 eggs

- 3 ½ cups flour
- 1 teaspoon baking soda
- 2 cups milk
- 2 teaspoon vanilla extract
- 3 teaspoon baking powder

For the cream:

- 6 tablespoon honey
- 4 cups sugar

- 1 cup butter; soft

Directions:

1. Put the milk in a pot, heat up over medium heat, add tea; stir well, take off heat and leave aside to cool down.
2. In a bowl; mix 1/2 cup butter with 2 cups sugar, eggs, vegetable oil, vanilla extract, baking powder, baking soda and 3 ½ cups flour and stir everything really well.
3. Pour this into 2 greased round pans, introduce each in the fryer at 330°F and bake for 25 minutes.
4. In a bowl; mix 1 cup butter with honey and 4 cups sugar and stir really well.
5. Arrange one cake on a platter, spread the cream all over, top with the other cake and keep in the fridge until you serve it.

Blueberry Scones Recipe

(Prep + Cooking Time: 20 Minutes | Servings: 10)

Ingredients:

- 1 cup white flour
- 1 cup blueberries
- 2 teaspoon vanilla extract
- 2 eggs

- 1/2 cup heavy cream
- 5 tablespoon sugar
- 1/2 cup butter
- 2 teaspoon baking powder

Directions:

1. In a bowl; mix flour, salt, baking powder and blueberries and stir.
2. In another bowl, mix heavy cream with butter, vanilla extract, sugar and eggs and stir well
3. Combine the 2 mixtures, knead until you obtain your dough, shape 10 triangles from this mix, place them on a lined baking sheet that fits your air fryer and cook them at 320°F, for 10 minutes. Serve them cold

Plum Cake Recipe

(Prep + Cooking Time: 1 hour and 20 Minutes | Servings: 8)

Ingredients:

- 1 ¾-pound plums; pitted and cut into quarters
- 5 tablespoon sugar
- 3-ounce warm milk
- 1-ounce butter; soft

- 1 egg; whisked
- 1 package dried yeast
- 7-ounce flour
- Zest from 1 lemon; grated
- 1-ounce almond flakes

Directions:

1. In a bowl; mix yeast with butter, flour and 3 tablespoon sugar and stir well.
2. Add milk and egg and whisk for 4 minutes until you obtain a dough
3. Arrange the dough in a spring form pan that fits your air fryer and which you've greased with some butter, cover and leave aside for 1 hour. Arrange plumps on top of the butter, sprinkle the rest of the sugar, introduce in your air fryer at 350 degrees F, bake for 36 minutes; cool down, sprinkle almond flakes and lemon zest on top, slice and serve

Mandarin Pudding Recipe

(Prep + Cooking Time: 60 Minutes | **Servings:** 8)

Ingredients:

- 1 mandarin; peeled and sliced
- 3/4 cup white flour
- 3/4 cup almonds; ground
- 4-ounce butter; soft
- 2 eggs; whisked
- Juice from 2 mandarins
- 2 tablespoon brown sugar
- 3/4 cup sugar
- Honey for serving

Directions:

1. Grease a loaf pan with some butter, sprinkle brown sugar on the bottom and arrange mandarin slices
2. In a bowl; mix butter with sugar, eggs, almonds, flour and mandarin juice; stir, spoon this over mandarin slices, place pan in your air fryer and cook at 360°F, for 40 minutes.
3. Transfer pudding to a plate and serve with honey on top

Berries Mix Recipe

(Prep + Cooking Time: 11 Minutes | **Servings:** 4)

Ingredients:

- 1-pound strawberries; halved
- 2 tablespoon lemon juice
- 1 ½ tablespoon maple syrup
- 1 ½ tablespoon champagne vinegar
- 1 ½ cups blueberries
- 1 tablespoon olive oil
- 1/4 cup basil leaves; torn

Directions:

1. In a pan that fits your air fryer, mix lemon juice with maple syrup and vinegar, bring to a boil over medium high heat, add oil, blueberries and strawberries; stir
2. Introduce in your air fryer and cook at 310°F, for 6 minutes.
3. Sprinkle basil on top and serve

Lemon Tart Recipe

(Prep + Cooking Time: 1 hour 35 Minutes | **Servings:** 6)

Ingredients:

For the crust:

- 12 tablespoon cold butter
- 2 tablespoon sugar
- 2 cups white flour
- 3 tablespoon ice water
- A pinch of salt

For the filling:

- 2 eggs; whisked
- 10 tablespoon melted and chilled butter
- 1 ¼ cup sugar
- Zest from 2 lemons; grated
- Juice from 2 lemons

Directions:

1. In a bowl; mix 2 cups flour with a pinch of salt and 2 tablespoon sugar and whisk
2. Add 12 tablespoon butter and the water, knead until you obtain a dough, shape a ball, wrap in foil and keep in the fridge for 1 hour.
3. Transfer dough to a floured surface, flatten it, arrange on the bottom of a tart pan, prick with a fork, keep in the fridge for 20 minutes; introduce in your air fryer at 360°F and bake for 15 minutes.
4. In a bowl; mix 1 ¼ cup sugar with eggs, 10 tablespoon butter, lemon juice and lemon zest and whisk very well.
5. Pour this into pie crust, spread evenly, introduce in the fryer and cook at 360°F, for 20 minutes. Cut and serve it.

Sweet Potato Cheese Cake

(Prep + Cooking Time: 15 Minutes | **Servings:** 4)

Ingredients:

- 3/4 cup milk
- 6-ounce mascarpone; soft
- 8-ounce cream cheese; soft
- 1 teaspoon vanilla extract
- 4 tablespoon butter; melted
- ⅔ cup graham crackers; crumbled
- ⅔ cup sweet potato puree
- 1/4 teaspoon cinnamon powder

Directions:

1. In a bowl; mix butter with crumbled crackers; stir well, press on the bottom of a cake pan that fits your air fryer and keep in the fridge for now.
2. In another bowl, mix cream cheese with mascarpone, sweet potato puree, milk, cinnamon and vanilla and whisk really well. Spread this over crust, introduce in your air fryer, cook at 300°F, for 4 minutes and keep in the fridge for a few hours before serving

Special Brownies Recipe

(Prep + Cooking Time: 27 Minutes | **Servings:** 4)

Ingredients:

- 1/3 cup cocoa powder
- 7 tablespoon butter
- 1 egg
- 1/2 teaspoon baking powder
- 1/2 teaspoon vanilla extract
- 1/3 cup sugar
- 1/4 cup walnuts; chopped.
- 1/4 cup white flour
- 1 tablespoon peanut butter

Directions:

1. Heat up a pan with 6 tablespoon butter and the sugar over medium heat; stir, cook for 5 minutes; transfer this to a bowl, add salt, vanilla extract, cocoa powder, egg, baking powder, walnuts and flour; stir the whole thing really well and pour into a pan that fits your air fryer.
2. In a bowl; mix 1 tablespoon butter with peanut butter, heat up in your microwave for a few seconds; stir well and drizzle this over brownies mix
3. Introduce in your air fryer and bake at 320°F and bake for 17 minutes. Leave brownies to cool down, cut and serve

Fried Apples Recipe

(Prep + Cooking Time: 27 Minutes | **Servings:** 4)

Ingredients:

- 4 big apples; cored
- 1 tablespoon cinnamon; ground
- Raw honey to the taste
- A handful raisins

Directions:

1. Fill each apple with raisins, sprinkle cinnamon, drizzle honey, put them in your air fryer and cook at 367°F, for 17 minutes. Leave them to cool down and serve.

Brown Butter Cookies Recipe

(Prep + Cooking Time: 20 Minutes | **Servings:** 6)

Ingredients:
- 2 teaspoon vanilla extract
- 1 teaspoon baking soda
- 2 eggs; whisked
- 1 ½ cups butter
- 2 cups brown sugar
- 3 cups flour
- ⅔ cup pecans; chopped
- 1/2 teaspoon baking powder

Directions:
1. Heat up a pan with the butter over medium heat; stir until it melts, add brown sugar and stir until this dissolves.
2. In a bowl; mix flour with pecans, vanilla extract, baking soda, baking powder and eggs and stir well.
3. Add brown butter; stir well and arrange spoonfuls of this mix on a lined baking sheet that fits your air fryer.
4. Introduce in the fryer and cook at 340°F, for 10 minutes. Leave cookies to cool down and serve

Lemon Bars Recipe

(Prep + Cooking Time: 35 Minutes | **Servings:** 6)

Ingredients:
- 2 ¼ cups flour
- 4 eggs
- 1 cup butter; soft
- Juice from 2 lemons
- 2 cups sugar

Directions:
1. In a bowl; mix butter with 1/2 cup sugar and 2 cups flour; stir well, press on the bottom of a pan that fits your air fryer, introduce in the fryer and cook at 350°F, for 10 minutes.
2. In another bowl, mix the rest of the sugar with the rest of the flour, eggs and lemon juice, whisk well and spread over crust. Introduce in the fryer at 350°F, for 15 minutes more, leave aside to cool down, cut bars and serve them

Tangerine Cake Recipe

(Prep + Cooking Time: 30 Minutes | **Servings:** 8)

Ingredients:
- 3/4 cup sugar
- 1/4 cup olive oil
- 1/2 cup milk
- 1 teaspoon cider vinegar
- 2 cups flour
- 1/2 teaspoon vanilla extract
- Juice and zest from 2 lemons
- Juice and zest from 1 tangerine
- Tangerine segments; for serving

Directions:
1. In a bowl; mix flour with sugar and stir
2. In another bowl, mix oil with milk, vinegar, vanilla extract, lemon juice and zest and tangerine zest and whisk very well.
3. Add flour; stir well, pour this into a cake pan that fits your air fryer, introduce in the fryer and cook at 360°F, for 20 minutes. Serve right away with tangerine segments on top

Rhubarb Pie Recipe

(Prep + Cooking Time: 1 hour 15 Minutes | **Servings:** 6)

Ingredients:
- 1 ¼ cups almond flour
- 8 tablespoon butter

For the filling:
- 3 cups rhubarb; chopped
- 1/2 teaspoon nutmeg; ground
- 1 tablespoon butter
- 1 ½ cups sugar

- 5 tablespoon cold water
- 1 teaspoon sugar

- 3 tablespoon flour
- 2 eggs
- 2 tablespoon low fat milk

Directions:
1. In a bowl; mix 1 ¼ cups flour with 1 teaspoon sugar, 8 tablespoon butter and cold water; stir and knead until you obtain a dough.
2. Transfer dough to a floured working surface, shape a disk, flatten, wrap in plastic, keep in the fridge for about 30 minutes; roll and press on the bottom of a pie pan that fits your air fryer.
3. In a bowl; mix rhubarb with 1 ½ cups sugar, nutmeg, 3 tablespoon flour and whisk
4. In another bowl, whisk eggs with milk, add to rhubarb mix, pour the whole mix into the pie crust, introduce in your air fryer and cook at 390°F, for 45 minutes. Cut and serve it cold

Sweet Squares Recipe

(Prep + Cooking Time: 40 Minutes | **Servings:** 6)

Ingredients:
- 1 cup flour
- 1/2 cup butter; soft
- 2 tablespoon lemon juice
- 1/4 cup powdered sugar

- 2 teaspoon lemon peel; grated
- 2 eggs; whisked
- 1 cup sugar
- 1/2 teaspoon baking powder

Directions:
1. In a bowl; mix flour with powdered sugar and butter; stir well, press on the bottom of a pan that fits your air fryer, introduce in the fryer and bake at 350°F, for 14 minutes.
2. In another bowl, mix sugar with lemon juice, lemon peel, eggs and baking powder; stir using your mixer and spread over baked crust. Bake for 15 minutes more, leave aside to cool down, cut into medium squares and serve cold.

Poppy Seed Cake Recipe

(Prep + Cooking Time: 40 Minutes | **Servings:** 6)

Ingredients:

- 1 ¼ cups flour
- 1 teaspoon baking powder
- 1 tablespoon orange zest; grated
- 2 eggs; whisked
- 1/2 teaspoon vanilla extract
- 3/4 cup sugar
- 2 teaspoon lime zest; grated
- 2 tablespoon poppy seeds
- 1/2 cup butter; soft
- 1 cup milk

For the cream:

- 1 cup sugar
- 1/2 cup passion fruit puree
- 4 egg yolks
- 3 tablespoon butter, melted

Directions:

1. In a bowl; mix flour with baking powder, 3/4 cup sugar, orange zest and lime zest and stir
2. Add 1/2 cup butter, eggs, poppy seeds, vanilla and milk; stir using your mixer, pour into a cake pan that fits your air fryer and cook at 350°F, for about 30 minutes.
3. Meanwhile; heat up a pan with 3 tablespoon butter over medium heat, add sugar and stir until it dissolves.
4. Take off heat, add passion fruit puree and egg yolks gradually and whisk really well
5. Take cake out of the fryer, cool it down a bit and cut into halves horizontally
6. Spread 1/4 of passion fruit cream over one half, top with the other cake half and spread 1/4 of the cream on top. Serve cold.

Air Fryer Cooking Charts

The below chart can be used for reference assuming that the food is flipped or basket shaken halftime during cooking.

POULTRY		
Type	**Temperature (Fahrenheit)**	**Cook Time (Minutes)**
Bone-In breasts (1.25 lbs.)	370	25
Boneless breasts (4 lbs.)	380	12
Drumsticks (2.5 lbs.)	370	20
Bone-In thighs (2 lbs.)	380	22
Boneless thighs (1.25 lbs.)	380	18 - 20
Bone-In Legs (1.75 lbs.)	380	30
Wings (2 lbs.)	400	12
Halved Game Hen (2 lbs.)	390	20
Whole Chicken (6.5 lbs.)	360	75
Tenders	360	8 - 10

BEEF		
Type	**Temperature (Fahrenheit)**	**Cook Time (Minutes)**
Burger (4-ounce)	370	16 - 20
Filet Mignon (8-ounce)	400	18
Flank Steak (1.5 lbs.)	400	12
London Broil (2 lbs.)	400	20 - 28
Meatballs	380	7
Bone-In Ribeye (8-ounce)	400	10 - 15
Sirloin Steaks (12-ounce)	400	9 - 14
Beef-Eye Round Roast(4lbs)	390	45 - 55

FISH & SEAFOOD

Type	Temperature (Fahrenheit)	Cook Time (Minutes)
Fish Filets (8-ounce)	400	10
Calamari (8-ounce)	400	4
Salmon filets (6-ounce)	380	12
Swordfish Steak	400	10
Tuna Steak	400	7 - 10
Scallops	400	5 - 7
Shrimps	400	5

VEGETABLES

Type	Temperature (Fahrenheit)	Cook Time (Minutes)
Asparagus (sliced)	400	5
Beets (whole)	400	40
Broccoli Florets	400	6
Brussels Sprouts(halved)	380	15
Carrots (sliced)	380	15
Cauliflower florets	400	12
Corn on cob	390	6
Eggplant (cubed)	400	15
Fennel (quartered)	370	15
Green Beans	400	5
Kale leaves	250	12
Mushrooms (sliced)	400	5
Pearl Onions	400	10
Parsnips (cubed)	380	15
Pepper (chunks)	400	15
Small baby potatoes	400	15

Potato (chunks)	400	12
Whole potatoes (baked)	400	40
Squash (chunks)	400	12
Sweet potatoes (baked)	380	30 - 35
Cherry Tomatoes	400	4
Tomatoes (halved)	350	10
Zucchini sticks	400	12

FROZEN FOODS		
Type	Temperature (Fahrenheit)	Cook Time (Minutes)
Thin French Fries (20-ounce)	400	14
Thick French Fries (17-ounce)	400	18
Onion Rings (12-ounce)	400	8
Mozarella Sticks (11-ounce)	400	8
Pot Stickers (10-ounce)	400	8
Fish Sticks (10-ounce)	400	10
Fish Filets (10-ounce)	400	14
Chicken Nuggets (12-ounce)	400	10
Breaded Shrimps	400	9

Made in the USA
Lexington, KY
25 February 2019